PROHIBITION

Also by Edward Behr

THE ALGERIAN PROBLEM

THE THIRTY-SIXTH WAY (with Sidney Liu)

"ANYONE HERE BEEN RAPED AND SPEAKS ENGLISH?"

GETTING EVEN

THE LAST EMPEROR

HIROHITO: BEHIND THE MYTH

THE COMPLETE BOOK OF *LES MISÉRABLES*

KISS THE HAND YOU CANNOT BITE: THE RISE AND FALL OF
      THE CEAUSESCUS

THE STORY OF MISS SAIGON (with Mark Steyn)

THE GOOD FRENCHMAN (THE LIFE AND TIMES OF MAURICE
      CHEVALIER)

PROHIBITION

THIRTEEN YEARS THAT CHANGED AMERICA

EDWARD BEHR

ARCADE PUBLISHING • NEW YORK

FIRST NORTH AMERICAN EDITION

Library of Congress Cataloging-in-Publication Data

Behr, Edward, 1926 –
    Prohibition : thirteen years that changed America / Edward Behr. —
1st North American Ed.
        p.   cm.
    Includes bibliographical references and index.
    ISBN 1-55970-356-3 (hc)
    ISBN 1-55970-394-6 (pb)
    1. Prohibition — United States — History. 2. Drinking of alcoholic
beverages — United States — History. 3. Alcoholism — United States —
History. I. Title
HV5089.B424. 1996
363.4.1.0973 — dc20   96 – 24063

Published in the United States by Arcade Publishing, Inc., New York
Distributed by Little, Brown and Company

10   9   8   7   6   5   4   3   2   1

PRINTED IN THE UNITED STATES OF AMERICA

CONTENTS

	Acknowledgments	vii
	Introduction	1
One	The Good Creature of God	7
Two	Fervor and Fanaticism	21
Three	The Women's War	35
Four	The Lineup	45
Five	Prohibition's First Victims	63
Six	America Goes Dry	77
Seven	The Providers	91
Eight	Harding and the Racketeers	105
Nine	Remus Unravels	121
Ten	The Adventurers	129
Eleven	"Prohibition Works!"	147
Twelve	"Prohibition Doesn't Work!"	161
Thirteen	Chicago	175
Fourteen	Remus on Trial	195
Fifteen	Remus Redux	209
Sixteen	A Fatal Triumph	221
Seventeen	The Aftermath	237
	Notes	245
	Bibliography	251
	Index	253

ACKNOWLEDGMENTS

Philip Guedalla once said that while history repeats itself, historians repeat each other—and all writers on Prohibition owe a huge debt to Herbert Asbury, whose *Great Illusion* remains the best record of its historical and evangelical origins. Another essential source book is *Wayne Wheeler: Dry Boss,* by Justin Stewart, Wheeler's former private secretary. I have also drawn heavily on the insider accounts of Prohibition by Roy Haynes, one of the first Prohibition Bureau commissioners, and Mabel Walker Willebrandt, who was deputy attorney general in charge of Prohibition law enforcement from 1921 to 1929.

I also want to thank the New York, St. Louis, Cincinnati, and East Hampton public libraries for their helpful cooperation, and the Library of Congress for its material on the Senate Investigative Committee on Attorney General Daugherty in 1924. I am especially beholden to a number of Cincinnati residents and experts: Jim Bruckmann, who reminisced about the pre-Prohibition fortunes of his family brewery; Jack Doll, gifted amateur photographer and organizer of a remarkable photo exhibition on George Remus; Geoffrey Giuglierino; Dr. Don H. Todzmann of the University of Cincinnati—and countless others, on Long Island and the East Coast, who were kind enough to share with me the family tales and reminiscences of not so long ago.

I would also like to thank my agent, Jean-François Samuelson, for his unfailing support, and my old friend and colleague Anthony Geffen for his constant encouragement. Thanks to him, what began as a vague telephone conversation ended up not only as a book but as an international, three-part television series.

PROHIBITION

Prohibition is better than no liquor at all.

—WILL ROGERS

INTRODUCTION

Early one fine autumn morning — October 6, 1927 — a stocky, middle-aged man named George Remus ordered George Klug, his driver, to overtake a taxi in Cincinnati's Eden Park. He had been tailing it ever since it had left the Alms Hotel with its two women passengers. After driving alongside, and motioning it to stop — it failed to do so — Remus got the driver to swerve suddenly, forcing the taxi off the road.

The cabdriver swore and hit the brakes, barely avoiding a collision, and the two women were shaken nearly off their seats. The older one, Imogene, was Remus's wife, and she was on her way to her divorce court hearing. By today's standards, she was distinctly on the stocky side, but her opulent figure, ample curves, and huge, gray-green eyes were typical beauty canons of the time, and her clothes — a black silk dress, patent leather black shoes, and black cloche hat from Paris — identified her as a woman of means. The younger woman, her daughter Ruth by an earlier marriage, was a slightly dumpy twenty-year-old.

As Ruth would later tell the court, at Remus's trial, Imogene gasped, "There's Remus," when she first spotted the overtaking car. Imogene got out of the stationary cab as Remus emerged from *his* car, a gun in his right hand (the defense later challenged this evidence, for Remus was left-handed). Ruth recounted: "He hit her on the head with his fist." Imogene said, "Oh, Daddy, you know I love you, you know I love you!" Remus turned to Ruth. "She can't get away with *that*," he snarled.

Imogene shrieked, "For God's sake, don't do it!" as Ruth, also spotting the gun, shouted, "Daddy, what are you going to do?" Then Imogene screamed, "Steve [the taxi driver], for God's sake, come over and help me!" But the driver stayed put. He heard George Remus shout, "Damn you, you dirty so-and-so bitch, *damn* you, I'll *get* you."

Imogene then rushed back into the cab, pursued by Remus. That was when he shot her, once in the stomach. She had the strength to get out of the other side of the car, running, her hands above her head, with Remus still in pursuit. She then got into another car, which had come to a halt behind the stalled taxicab, and collapsed.

Rather than confront the driver, Remus walked away. Shortly afterward, he gave himself up. As the *Cincinnati Enquirer* wrote the following day (October 7, 1927), "Thus did the much tangled domestic affairs of George Remus, once the multi-millionaire bootlegger king of Cincinnati, come to a sudden — and dramatic — climax."

The trial of George Remus for his wife's murder — and its spectacular conclusion — became the 1920s equivalent of the O. J. Simpson case. Reporters arrived from all over the United States, Canada, and even Europe — a special press room was set aside for them in the tiny courthouse. Proceedings were reported extensively in newspapers nationwide, the *Cincinnati Enquirer* running an almost verbatim account of the trial, from beginning to end.

George Remus would have remained an obscure Chicago criminal lawyer with an interest in law reform and a passionate opposition to the death penalty had Prohibition not turned him, in the space of four years, into a megastar millionaire. His *crime passionnel* stemmed not only from this sudden change in fortune, but from Imogene's sudden passion for Remus's nemesis, handsome young Justice Department agent Franklin Dodge, and her own considerable greed. Overwhelmingly, American men sided with George Remus, and even many staid, middle-class American matrons felt that Imogene "had had it coming to her."

For all the sordid details revealed during the trial, enabling Remus to present his case as an avenger rather than a murderer, Prohibition itself was the real culprit. Had there been no Volstead Act, he told the court, "I would not be here." The "greatest social experiment of modern times," as President Calvin Coolidge described it, brought with it irresistible temptations in the wake of unprecedented corruption.

The story of George and Imogene Remus is all part of that "noble experiment." George Remus's background, as a German-born "new American," was relevant to the unprecedented (and, to most Europeans, at least, deluded) attempt at the regulation of social behavior, for with hindsight, the Prohibition phenomenon can be seen not just as a well-meaning, albeit absurd, attempt to stamp out drunkenness, then regarded as society's most devastating scourge (graver even than TB, the other great affliction of the time, for it affected the mind as well as the body), but as a watershed marking the end of one American era and the beginning of another.

Beyond the debate on the rights of reformers to regulate social behavior by force, restricting individual freedom in the name of better health, morality, and godliness, Prohibition was the rearguard action of a still dominant, overwhelmingly rural, white Anglo-Saxon Protestant establishment, aware that its privileges and natural right to rule were being increasingly threatened by the massive arrival of largely despised (and feared) beer-swilling, wine-drinking new American immigrants.

Old-established Americans, most of them Protestants, of overwhelmingly British lineage, regarded themselves as the natural guardians of traditional values, and were determined to maintain their moral and religious standards by almost any means. They were also intent on preserving their own considerable privileges. As historian Andrew Sinclair later wrote,[1] the Prohibitionists' victory in 1920, turning the whole of the country dry, was "the final victory of the defenders of the American past. On the rock of the 18th Amendment, village America made its last stand."

America's Marxists, a very small minority even in the heyday of Marxism, saw Prohibition in a very different light. For them it was a deliberate attempt on the part of the "dominant bourgeoisie" to duck the *real* issues — poverty, slum housing, economic exploitation of all kinds — using the Prohibition campaign as a pretext to deflect attention from the fact that the working classes were paying a huge price for the American industrial revolution. They argued that the ideals the Prohibitionists considered most important — godliness, industry, sobriety, thrift — were deliberately, and with consummate hypocrisy, advocated to compel the underprivileged to accept their fate and inferior status. Sobriety was simply a "plutocratic weapon" employers used to make wage slaves work harder and faster on the factory assembly lines. The underlying assumption was that if the workers refrained from drink, their one easily available pleasure, they could then get by on their miserable wages.[2]

The story of Imogene and George Remus, and of their nemesis, Prohibition — in retrospect one of the greatest of American disasters, and in its day "without a doubt the most important question in American life"[3] — is oddly relevant today. In its simplistic determination to strike at the root of a "social evil" without any thought of the consequences, or of the means required to enforce it, Prohibition was a striking example of the American propensity to believe that society was infinitely malleable and that all it would take to rid America of its blemishes and turn it into a promised land would be a few well-meaning laws.

It also embodied a number of righteous beliefs — in the perfectibility of human nature and the legitimacy of the moral imperative to improve the health and well-being of the masses whether they liked it or not — that revealed a perennial American naiveté of the type embodied by successive generations of idealist-politicians.

The persistence and skill with which the architects of Prohibition pleaded their cause over most of a century, winning state after state until an overwhelming majority in Congress voted for the Eighteenth Amendment, was a textbook example of successful lobbying. All practitioners of that art have since, consciously or unconsciously, emulated the tactics of the Anti-Saloon League and its ruthless legal adviser and political power broker Wayne Wheeler. But the incompetence that followed was equally exemplary — as if the very politicians who had brought Prohibition into being were determined to do everything in their power to ensure its failure.

Despite its almost risible collapse, Prohibition's lessons are valuable — and have still not been learned. Some of its methods were strikingly similar to those used today to fight drug abuse, with equally disappointing results, and today's controversy over drugs could, with only minor semantic changes, apply to the Prohibition controversy almost a century ago. "Prohibition is what makes drugs so profitable, yet the thought of legalizing their distribution, even with rigid controls and treatment programs, arouses the fear of infecting millions of addicts," wrote Max Frankel in the *New York Times* Sunday magazine recently.[4] That fear, if valid, explains the central dilemma expressed two years ago by Senator Daniel Patrick Moynihan. "The nation's choice of policy," he wrote — legalization or prohibition — "offers a choice of outcomes." Neither alternative seemed to him entirely satisfactory: legalization entailed increased public health problems, whereas prohibition led to an enormous increase in crime. Identical concerns were expressed by equally baffled social reformers as far back as 1890.

For all its outrageously intolerant overtones, its hypocrisy and double standards, Prohibition represented a genuine attempt to better the lives of people. That it did them instead untold harm — that America has never fully recovered from the legacy of those thirteen years — should come as no surprise. As history keeps telling us — but do we ever listen? — the road to hell is paved with good intentions.

1

THE GOOD
CREATURE OF GOD

There was a time in America when liquor was regarded as God's gift to mankind and a panacea for almost every type of ailment. The last half of the eighteenth century was "the most intemperate era in American history."[1] The going price for a muscular slave was twenty gallons of whiskey; farmers found whiskey distillers gave them a far better price for grain than millers; and the "good creature of God" — *aqua vitae,* the very stuff of life — was food, medicine, and, even more than in Europe, the indispensable lubricant for civilized, enjoyable social intercourse.

From the time they were born, Americans acquired a taste for liquor: as babies, their bottles were laced with rum to keep them "pacified"; later, "able-bodied men, and women, too, for that matter, seldom went more than a few hours without a drink." Here is the *Old American Encyclopedia* (1830) describing pre-independence drinking habits:

> A fashion at the South was to take a glass of whiskey, flavored with mint, soon after waking. . . . At eleven o'clock, while mixtures, under various peculiar names — sling, toddy, flip, — solicited the appetite

at the bar of the common tippling-shop, the offices of professional
men and counting rooms dismissed their occupants for a half hour to
regale themselves at a neighbor's or a coffee-house with punch. . . .[2] At
the dinner hour . . . whiskey and water curiously flavored with apples,
or brandy and water, introduced the feast; whiskey or brandy and water helped it through; and whiskey or brandy without water secured
its safe digestion. . . . Rum, seasoned with cherries, protected against
the cold; rum, made astringent with peach-nuts, concluded the repast
at the confectioner's; rum, made nutritious with milk, prepared for
the maternal office.

Most early settlers were hard drinkers, and while the Puritans
preached against every form of pleasurable self-indulgence, they
outlawed drunkenness, not drinking. This would have been unthinkable, for the Bible itself was full of references to the joys, and blessings,
of liquor. The Book of Proverbs contains this eulogy, that would have
been in its place on the wall behind every bar in the land: "Give strong
drink unto him that is ready to perish, and wine unto those that be of
heavy heart. Let him drink, and forget his poverty, and remember his
misery no more."

With this type of biblical *leitmotif*, it was no surprise that clergymen were among the biggest tipplers of all. At every housecall they
were offered drinks, rum or cider was served almost continuously during their stay, and when they left they had to take a farewell drink for
politeness' sake. Some clergymen made twenty such calls a day. No
wonder a noted Temperance figure in Albany noted in 1857 that to his
knowledge, "fifty percent of the clergy, within a circuit of 50 miles, died
drunkards." The Reverend Leonard Woods, professor of theology at
Andover Seminary, recalled in 1880 that among his acquaintances were
at least forty ministers, "who were either drunkards, or so far addicted
to drinking, that their reputation and usefulness were greatly impaired,
if not utterly ruined."

City authorities invariably granted licenses to saloons close to
churches, the rationale being that the priest and his flock would meet
there between services. All ordinations, weddings, and especially funerals turned into prolonged drinking bouts, some of them phenomenal. In *The Great Illusion* Herbert Asbury cites the cost of liquid
refreshment at a Virginia funeral at four thousand pounds of tobacco,
and at a preacher's widow's funeral in Boston, the mourners put away

over 51 gallons of Malaga. Any communal physical effort — whether harvesting, road-building, or wood-cutting — was an excuse for a binge. Workers' wages came, in part, in the form of liquor, and days off to get drunk were part of an unwritten agreement between employer and laborer.

The massive consumption of hard liquor had been a feature of "New Continent" life ever since the earliest colonization stages: as early as 1630, Peter Stuyvesant noted that "one quarter of New Amsterdam (as New York was then called) is devoted to houses for the sale of brandy, tobacco and beer." In pre-independence times, the colonies' judges were so frequently drunk at the bench that heavy fines were instituted for those proved incapable during court proceedings.

In some parts of rural America, liquor was used as currency, with prices displayed in terms of whiskey pints or gallons. Farm laborers, including slaves, got ample liquor rations. Kegs of whiskey, with tin cups attached, were at the disposal of ships' crews and passengers on flatboats on the Ohio and Mississippi Rivers. There were barrels of rum on tap in shops for favored customers, and even court sessions were an excuse for drinking: the liquor consumed by judge and jury during proceedings was a legitimate court expense. With rum, applejack, and blackstrap (rum and molasses) a few pence a quart, eighteenth century Americans, whether rich or poor, slaves or free men and women, appear to have gone through life in a semiperpetual alcoholic haze. In the early nineteenth century, Asbury noted, "so much rum was available in the Massachusetts metropolis that it sold at retail for fourpence a quart. West Indian rum, supposed to be better than the New England product, was only twopence more."

The New Continent passion for liquor reflected the settlers' own cultural origins — in no way was it *sui generis*. The early immigrants came from a land — Britain — where eighteenth-century pub owners routinely displayed the notice "Drunk for a penny, dead drunk for twopence." Hogarth's "Gin lane" immortalized the degradation of London's wretched "lumpen proletariat." Cheap gin first made its massive appearance in London in 1724, and became an immediate addiction (much like crack or heroin today) to wretched, underpaid, unrepresented slum dwellers, so much so that the "Gin Act," passed by Parliament, attempted to contain this plague — to little effect, for, as Henry Fielding, the writer and social reformer, noted in a pamphlet published in 1751, "should the drinking of this poison be continued at its present height, during the next twenty years, there will be by that time very few of the common people left to drink it." Some at least of Fielding's "common people," intent on a different, less miserable life, must later have joined the ranks of America's eighteenth-century settlers.

The taverns where Americans did their drinking were little different in their squalor from the inns described by eighteenth- and early nineteenth-century travelers in Europe, with the exceptions that at first rum, and not gin, was the staple liquor; that hard liquor and beer (not wine) prevailed; and that it was all absurdly inexpensive. At first no licenses of any kind were required, no taxes imposed. The only proviso was that, as in Europe, saloons and bars had to be lodging houses as well — all drinking establishments were expected to provide meals and living quarters. These were, almost invariably, as in Europe, on the sordid side.

Long before the Revolution, there were big differences between European and American attitudes as far as drinking practices were concerned. Temperance — and later, Prohibition issues — from the eighteenth century on, rapidly became "the most important question in American life." The reason why is still a matter for endless debate. The puritan ethic largely explains why the Temperance issue was to become a constant religious obsession. But perhaps the simple, largely overlooked answer is that unlike Europe there were no other major issues that warranted equal concern — no wars (until the Civil War), no major social upheavals, no immediate, overwhelming cause around which public opinion might be mobilized in the interests of justice and freedom. The Prohibition issue became America's lasting preoccupation largely by default.

New Continent saloon keepers had far more clout and from the start were far more involved in the political process than their European counterparts. This, too, was an example of the idiosyncratic social context of the land, where political ideology mattered far less than in Europe.

In America, from independence onward, the saloon keeper became a key figure in local politics. He delivered the vote — usually to the highest bidder, whose political views mattered far less than his personality, his prejudices, and the amount of jobs and money at his disposal. As John Adams, America's second president, wrote of saloons in his diary in 1760:

The worst effect of all [is that] these houses are become the nurser-
ies of our legislators. An artful man, who has neither sense nor sentiment, may, by gaining a little sway among the rabble of a town, multi-
ply taverns and dram-shops and thereby secure the votes of taverner
and retailer and all; and the multiplication of taverns will make many,
who may be induced to flip and rum, to vote for any man whatever.

This lasting connection between politics and liquor, predating the
Prohibition era by 150 years, was what made American drinking habits
unique. In eighteenth- and nineteenth-century European literature,
there are few references to the *political* clout of English publicans, or
of French café or German *Bierstube* owners, though there are endless
examples of European social, literary, and political groups meeting in
drinking places, from Dr. Samuel Johnson's London pubs to Hitler's
Munich *Bierstuben*.

The drinking habits of Americans in the eighteenth and early nineteenth centuries must be seen in this special social context. America
was an overwhelmingly rural, vastly underpopulated country. Unlike
Europe, it was not permanently wracked by bitter ideological con-
flicts (except for the issues culminating in the Civil War). The social
and political life of small communities, scattered over a vast expanse
of land, centered, far more than in Europe, around those twin meeting places, the church and the tavern, and it was no coincidence in an
age devoid of radio, television, mass advertising, and mass-circulation
newspapers that tavern keeper and preacher were key community opinion makers — influential figures whose views were taken seriously and
discussed interminably. (The status of the saloon keeper would change
in the second part of the nineteenth century, as increasingly they were
foreign-born, reflecting the urban immigration waves that changed the
composition of American society so dramatically from 1850 on.)

The early political clout of the tavern owner — and later of the
brewing or liquor conglomerates that would take them over — was intolerable to idealists such as Adams. In a letter to a friend in 1811, he
wrote:

I am fired with a zeal amounting to enthusiasm against ardent
spirits, the multiplication of taverns, retailers, dram-shops and tip-
pling houses, and grieved to the heart to see the number of idlers,
thieves, sots and consumptive patients made for the physician in these
infamous seminaries.

With time, drinking habits changed. Americans continued to drink inordinately, but, as also happened in Europe, rum and gin became working-class staples, whereas the wealthy indulged in increasingly fashionable Madeira, port, and Malaga. (Beer was not consumed in large quantities until much later, with the nineteenth-century arrival of German immigrants.) Hard cider had been a staple since the early eighteenth century, and whiskey made its first appearance about 1760 (the first distillers were in western Pennsylvania, but many farmers made their own). The Whiskey Rebellion occurred in 1794 when the federal government, discovering for the first time the *milch-cow* opportunity of liquor taxation as a source of revenue, imposed a small excise tax on distilled spirits.[3] The "whiskey war" was brutally put down by the militia. Although the farmers eventually paid the tax, "every family in Western Pennsylvania operated its own (illegal) still."[4]

In 1810, the total population of the United States was still only slightly above the 7 million mark, and though statistics were, by today's standards, primitive, they reveal that per capita consumption of liquor was huge. According to a report published in 1814 by the Massachusetts Society for the Suppression of Intemperance (one of the first of the Temperance movements), "the quantity of ardent spirits consumed in the country surpasses belief." Over 25 million gallons were consumed locally, it claimed, but

> considering the caution with which accounts of property are rendered to government through fear of taxation; considering also the quantities distilled in private families . . . there is a high probability that millions might be added to the account rendered by the marshals. Let it stand, however, as it is, and add to it eight million gallons of distilled spirits in the same year imported, and the quantity for home consumption amounts to 33,365,559 gallons (or 4.7 gallons per person).

Another Temperance society (Connecticut, May 19, 1830) reported that "in one of the most moral and regular towns of Lichtfield County, whose population is 1,586, the amount of distilled liquors retailed during the last ten years has been 36,400 gallons." Later reports from other local temperance societies claimed that the "1,900 inhabitants of Dudley, Massachusetts, drank ten thousand gallons of rum" and that "the population of Salisbury, Connecticut, consumed 29.5 gallons of rum for each of its thirty-four families" in 1827.

According to the Albany (New York) Temperance Society, its 20,000 inhabitants (in 1829) "consumed 200,000 gallons of ardent spirits" — ten gallons a head of what must have been mostly whiskey, rum, or gin. The average (white, adult, male) *yearly per capita* consumption, in the years 1750–1810, has been roughly estimated at between ten and twelve gallons of "ardent spirits."

Long before American independence, local authorities and their London masters made sporadic efforts to reduce the scale of drinking, with little success. In theory, regulations abounded: drinking shops could serve only limited quantities to each customer, who could remain there for only an hour or two (both times and quantities varied from place to place). However, the rules were rarely enforced. In Massachusetts, habitual offenders were pilloried, and made to wear hair shirts inscribed with a large D or the word *Drunkard*.

In Georgia, when drinking assumed such alarming proportions that news of it reached London, an Act of Parliament was passed in 1734 enforcing Prohibition (though beer was exempt), and a ban on exports of rum and brandy to Georgia, regarded by London's colonial authorities as the most turbulent part of the colony, was put into effect. Effective in 1735, it lasted eight years and was only rescinded in 1743 after reports reached London that Georgian farmers were abandoning their crops to concentrate on moonshining, and that contraband liquor from South Carolina was entering Georgia on a huge scale. This earliest Prohibition experiment revealed, in this Georgian microcosm, almost all of Prohibition's inherent failings: bootlegging[5] and moonshining apart, Georgian juries systematically refused to convict offenders, and some colonial enforcers of the law took bribes to look the other way. Over a century and a half later, history would repeat itself on a much vaster scale.

From the very earliest settler times, a small minority of Temperance activists tried to fight the tide. These were invariably Puritan leaders, such as Increase Mather and his more famous son Cotton, whose concern was less the physical than the religious health of their parishioners, Increase Mather preaching, for instance, in 1673, that "the flood of excessive drinking will drown Christianity." But even Cotton Mather was unable to fight the tide completely: at a "private fast" in Boston, he noted in his journal, after prayers, "some biskets, and beer, cider and wine were passed round."

The Methodists were to become the avant-garde of the Temperance movement, but their use of the word *excessive* was significant: social drinking was so prevalent that outright Prohibition was unthinkable, except to a few mavericks. So strong were the rules of social behavior that even the most abstemious preachers found it difficult to refuse a drink. Increase Mather himself put it eloquently in his sermons: "Wine is from God but the drunkard is from the devil."

The most revered American of all, George Washington, was no role model for Temperance activists. A notorious drinker — in his first few months as president, about one fourth of his household expenses were spent on liquor — he may well, if his generals' testimony is to be believed, have conducted part of the war against the British in an alcoholic haze, for, as General Marvin Kilman, a commander in the Continental Army, was to write, "Much of George Washington's continuing good cheer and famed fortitude during the long years of the war, caused to some extent by his overly cautious tactics, may have come from the bottle."

Temperance activists were still harping on the religious note seventy-one years later. Excessive drinking, they were convinced, went hand in hand with spiritual neglect — it "obliterated the fear of the Lord." In 1744, a Philadelphia grand jury, chaired by Benjamin Franklin, claimed that the greatest danger facing intemperate drinkers was "Godlessness," and that excessive drinking was responsible for the increasing evils of "swearing, poverty, *and the distaste for religion*." Thirty-five years later (February 27, 1777), a Constitutional Congress in newly independent America pressed, unsuccessfully, for a total ban on the manufacture of whiskey.

But it was Dr. Benjamin Rush, the former surgeon general of the Continental Army during the Revolution and one of the heroes of the war against the British (his signature is on the Declaration of Independence), who introduced the first scientific note in the still largely ineffective, minority campaign against excessive drinking. Rush, who had graduated from the College of New Jersey (later renamed Princeton) at the early age of fifteen, was an intellectual giant as well as the country's best-known doctor and the founder of America's first antislavery society. A Quaker, he numbered Benjamin Franklin among his close friends, and in his youth had become a disciple of another Quaker luminary, Anthony Benezet, an eccentric Temperance campaigner who was also a convinced abolitionist.

It was Benezet who aroused Rush's interest in liquor, and his later "revisionist" views. Based on his own vast medical experience, including his treatment of war casualties, his book *An Inquiry into the Effect of Spirituous Liquours on the Human Body and Mind* (published in 1785) called into question the widely held belief that alcohol was a healthy stimulant, the "good creature of God." On the contrary, he wrote, alcohol had no real food value; administered to the sick or wounded, it worsened their condition; and even moderate drinking of "ardent spirits" (by which he meant whiskey and rum, for there was little gin at the time in America) was habit-forming, leading first to memory loss, then to progressive physical and moral degradation. The addict's descent was described in Hogarthian rhetoric: "In folly it causes him to resemble a calf; in stupidity, an ass; in roaring, a mad bull; in quarreling and fighting, a dog; in cruelty, a tiger; in fetor, a skunk; in filthiness, a hog; and in obscenity, a he-goat."

Losing all moral sense, his downward path was inevitable: first came burglary, then murder, then madness and despair, and, in the end, the gallows. Rush's "Inquiry" included a chart, a "moral and physical thermometer of intemperance," that became a fixture in thousands of homes. Milk and water guaranteed "serenity of mind, reputation, long life and happiness." Wine, porter, and beer could be absorbed "only in small quantities and at meals." But the fated downward path was revealed in the following chart, on a scale of 0 to 80:

Intemperance

0		Vices	Diseases	Punishments
10	Punch	Idleness	Sickness	Debt
20	Toddy, egg rum	Gaming, peevishness	Tremors of the hands	Jail
30	Grog, brandy and water	Fighting, horse-racing	Inflamed eyes, red nose and face	Black eyes and rags
40	Flip and shrub	Lying and swearing	Sore and swelled legs	Hospital or poorhouse

50	Bitters, infused in spirits & cordials	Stealing & swindling	Jaundice, pains in hands & feet	Bridewell
60	Gin, brandy & rum in mornings	Perjury	Dropsy, epilepsy	State prison
70	The same in mornings & evenings	Burglary	Melancholy, palsy, apoplexy	Ditto for life
80	The same during day & night	Murder	Madness, despair	Gallows

The symptoms of "this odious disease" included "certain immodest actions" and other "extravagant acts: singing, hallooing, roaring, imitating the noises of brute animals, jumping, tearing off clothes, dancing naked, breaking glasses and china." The specific diseases caused by liquor were listed as follows:

1. Decay of appetite, sickness at stomach, puking of bile and discharging of frothy and viscous phlegm.
2. Obstruction of the liver.
3. Jaundice and dropping of belly and limbs, and finally every cavity of the body.
4. Hoarseness and a husky cough, leading to consumption.
5. Diabetes, i.e., a frequent and weakening discharge of pale or sweetish urine.
6. Redness and eruptions in different parts of the body, rumbuds, a form of leprosy.
7. A fetid breath.
8. Frequent and disgusting belchings.
9. Epilepsy.
10. Gout.
11. Madness — one third of patients confined owed their condition to ardent spirits. *Most of the diseases are of a mortal nature.*

Rush's renown and the apocalyptic imagery of his prose had an enormous effect on ordinary people, and on physicians and clergymen around the country, as well as on congressmen in Washington — though President James Madison continued to drink a pint of whiskey before breakfast. Rush himself was no Prohibitionist: on the contrary, the core of his argument was that consumers should be made to switch from hard liquor to wine and beer. To wean addicts, he even suggested mixing wine with opium to calm them down until they were cured — for opium then was no controlled substance but an innocuous, effective drug, almost as widespread as aspirin today.

Rush saw hard liquor as a "temporary aberration." The moderate consumption of wine and beer, ensuring health and lasting happiness, would ensure a radiant future for generations to come. Some cynics, such as Boston's Fisher Ames, who had defeated Samuel Adams for Congress in 1788, were more cynical, and realistic: "If any man supposes that a mere law can turn the taste of a people from ardent spirits to malt liquors, he has a most romantic notion of legislative power." This was a warning later Prohibition advocates would dismiss or ignore.

There was one issue that united both laissez-faire advocates and hands-on Temperance interventionists: all those in authority, in Indian territories and reservations, banned the sale of liquor to the "native American" survivors, or at least issued orders that liquor was not to be used as a medium of exchange. Earlier traders bartered cheap rum for valuable otter furs, and witnessed the consequences: Indian tribes became so addicted that their interest in trapping animals waned.

But such orders were systematically ignored. Liquor was introduced in the Northwest by John Jacob Astor's Pacific Fur Company in 1807, at first with disappointing results — to the traders. A company employee, Gabriel Franchere, noted that the "mild and inoffensive" Pacific Northwest Indians did not know how to make liquor, and despised those who drank. "These savages," he wrote, "are not addicted to intemperance, regard liquor as poison and consider drunkenness disgraceful."[6] Strong drink, noted another Northwest company trader, Ross Cox, was anathema to them: "All the Indians on the Columbia River entertain a strong aversion to ardent spirits." Liquor, they believed, was only fit for slaves.

Sir George Simpson, head of the Hudson's Bay Company in London, and a highly moral man, was aware of this and issued instructions that on no account should liquor be used as barter. But by 1824, the battle had been lost: rival traders, including Russians from across the Siberian border, had no such qualms, and although the Indian chiefs at first sent them packing, younger members of the Pacific Northwest tribes eventually challenged the elders' authority. The traders were cunning, devious — and patient. Some provided the Indian hunters with slaves, bought from other tribes, to sweeten their deals. The Hudson's Bay Company directives were still observed, at least in principle: strong drink was not used as a medium of exchange. It *was*, however, used to celebrate a deal. First the traders and the Indians drank together, to seal their contract. Then liquor became a bonus package, along with money, that accompanied every transaction. Soon afterward, this fiction went by the board, and liquor replaced money. Ten otter pelts could be had for a bottle of whiskey. Russian traders used vodka.

The result was a holocaust: liquor addiction went hand in hand with mortal disease. The Columbia River Indians died en masse, and some, such as the Chinooks, were virtually wiped out. The tragedy was recorded in extraordinarily lyrical poems, passed down from generation to generation by survivors. Here is the piteous cry of an Indian chief as he simultaneously chronicles his decay and finds solace in the whiskey that enables him to forget his plight:

> I am afraid to drink but still I like to drink.
> I don't like to drink, but I have to drink whiskey.
> Here I am singing a love song, drinking.
> I didn't know that whiskey was no good.
> And still I am drinking it.
> I found out that whiskey is no good.
> Come, come closer to me, my slaves,
> And I'll give you a drink of whiskey.
> Here we are drinking now.
> Have some more, have some more of my whiskey.
> Have a good time with it.
> Come closer to me, come closer to me, my slaves,
> We are drinking now, we feel pretty good.
> Now you feel just like me.[7]

Once the drinking habit started, Edwin Lemert,[8] a native-American specialist, noted the Indians drank until they dropped. Massacres, blood feuds, and killings all became endemic after 1820. And though the Hudson's Bay Company reiterated its instructions in 1831, unregulated competition proved too strong: the whiskey-for-skins barter continued, with fearful consequences.

Most Temperance activists, of course, were unaware of the Indians' tragic predicament. But whether as a result of Dr. Rush's writings, or because of the growing spectacle of "immoderate" drinking among increasing numbers of manual workers, Temperance societies mushroomed throughout America at the turn of the century. Active at first on the East Coast, and stimulated by campaigns conducted by puritan theologians such as the Reverend Lyman Beecher and his more famous daughter, Harriet Beecher Stowe, they formed, split, and amalgamated, but invariably thrived. *The Philanthropist,* the first Temperance newspaper, began publication in Boston in 1826. By 1829, there were a thousand Temperance societies throughout America, and *The Philanthropist* chronicled their spectacular successes: liquor dealers pledging to stop selling hard liquor and drunkards pledging no longer to drink the stuff. In 1831, Lewis Cass, a prominent Temperance advocate appointed secretary of War, put an end to the army's liquor ration, also banning the sale of "ardent spirits" in all military installations. By 1836, a web of Temperance societies — some affiliated, others single-mindedly autonomous — blanketed inhabited America. No preacher — whether Methodist, Presbyterian, or Catholic — could ignore them, and many clergymen became totally committed to these movements, providing venues, and in some cases actively using the pulpit to raise funds. They were not yet politically important, at least not in the sense that "wet" or "dry" advocacy might determine election outcomes. But they were becoming bolder, more extreme — and more intolerant. By 1836, Rush's vision of a healthy community enjoying moderate quantities of beer and wine was largely forgotten: the new Temperance leaders were on the warpath against wine, beer, and cider drinkers as well. For the first time, from the 1830s on — in pulpits, pamphlets, and medical journals — total Prohibition was being openly advocated.

2

FERVOR AND
FANATICISM

A new generation of puritanical Temperance advocates, from the early nineteenth century on, discovered — and richly mined — a new theme, both simple and compelling, designed to put an end to yet another avenue of pleasure: drinking, they decided, was a mortal sin. A leading Boston preacher, the Reverend Justin Edwards, was among the first to spread this doctrine. Others quickly took it up. The evils of drink were no longer to be found, exclusively, in physical and mental deterioration: what was at stake, from the 1830s onward, was the human soul itself.

The puritan ethic has always required a "sign," an incontrovertible, *visible proof* of salvation, among its elect. In earlier days, material prosperity — as Tawney showed in *Religion and the Rise of Capitalism* — had been proof enough. But in the 1830s, it became fashionable to invoke another "sign," another kind of proof: preachers all over America began equating drunkenness with damnation, abstinence with salvation. And salvation, according to an editorial in the *Temperance Recorder,* one of a spate of new prohibitionist journals, would bring about "unprecedented peace, happiness, prosperity." Lyman Beecher, Harriet Beecher Stowe's father, repeatedly relayed the terrifying message: "Drunkards, no more than murderers, shall inherit the Kingdom of God."[1] The message became increasingly vituperative, increasingly extreme. Here, for instance, is the Reverend Mark Matthews, moderator of Seattle's First Presbyterian Church: "The saloon is the most fiendish, corrupt, hell-soaked institution that ever crawled out of the slime of the eternal pit. . . . It takes your sweet innocent daughter, robs her of her virtue, and transforms her into a brazen, wanton harlot. . . . It is the open sore of this land." It was a tone that would retain its power right up to the imposition of Prohibition in 1920.

With the new religious fervor, even Rush acknowledged that his scientific evidence had taken second place. Given that the huge majority of Americans still indulged in liquor with evident enjoyment, and little care for their health, "I am disposed to believe," he wrote, "that the business must be affected finally by religion alone."

Not that medical evidence was neglected. As so often happens, Rush's learned treatise spawned a rash of pseudoscientific, alarmist nonsense. A Dr. Thomas Sewell of Columbian College, Washington, alleged that liquor was responsible for most human afflictions: "Dyspepsia, jaundice, emaciation, corpulence, rheumatism, gout, palpitation, lethargy, palsy, apoplexy, melancholy, madness, delirium tremens, premature old age. . . ."

These were but a "small part of the endless catalogue of diseases produced by alcohol drinking." Physicians also began propagating as scientific fact a myth that became accepted, for decades, as verifiable truth: that excessive drinking could lead to the body's spontaneous combustion. Case after case, recorded not only in American but in French and British nineteenth-century medical journals, involved individuals bursting into flames from close contact with a candle, suddenly and inexplicably exploding, or even ". . . quietly simmering, while smoke poured from the apertures of the body. . . . Vivid accounts of the terrible sufferings of drunkards whose insides had been transformed into roaring furnaces were published in most of the leading temperance papers. . . . and temperance lecturers were quick to point out that such an unusual experience was but a mild foretaste of what awaited the drunkard in hell."[2] Dr. Eliphalet Nott, President of Union College,

Schenectady, New York, was an expert on this form of "spontaneous combustion," and firmly believed that

> . . . these causes of death of drunkards by internal fires, kindled often spontaneously in the fumes of alcohol, that escape through the pores of the skin, have become so numerous and so incontrovertible that I presume no person of information will now be found to call the reality of their existence into question.

No one delivered these grim messages more eloquently than the Reverend Justin Edwards, a prolific writer and speaker, whose fulminating, alliterative style made him the most sought-after preacher of his day, and the Prohibitionists' chief attraction. His "Temperance Manual," originally devised as a sermon, widely distributed throughout America,[3] began with the grim premise that any human activity that did not directly involve religious worship was a misappropriation of the brief time on earth allotted to human beings, for "Ever since man turned away from God as a source of enjoyment, and from his service as a means of obtaining it, he has been prone to seek it in some improper bodily or mental gratification."

It was necessary, first of all, to demolish the theory that liquor was "the good stuff of life." Edwards ridiculed Holinshed's sixteenth-century chronicles, which claimed that

> It sloweth age; it strengtheneth youth; it helpeth digestion; it cutteth flegm; it abandoneth melancholia; it relisheth the heart; it highlighteth the mind; it quickeneth the spirits; it cureth the hydropsie; it expelleth the gravel; it puffeth away ventosity; it keepeth and preserveth the head from whirling, the eyes from dazzling, the tongue from lisping, the teeth from chattering, the hands from shivering, the sinews from shrinking, the veins from crumbling, the bones from aching, the marrow from soaking. . . .

But the core of Edwards's argument was that liquor never had been, and never could be, part of the kingdom of God, for "The ingredient [vinous fermentation] is not the product of creation, nor the result of any living process in nature. It does not exist among the living works of God." On the contrary,

. . . it is as really different from what existed before in the fruits
and the grains as the poisonous miasma is different from the decom-
position and decay of the vegetables from which it springs. It is as
different as poison is from food, sickness from health, drunkenness
from sobriety . . . they are as really different in their natures as life is
from death.

He was on tricky ground here. How could God, creator of all
things, not be held responsible for this "poisonous miasma"? After all,
as even his most devoted parishioners must have observed, fruit and
vegetables rotted with age, in a natural fermentation process.

In his zeal to deny liquor any organic authenticity whatever, his
metaphors became increasingly mixed, his arguments more extreme:

To conclude that because one is good as an article of diet, and
therefore the other must be good, is as really unphilosophical and
false as it would be to conclude that because potatoes are good as an
article of food, that therefore the soil out of which they grow is good
for the same purpose.

Without a single redeeming quality, liquor

. . . has been among the more constant and fruitful sources of all
our woes. Yet such has been its power to deceive men that while evil
after evil has rolled in upon them, like waves of the sea, they have
continued till within a few years knowingly and voluntarily to increase
the cause. . . . Ministers preached against drunkenness and drank the
drunkard's poison.

Conventional wisdom, in short, was that "to take a little now and
then does a man good." But, Edwards continued, between 1820 and
1826 "it was realized that if drunkenness was to be done away with,
men must abstain not only from abuse but from the use of what in-
toxicates — that is one of the first principles of moral duty." The result
would be immediately forthcoming: "They will enjoy better health; *they
can perform more labor;*[4] they will live longer."

Alcohol was a drug that altered perceptions. Sometimes, he
admitted, "men take alcohol to drown present sorrow." Thus,

A man lost his wife, the mother of his children, and he was in great distress. He took alcohol, and under its influence grew cheerful, and seemed full of mirth. He seized the dead body of his wife, and with high glee dragged her across the room by the hair of her head, and threw her into the coffin.

Likewise, "auctioneers, merchants and others have often furnished it to their customers, gratis, to make them feel more rich, and thus induce them to purchase more goods and at higher prices, and thus cheat them." It was, of course, the Reverend Justin Edwards's intention to strike the fear of God into his listeners, and his diatribe ends with a horrific description of the impact of alcohol on the human body.

> Why does alcohol cause death? Were the human body transparent, every man might answer this question. Alcohol inflames the sinews of the stomach. The surface becomes inflamed and begins to grow black. The coats become thickened. Ulcers begin to form and spread out till . . . the whole inner coat of that fundamental organ puts on an appearance of mortification, and becomes in color like the back of the chimney. Not infrequently cancers are formed and the whole surface becomes one common sore. The man cannot digest his food. The system is not nourished. Other organs become diseased, till the body itself is literally little else than a mass of putrefaction.

The "spontaneous combustion" theory was a fact.

> Take the blood of a drunkard, from his head, or his liver, and distil it. You have alcohol. It has actually been taken from the brain, strong enough, on application of fire, to burn. Dr. Kirk of Scotland dissected a man who died in a fit of intoxication. From the lateral ventricles of his brain he took a fluid distinctly sensible to the smell as whiskey. When he applied a candle to it, it instantly took fire and burnt blue.

However absurd, such tales were of considerable symbolic importance to a devout Christian audience. The point was made that the drunkard was not only destroyed by fire in his own lifetime: his hideous fate reminded them of the eternal hell-fire that awaited him in the thereafter.

This, and other apocalyptic vignettes designed to strike fear in the hearts of all its readers, was the theme of an 1850s best-seller. Timothy

Shay Arthur's *Ten Nights in a Bar Room and What I Saw There* — an immensely popular, mawkish tearjerker — described the appalling fate, the "road to hell," of all those who succumbed to the temptation of ardent spirits. Interestingly, though such potboilers were dutifully written by profit-seeking hacks, no truly great American literature used the ravages of alcohol as a pretext to examine current social issues on a broader canvas.

But there was no nineteenth-century American writer comparable to Emile Zola (Jack London is his nearest equivalent, at any rate in terms of subject matter), whose favorite theme was the destruction of human lives through alcohol — the only drug that enabled the dispossessed to endure the monstrously cruel social system exploiting them. In America, alcohol was a religious rather than political or social problem. The Puritans' view of habitual drunkards was singularly uncharitable: they were perceived as weak, self-indulgent, profoundly flawed individuals, not, as in Zola, as victims of an unjust society, alcohol merely accelerating their doom.

In early nineteenth-century American literature there is almost no hint that excessive drinking may have been the only solace of desperate men and women for whom there was no other release — that for underprivileged males (women were not admitted) the saloon was at once refuge, club, library, employment agency, and sole source of local news. Jack London is an exception, but his descriptions of America's saloon culture show a mixed attitude. Although he was fascinated by the working-class companionship and sense of belonging that only the saloon could provide, he nevertheless regarded liquor as an intrinsic evil, never bothering to ask why working-class people became drunkards in the first place.

The thrust of the new, hard-line Temperance preachers was very different, and the impact of men such as the Reverend Justin Edwards was enormous because the message they imparted was far more ominous: they were convinced that the liquor industry was nothing less than a vast, godless conspiracy intended to undermine society. Their message struck an immediate chord, for any conspiracy theory — whether it has to do with witchcraft, communism, satanic child abuse, or even more recently the United Nations — has always found a ready, credulous American audience.

As the Reverend Justin Edwards constantly reminded his listeners,

Judge Jaggett says: "Over every grog shop ought to be written in great capitals: THE ROAD TO HELL, LEADING DOWN TO THE CHAMBERS OF DEATH. You sell to the healthy, and you poison them. So by the time the father is dead, the son is ready to take his place." So with men who sell poisonous drink. If they sold it to none but drunkards, they would soon kill them and the evil would cease. But the difference is: they sell to sober men. No sooner have they killed one generation than they have prepared another to be killed in the same way. That is abominable, and ought to receive universal execration.

He conceded that not *all* those involved were necessarily conscious conspirators. Some (relatively innocent) saloon keepers might plead: "But in that case I must change my business?" To which he replied, with the earnestness of the truly saved: "So must the thief, the highway robber, the murderer."

The American Temperance Society, though silent on Christian dogma, was even more intransigent. One of its booklets, *"Medico-legal Considerations upon alcoholism, and the moral and criminal responsibility of inebriates,"* by Paluel de Marmon, M.D. (reproduced in 1872 in the *Medical World*), asserted that liquor

> . . . modifies, perverts or abolishes the functions of the nerve centers. In the first stage, the drunkard is jolly good-natured, witty. His natural timidity has been changed to boldness. He is kind, generous, friendly. . . he is social and obliging. The words flow out of his mouth like a stream.

This was followed by gradual loss of physical control, ending in "brutishness and somnolence." In a tougher vein, M. W. Baker, M.D., in the *Journal of Inebriety* (April of 1887) advocated establishing

> . . . special asylums for the inebriates on a par with criminal lunatic asylums. They should resemble those provided for the insane in being under medical care; and in possessing equal powers of detention and control, and will differ from insane asylums in their stricter discipline and in the constant employment of their patients.

He recommended a mandatory one-year term for those found drunk, and a two-year term for a second offense. The magazine claimed that "300 physicians have subscribed $6300 to the U.S. inebriate asylum plan."

Ironically, as Temperance movements of all types gathered strength throughout America, the actual *consumption* of liquor decreased considerably. Data show that in 1850, per capita yearly consumption was little more than two gallons — proof that the "spiritual" health of the nation was by now a far more important consideration than the physical health originally advocated by Dr. Rush.

The growing power of church movements, especially on the East Coast, spawned a generation of new lay activists. The 1830s and 1840s saw the rise of the first great tub-thumping prohibitionist advocates — not just clergymen but men such as General James Appleton of Massachusetts, who first advocated total Prohibition in the *Salem Gazette* in 1832 and entered politics solely to further its cause, becoming a member of the Massachusetts state legislature in 1836.

There were politicians who never achieved national status but nonetheless became immensely influential in their own states: Neal Dow, a prominent Quaker, and a tanner and timber speculator from Portland (Maine), alternately cajoled and bullied his fellow citizens, lecturing them relentlessly on the evils of drink, until in 1840 this small town became America's first "dry" city (though illegal, unlicensed grog shops abounded).

In 1847, an important Maine Supreme Court ruling restricted drinking hours throughout the state, setting the scene for future legislation. This gave Dow a new importance: he had lobbied for it for years. Saloon keepers and liquor retailers argued that such measures were illegal, threatened individual liberty, and were in restraint of trade. They lost their case.

The ambitions of Neal Dow, this "pretty dapper little man," as his political opponents described him, did not stop there. Although nominally a Republican, he was no party hack, and was convinced he was if not presidential material at least qualified to be vice president of the United States, regardless of the winning party. (He partially fulfilled this goal, in 1880 becoming the tiny Prohibition party's presidential candidate.)

A brilliant lobbyist, drawing on his own considerable funds, and unfazed by repeated defeats in the Maine legislature, he constantly urged that "traffic in intoxicating drink be held and adjudged as an infamous crime."

By 1851 his persistence was rewarded, and he scored a famous victory: on June 2 that year, the Maine State Legislature finally passed the bill he had proposed so many times, making the sale of liquor illegal throughout the state. It was a law with teeth. Its provisions contained fines, prison for repeat offenders, searches, seizures, and raids on liquor stocks. Almost the entire paraphernalia of the later (1920) Eighteenth Amendment was to be found in this early Maine law.

Dow reveled in his new fame. He was now the independent mayor of Portland, welcoming Republican *and* Democratic supporters provided they held pro-Temperance views and initiating a policy that would prove so useful to the later Anti-Saloon League. He began staging much-publicized raids in his hometown, watching with evident glee as thousands of gallons of illegal liquor were poured down the gutters in front of the local town hall.

The climate of blind hate between Temperance advocates and their opponents extended to other matters. The "wets" were, by and large, dyed-in-the-wool conservatives: backed by the brewers, the distillers, and the saloon keepers, they not only opposed any form of legislation restricting drinking but were in favor of maintaining slavery. They regarded Temperance activists and abolitionists as fanatics, tarred with the same brush. This explains the violence of the attack made on Dow by his principal opponent, Democratic Senator Shepherd Cary, on the eve of the Civil War.

"I train in a different company," said Cary,

and I do not expect to have any influence in the party until the reign of niggerism and fanaticism is over. A few years ago the jack-daw Mayor of Portland, this man with the fancy vest, was at the head of the nigger movement in that city. . . . Even Abolitionism was not strong enough for his diseased palate, and he has added temperance to his former stock of humbugs. Is this Federal-abolition wringneck to be allowed to dictate to a Democratic legislation what enactments it shall pass?

For all his "liberal" antislavery convictions, Dow was also, by current standards at least, a notorious racist: he had a visceral hatred for

Irish Catholics. Their growing presence was "a permanent threat to destroy law-abiding America." After a riot in front of his town hall, in which one man was killed by the police, his first question was: "Was he an Irishman?" This atypical Quaker, who fought with his fists and flaunted his wealth, was capable of the most un-Christian callousness, happily touring the most wretched street slums of his beloved Portland with his friends, gesturing to children in rags and broken-down shacks. "Rum did that," he would say, with evident relish. Blinded by his obsession, he believed his role as mayor was to wage war not on slums but on liquor. The maniacal zeal with which his minions carried out raids on illegal liquor stocks made him so unpopular with tradespeople that he was repeatedly mugged, his windows smashed, his family threatened.

Although it banned saloons, "Dow's law" did not ban drinking: liquor could still be freely imported and consumed at home. It could also be home-brewed. The new law also proved how easily proscription could be circumvented. In Maine, as in other states with early Prohibition laws, shopkeepers started charging five cents for a soda cracker — the accompanying glass of rum was free. The early code phrase used was "Do you want to see the blind pig?" That is, do you want a glass of rum? "Blind pigs" would later become one of the slang terms for the speakeasies of the Prohibition era.

Prohibitionist fervor was not confined to Maine. In one form or another, Oregon, Minnesota, Rhode Island, Massachusetts, Vermont, and Michigan voted in *their* laws by 1852. Michigan followed in 1853, Connecticut in 1854, and Indiana, Delaware, Nebraska (a territory, not yet a state), Pennsylvania, New York, and New Hampshire in 1855.

These years coincided with the apogee of the Washingtonian Revival, a movement actually established not in Washington but in nearby Baltimore. In that town, six well-known drunkards, all of them artisans or shopkeepers, became the disciples of the Reverend Matthew Hale Smith, a noted Temperance orator. In 1840, they decided to take the pledge and campaign for abstinence, which they did with the same devotion they had previously shown for drinking.

Their movement spread, thousands of former heavy drinkers signed up, and Timothy Shay Arthur, the same potboiling author who had penned *Ten Nights in a Bar Room and What I Saw There*, praised the reformed Baltimore drunkards with his *Six Nights with the*

Washingtonians. (Another best-seller was the Reverend John Marsh's *Hannah Hawkins, or, The Reformed Drunkard's Daughter,* a tear-jerker telling the story of the conversion of Hannah's father after listening to her tearful plea "Papa, please don't send me for whiskey today!")

The Washingtonian Revival spawned a host of rival societies, such as the Independent Order of Good Templars, which increased its membership from 50,000 in 1859 to 400,000 in 1869. Some of them, somewhat condescendingly, sought out black members for the first time — segregating them in separate groups, of course. The black affiliate of the Friends of Temperance was called the Sons of the Soil.

Then, dramatically, Temperance movements all over America lost their momentum, and in time, one by one, except for Maine, state Prohibition laws were repealed. The reason was simple: for the first time since the overthrow of British rule, more pressing issues were attracting American attention.

As the abolitionist movement, leading to the Civil War, gathered momentum, priorities shifted, and for the next 25 years, all prohibitionist progress halted. The cause was also jolted by a prominent Massachusetts politician, John A. Andrew, who later became its wartime governor. Shortly before the Civil War began, he headed a legislative committee whose report totally refuted the Prohibitionists' claims. Liquor was not "sinful or hurtful in every case." More important, it was "the right of every citizen to determine for himself what he will eat or drink."

> A law prohibiting him from drinking every kind of alcoholic liquors, universally used in all countries and ages as a beverage, is an arbitrary and unreasonable interference with his rights, and is not justified by the consideration that some men may abuse their rights, and may, therefore, need the counsel and example of good men to lead them to reform.

It was an argument that "wets" would later claim to be so self-evident that they assumed, wrongly, that it must ultimately prevail. Even as the Civil War began, Maine became famous for its "temperance regiments." Neal Dow himself raised and commanded the Thirteenth Maine (Temperance) Regiment. Hundreds of families begged him to take their sons, so that they would not have to mix with volunteers of

Scottish or Irish descent, known for their hard drinking and immoral ways.

The Civil War put a stop to the onward march of the Temperance movement — it was a time of excessive alcoholic indulgence. Abraham Lincoln himself, though a temperance advocate and lifelong teetotaler, turned a blind eye to Ulysses S. Grant's excessive drinking. When called upon to remove him from his command, Lincoln replied, with his usual irony: "Can you tell me where General Grant gets his liquor? If you could, I would direct the Chief Quartermaster to lay in a large stock of the same kind of liquor, and would also direct him to furnish a supply to some of my other generals who have never yet won a victory."

But Prohibition activists would later claim that had he lived Lincoln would have proved a formidable Prohibition ally. On the very last day of his life, they recalled, it was claimed he had agreed that "after reconstruction the next great question will be the overthrow and suppression of the legalized liquor traffic."

Although Lincoln had in early life acquired a store in New Salem, Illinois, that sold liquor, he had some sympathy for the Washingtonian movement, and in his famous (1842) Temperance address, eloquently supported the Temperance cause: "We found intoxicating liquor used by everybody, repudiated by nobody. It commonly entered into the first draught of an infant, and the last thought of the dying man."

On public occasions, he noted, it was "positively insufferable" to be without it. Liquor, "the devastator, came forth in society like the Egyptian angel of death, commissioned to slay if not the first, the fairest born of every family. . . . Social and personal disasters brought by liquor come not from the abuse of a very good thing but from the use of a very bad thing."

The drys, and especially the Anti-Saloon League (ASL), would later exploit Lincoln's views with considerable effect. As the struggle for Prohibition became increasingly fierce, the ASL appropriated carefully selected Lincoln quotes. Millions of small metal buttons showed an effigy of Lincoln, circled by his words: "The legalized liquor traffic is the tragedy of civilization." A hugely popular youth movement, devised and administered by the ASL, was the Lincoln Legion for the young. Each enrolled member (and though no accurate statistics exist, they probably numbered in the millions eventually) signed a pledge and received an elaborately printed certificate. Headed "Love-Sacrifice-Service," it read:

LINCOLN LEGION

I hereby enrol in the Lincoln Legion and promise, with God's help, to keep the following pledge, written, signed and advocated by Abraham Lincoln. "Whereas the use of intoxicating liquors as a beverage is productive of pauperism, degradation and crime; and believing it is our duty to discourage that which produces more evil than good, we therefore pledge ourselves to abstain from the use of intoxicating liquors as a beverage."

What Prohibition activists conveniently ignored was that Lincoln's innate tolerance, humor, sense of irony, and, above all, concern for individual freedom would never have allowed him to support, much less impose, Prohibition legislation. In 1840, he had made his position clear when he said: "Prohibition will work great injury to the cause of temperance. It is a species of intemperance within itself, for it goes beyond the bounds of reason by legislation and makes a crime out of things that are not crime. A prohibition law strikes at the very principle upon which our Government is founded."

Even in his 1842 Temperance address he stigmatized the dogmatists' "thundering tone of anathema and denunciation." Liquor taxes were essential to pay for the huge costs of the Civil War. Reluctantly, Lincoln imposed what some regarded as crippling levies on breweries, distilleries, and saloons: a manufacturing tax of $1 per barrel of beer, 20 cents a gallon on distilled liquor, and an annual $20 tax on retail liquor outlets. To outraged Prohibitionists, Lincoln was simply perpetuating the liquor traffic.

3

THE WOMEN'S WAR

The next step in the long march toward Prohibition was very different. American women spearheaded what briefly turned into a nation-wide movement, discovering their formidable power for the first time.

The Women's War against liquor was the first women's mass movement in American history. It was also the modern world's first large-scale, nonviolent protest movement. Long before Mahatma Gandhi invented the passive but effective form of protest known as Satyagraha, those waging the Women's War used their "gentle sex" and their only other weapons — passivity and Christian forbearance — to gain their ends, kindling imaginations all over America and making for compelling media coverage at a time when newspapers were assuming an increasingly influential role. Like Gandhi's followers, its "crusaders" courted arrest, welcoming blows and insults, with the deliberate intention of shaming their adversaries and turning them into guilt-ridden converts — and they succeeded, for a time, beyond their wildest dreams.

But if women were the shock troops at the forefront of this new crusade, deliberately excluding men from the actual battle, their behind-the-scenes mentors were men, and the logistics of the war were furnished by the male-dominated Protestant churches.

The Prohibition portrait gallery includes many notorious eccentrics, but few are as odd as the man who inspired the Women's War. Dr. Dioclesian Lewis was a preacher, social reformer, feminist, and health faddist whose targets included not only liquor but corsets and male chauvinism. In an age when women were still regarded as chattels, he campaigned for their freedom, not only in regard to the vote but to their physical selves. Heavy, constraining garments, he preached, were among the greatest dangers to health. In considerable advance of his time, he insisted that light clothing and short skirts were a prerequisite for better health and that "A clean tooth never decays." He advised women to walk, daily, with 20-pound sandbags perched on their heads to improve their posture.

This physical giant of a man, impervious to ridicule or threats, was a forceful personality with a distinct oratorical gift. He was also a prolific writer on hygiene and women's health problems, and was regarded by many as a charlatan because, though he used the title Doctor, he had in fact earned only a degree in "homeopathic studies" at Harvard. Although no Prohibitionist (he was too much of a libertarian for that), he was a firm believer in the evils of drink, his own father having been a notorious drunkard. It was Lewis who in the 1860s initiated the practice of walking into saloons at the head of his followers (mostly women) to pray for the souls of saloon keepers and bartenders, later lecturing in church halls on the effect of these "visitation bands," claiming that the results had been spectacular.

His message reached Elizabeth Thompson, in Hillsboro, Ohio, in 1873. Braving the sarcasm of her husband, this sixty-year-old housewife, encouraged by one of her sons, who had attended one of Dr. Lewis's meetings, summoned a group of townswomen — like her, respectable middle-class wives and mothers. After a warm-up meeting in a church hall, the women, in procession, made for Hillsboro's best-known liquor dealer, Dr. William Smith's Drug Store. After watching them picketing and praying outside his store, a contrite William Smith went up to "Mother Thompson," as she later became known, and publicly pledged to stop liquor sales, even agreeing to pour his liquor reserves into the gutter.

It was a "sign." A few days later, in the snow, Mother Thompson marshaled her troops again. This time the target was a saloon. Here too, though the wait was longer, and the praying more intense, the saloon keeper gave in to the women, and pledged to close his establishment. A beer garden run by a German, Charley Beck, was a tougher proposition. Picketing lasted two weeks, but by now the movement was in full swing, and many more volunteers were available to swell Mother Thompson's ranks and maintain a 24-hour hymn-singing marathon. "Ach, vimmins, shut up vimmins, I quits," he finally told the group.

The crusade, gathering strength all over the state, now staged more ambitious incursions further afield. In Clinton City, Ohio, the villainous John Calvin van Pelt, owner of the Dead Fall saloon, famous for its disreputable clientele, at first mobilized some of his patrons to get rid of the women by force. They remained where they were until forced to flee under a hail of stones and brickbats. Many suffered cuts and bruises, and, as a result, Pelt was jailed for a week. There he underwent a dramatic conversion, for on his release, before an audience of praying, hymn-singing crusaders, he smashed his liquor casks himself, announcing he was doing so "to sacrifice that which I fear has ruined many souls."

For several months, the "Women's Crusade" became an itinerant wonder, attracting crowds similar to those that flock to self-proclaimed saints claiming miraculous powers. On Dr. Lewis's advice, Mother Thompson restricted her activities to villages and small towns. Other, related "women crusaders" attempted, without success, to emulate her in New England (Dr. Lewis noted that this part of America was "not adapted to this new method of warfare") and in larger towns, such as Cincinnati, a liquor stronghold. Invariably in these big cities the crusade was a total failure. But though its greatest impact was on the Midwest, there were instances of successful women's crusades picketing as far away as California. Mrs. Annie Wittenmayer, a later president of the National Women's Christian Temperance Union, who was to chronicle the crusaders' movement, wrote of further "miracles." In Cleveland, a saloon keeper's wife loosed three fierce dogs on a kneeling "crusader," Mrs. Charles Wheeler, who never stopped praying but simply extended her hands to pat the animals on the head: they curled up at her feet. In Ohio, another saloon keeper's wife hurled a torrent of vile abuse at the kneeling, praying women. Their leader cried out: "Lord, silence this woman," and "immediately, the woman's mouth was shut like a steel trap, and she never spoke another word as long as she lived."

In retrospect, Mother Thompson's Women's Crusade proved to be more of a media triumph than a lasting contribution to the Prohibition cause. After its initial successes, it lost its momentum. Between 1873 and 1875, Ohio and Indiana state revenues dropped considerably. The *New York Tribune* reported that over $300,000 in liquor taxes had been forfeited because so many breweries and saloons had closed. But this proved only temporary. One by one, breweries and saloons reopened as media interest waned and the crusaders returned to their home activities.

The crusade not only brought the by-now almost moribund Temperance issue back on the front pages but kick-started the churches into a further round of activity. Presbyterian Church organizers in Cleveland, who had closely followed the crusade phenomenon from afar, were well aware that many of their parishioners had been erstwhile crusaders. They convened a meeting in the winter of 1874 that led to the establishment of the National Woman's Christian Temperance Union (WCTU). Representatives came from seventeen states, and this brand-new organization was to prove far more effective than any ephemeral, emotional crusade. Crucial, too, to its success was the election as first WCTU President of the formidable Frances Elizabeth Willard — a former university professor and a born organizer (and ex-crusader) — who soon had chapters of the movement in every state. Willard herself was the child of rigidly puritan Methodist parents. On Sundays, "the activities of the otherwise industrious family slowed down almost to the point of immobility. Willard Sr. would not shave, black his boots, write or read a letter, even look up a word in a dictionary, receive or make a visit."[1]

A tomboy, she developed "wild crushes on girls" as an adolescent, and her later friendships were exclusively with the same sex (an early engagement was rapidly terminated, and she never married). Needless to say, Frances Willard was brought up to believe that liquor was evil incarnate, promoting Godlessness and the "devil's works." The notion that liquor, in moderation, could be harmless, and even beneficial, was always anathema to the WCTU. Moderation was "the shoddy life-belt, which promises safety, but only tempts into danger, and fails in the hour of need. . . . the fruitful fountain from which the flood of intemperance is fed. . . . Most men become drunkards by trying to drink moderately and failing." When she began making Temperance speeches, Willard used a bung starter from a saloon as a gavel. She almost invariably dressed as a man, and her strict, humorless abstinence and crusading zeal marked her throughout her life.

She was one of the earliest activists to work for nationwide Prohibition, and it was under her leadership in 1875 that the WCTU petitioned Congress to do so. The WCTU's leaflets were designed to teach children about the evils of drink from the earliest possible age. Sunday school literature included "Counting Fingers." Its contents may seem laughably simplistic today, but in the 1870s, at a time when the WCTU was increasing its hold on such schools all over America, it had a huge impact on children — and on all God-fearing parents. The cover was an outspread hand, with numbered fingers, and its jingle was:

One, two, three, four, five fingers on every little hand.
Listen while they speak to us; be sure we understand.

1- THERE IS A DRINK THAT NEVER HARMS It will make us strong.

2- THERE IS A DRINK THAT NEVER ALARMS Some drinks make people wicked.

3- A DRINK THAT KEEPS OUR SENSES RIGHT There are drinks that will take away our senses.

4- A DRINK THAT MAKES OUR FACES BRIGHT We should never touch the drinks that will put evil into our hearts and spoil our faces.

5- GOD GIVES US THE ONLY DRINK — 'TIS PURE, COLD WATER.

Other effective children's teaching devices were APPLES ARE GOD'S BOTTLES ("Do you want to open God's bottle? Bite the apple with your teeth and you will taste the sweet juice God has put in His bottle for you.") and GRAPES ARE GOD'S BOTTLES (in the same vein).

The WCTU's first major triumph was to compel all public schools to teach a course on the evils of drink. Standard teaching practices included demonstrations of little scientific value but of startling impact.

Teacher would place part of a calf's brain in an empty glass jar. After discoursing on the nature of the brain and the nature of alcohol, she would then pour a bottle of alcohol into the jar. The color of the calf's brain would turn from its normal pink to a nasty gray. And that, the teacher would conclude in sepulchral tones, is what would happen to her pupils' little brains if ever they drank Satan's brew.

Along with the later secular Anti-Saloon League, the WCTU would be the formidable lobbying instrument that would in time make nationwide Prohibition inevitable. It was largely due to the WCTU that the Prohibition party made its ephemeral appearance on the political scene.

But twenty-five years later, while the WCTU was already hard at work, another woman was to lead a media blitz on the "devilish forces of liquor," and for a while her exploits completely overshadowed the more serious, academically inclined WCTU.

In the portrait gallery of Prohibition eccentrics, Carry Nation, still a legend in Kansas (where a small museum commemorates her activities), stands out as the wildest, maddest, most frenzied crusader of all. Although she was nominally a member of the WCTU, hers was a one-woman war, and she was determined to wage it on her own terms.

Born Carry Moore in 1846, in Garrard City, Kentucky — a town famous for its revivalist meetings — she became a rebel and a misfit while still a child. She has been dismissed as a freak, her detractors noting her own family's insanity. Her crusade against liquor, sex, and tobacco accurately reflected the tragic circumstances of her own disturbed emotional life. So unbalanced and out of control was she that in other circumstances, like some members of her mother's family, she might well have been confined to a mental institution. Her own mother, committed to a psychiatric hospital in old age, believed she was Queen Victoria, and even had her long-suffering husband build her a gilded royal carriage, from which she airily waved a white-gloved hand at bemused slaves on her husband's near-bankrupt Kentucky plantation.

A born rebel, Carry Nation was rejected by her eccentric mother, spending most of her time with blacks and slaves, and this closeness with them would remain with her all of her life. She became a firm believer in slave folklore, with special emphasis on clairvoyance and ghosts. Her first vision — of her grandmother — occurred at the age of eight. Subsequently, as she noted in "The Use and Need of the Life of Carry Nation," a largely incoherent record of her life, she frequently conversed with Jesus Christ and claimed her powers as a rainmaker had ended many a local drought.

The Civil War ruined the Moore family, turning them into wandering refugees who eventually settled in Cass County, near Kansas City. There, Carry, now a towering but plain and excessively bony 19-year-old — subject to fits, convulsions, and bouts of manic depression — fell in love with a handsome young doctor, Charles Gloyd, who married her in 1867 after a whirlwind courtship. Gloyd, she found out only on her wedding day, was an alcoholic. After the birth of a handicapped daughter, the couple separated, and Gloyd died shortly thereafter.

It was this first husband — a heavy smoker as well as a heavy drinker, and a Freemason to boot — who fired her rage against liquor, tobacco, and Freemasonry[2], in that order. For the rest of her life she would wage a relentless campaign against all three. As she later wrote:

> I believe that, on the whole, tobacco has done more harm than intoxicating drinks. The tobacco habit is followed by thirst for drink. The face of the smoker has lost the scintillations of intellect and soul. The odor of his person is vile, his blood is poisoned. . . . The tobacco user can never be the father of a healthy child.

Despite her unfortunate marital experience — which left her with such a hatred of sex that she took to stalking terrified courting couples, cursing and lunging at them with her umbrella — she married again. This time she was convinced that "David Nation was the husband God had selected for me." His family name may have had something to do with it. Anticipating the theories of French psychiatrist Jacques Lacan concerning the hidden meaning of words, she attributed considerable significance to the fact that as a married woman she would at last be empowered to "Carry a Nation."

Her second marriage was almost as unsatisfactory, but for other reasons. A henpecked preacher, lawyer, and occasional journalist, Nation was a dismal failure. He farmed cotton for a while, then ran a small hotel. Eventually he established a small law practice in Medicine Lodge, Kansas, where Carry, by now a WCTU member, was a prison visitor. Her husband occasionally officiated as a preacher, but unsuccessfully, for his delivery was poor and his material stereotyped. His halting delivery was further marred by Carry Nation, sitting in the front row of the church, prompting, interrupting, and sometimes bringing his sermon to an end with a peremptory "That will be all for today, David."

Kansas had been an officially dry state since 1880, but the local law was a joke, the state a drinker's paradise, and the local politicians hand in glove with liquor vendors and saloon keepers. In the 1890s, the small town of Medicine Lodge had seven saloons. Periodically, the WCTU picketed them, in the manner of the former "crusaders," and Carry Nation herself composed — and delivered — poems, half songs, and half hymns as the crusaders kneeled and prayed outside.[3]

But the propensity for violence in her huge frame (she was over six feet tall), together with her disturbed temperament, compelled more direct, physical action. Emulating her heroine, Joan of Arc, she claimed to have received a divine message from Jesus, the "big brother" she talked to regularly, and who now commanded her to act. Aged fifty-three, and with only one WCTU follower at her side, she burst into a Medicine Lodge drugstore illegally selling liquor, and, with a sledgehammer, smashed a keg of whiskey to smithereens, accompanying her action with a mixture of invective and appeals to the Lord. Understandably, no one dared confront her formidable, flailing rage.

It was the beginning of a whirlwind war: loading up a buggy with hammers and rocks, she drove to nearby Kiowa, another wide-open town, storming three saloons in a row in sudden hit-and-run raids. When she was through, Dobson's Saloon, its largest, most famous establishment, was completely wrecked, littered with splintered furniture, broken bottles, and shattered kegs. She lobbed billiard balls into plate glass windows and expensive mirrors with devastating effect. The bartenders and clientele were mesmerized, powerless to react.

Back in Medicine Lodge, she bought a large hatchet — an instrument of destruction that was to become her emblem, and enrich the American vocabulary with the word *hatchetization*. Her message was now painfully direct: "Smash! Smash! For Jesus' sake, smash!"

In a series of raids all over Kansas, she continued the good work, leaving in her wake wrecked cherrywood bars, smashed plate glass windows, and slashed, defaced paintings — "hatchetizing" kegs of rum and whiskey and reducing heavy barroom furniture to firewood. Her raids were so sudden, her violence so frightening, that few dared face her directly.

Local authorities were in a quandary: though she was inflicting huge losses on saloon keepers, the saloons (or "joints") were, after all, unauthorized. She was, admittedly illegally, destroying valuable property, but the property was part and parcel of an illicit activity. Consequently, she seldom spent more than one night in jail, and reveled in the publicity — posing, kneeling in her cell, conversing with Jesus, and clasping a Bible as press photographers crowded around her. The jailers became her friends, for she was also capable of considerable charm.

Kansas was soon too small for her. Soon she was showing up, always without warning, all over America, wrecking saloons in St. Louis, Cincinnati (where she refrained from hatchetization; the joints, she claimed, simply too numerous), Philadelphia, and New York. She became, overnight, a media star. Songs were written about her, and saloon keepers, dreading her hit-and-run tactics, securely padlocked their establishments until she was known to have left town.

At intervals, back in Kansas, she published "The Smasher's Mail," a wildly intemperate news-sheet full of invective against President McKinley and all other drinkers, smokers, and Freemasons. After McKinley's murder, she even wrote a disjointed editorial reviling both McKinley and his anarchist assassin. A series of lucrative lecture appearances had to be canceled because her audiences turned against her for condoning the President's murder. But she continued to raise funds, selling autographed postcards of herself by mail, as well as miniature hatchets.

Her outrageous conduct caused the WCTU, which had earlier provided her with legal and financial assistance, to keep her, increasingly, at arm's length. In the end, when her money ran out, and the media finally lost interest in her, she no longer destroyed *real* saloons but reenacted her raids on stage, reciting her poems and spouting her rage. In one play specially written for her, she "hatchetized" a bar, breaking 29 bottles.

An unscrupulous agent, who drank but concealed the fact from her, booked her for a series of appearances in England. The visit was not a success. Her lectures were ill-attended, and when she attempted to "hatchetize" some pubs, she was promptly fined. She was unaware that she had become a figure of fun — a female Professor Unrath out of Josef Von Sternberg's film classic *The Blue Angel*. After a final mental breakdown, she died in a mental institution, aged 65. As newspapers later gleefully recorded, Prohibition agents carried out a raid on a huge still that bootleggers had installed on what had once been Carry Nation's family farm.

4

THE LINEUP

Carry Nation and the Women's War had revealed the power, but also the limits, of individual emotional fervor where the war against liquor was concerned. As America slowly recovered from the physical and moral wounds of the Civil War, the lines of a new, more protracted war were slowly being drawn up. In the Reconstruction era, there was less room for individual eccentrics: society was becoming more organized, more complicated, and vested interests, on both sides, more formidable. Both the Prohibition activists and their bitterest enemies, the brewers and distillers, became increasingly institutionalized, increasingly manipulative.

The Prohibitionists' object now was not so much public opinion as the fluctuating mass of constantly wavering, opportunistic or blatantly corrupt politicians. It would be unfair to dismiss all of them as puppets in the hands of powerful vested interests. But the stakes were high, the temptations often irresistible. Most surprising of all, in retrospect, was the intensity of the battle: although Temperance issues became important in Europe, they never affected the political mainstream, except, briefly, perhaps, in Scotland and Scandinavia. In America, from 1810 on, Prohibition became a hugely important political issue, and would remain so for the next 130 years.

Prohibition illuminated the fundamental differences in political agendas on opposite sides of the Atlantic. To Europeans, the American obsession with Prohibition was — and remains — difficult to understand. European issues were very different. The failed Revolutions of 1848, the Paris Commune of 1871, the violent anarchist movements, the Marxist-Leninist explosion and the spread of communism, and the rise of fascism in the 1920s and 1930s: these were the seminal issues of the 1810–1933 period. Ironically, even America's most militant labor unions, which took their ideological cue from European events, found themselves caught up in the Prohibition dispute. At first, the only well-organized Prohibition lobby was Frances E. Willard's WCTU. Its impact, on as yet unenfranchised American women, and on all children going to Sunday schools, was huge. But the very cloistered, housewifely constraints imposed on them compelled the WCTU to strike out in many different directions. With American women enthusiastically embracing every worthy cause, from prison reform to adult education for growing numbers of foreign-born illiterates, the WCTU was compelled to extend its activities, inevitably diluting its strength with the pursuit of too many good causes. Its Department of Social Purity campaigned against prostitution and the white slave trade; the Department for the Suppression of Social Evil was intent on proving that alcohol was the cause of all major crime; and the Department of Unfermented Wine lobbied for the use of the unfermented grape in church services. The name Department for Inducing Corporations to Require Total Abstinence on Their Employees speaks for itself.

The WCTU was predominantly middle class. Its members were largely the wives of doctors, lawyers, merchants, and wealthy farmers. They wanted to better the working class economically, socially, and morally — even against its wish and inclination. They had plans (which, predictably, failed) to replace the hated saloon by the innocuous coffeehouse — a typically paternalistic, middle-class ambition that showed how out of touch they were with the working class.

There *were* a few working-class Prohibitionists, in a handful of trade unions, but they were mostly left-wingers who wanted to educate the workers politically and found that the lure of the saloon interfered with their indoctrination attempts. The International Workers of the World (IWW) did later claim that "the capitalists use saloons to tranquilize and humiliate the proletariate," but working-class Americans showed no signs that they were averse to such humiliation.[1]

Almost as worthy a cause, to WCTU members, as Prohibition was women's suffrage, and this proved a double-edged, confusing issue, for not all Prohibitionists were in favor of the vote for women, and anti-Prohibitionists were overwhelmingly against it. The Women's War triggered a fundamental change in attitudes. While it was at its height, an anonymous suffragist wrote in a letter to the New York *Herald Tribune,* which published it in 1874:

> To deny her the use of that most efficient weapon, a vote, and then urge her into contest with the liquor trade is like saying that women cannot use artillery . . . but ought to form the advance in an attack on an army well drilled in their use, sending them forward with broadswords, javelins and other implements of medieval warfare.

Much more averse to publicity than the WCTU, another lobby, established at the start of the Civil War, became increasingly active in the Reconstruction period. Understandably shocked by what they regarded as discriminatory taxes in 1862, the brewers formed the United States Brewers Association to ensure that they would never be taken by surprise again. Their dues (from $25 to $1,000, according to their size) enabled them to use considerable slush funds on cooperative politicians and consumers alike.

The most vocal opponents of Prohibition were the "new Americans." From 1840 onward, millions of Germans, Irish, and Italians entered the country, bringing their wine-, whiskey-, and beer-drinking culture with them, fueling a brewers', distillers', and winemakers' boom. At the Brewers Association's first meeting in 1862, many of its members spoke in German — the only language in which they were fluent. In increasingly expensive lobbying and newspaper campaigns, they quickly focused on the issue of women's suffrage: the brewers and distillers knew that women were the Prohibitionists' chief allies and saw the WCTU as its most formidable foe. The repeated failures of many state legislatures to bring about women's suffrage must be laid at their door. Wherever state suffrage amendments were introduced, they went into action. In Oregon in 1853, for instance, Arthur Denny, a leading Prohibitionist, introduced legislation to give the vote to (white) women. He failed by one vote. Some thirty years later, the Supreme Court of Washington State, invoking "technicalities," declared the newly passed women's suffrage law invalid. Insiders knew that the behind-the-scenes artisan of this decision was Tacoma's Harry Morgan — gambler, local political boss, and saloon supporter — an early precursor of the "mobster generation" of the 1920s and 1930s.

The Prohibition drive was mixed. Among its advocates were both "liberals" — with a left-wing political agenda that included women's suffrage, abolitionism, labor law, and other reforms, and trade unionism — and members at the opposite end of the political spectrum. These were the increasingly vocal opponents of unrestricted immigration and railroad and farm support grants; in other words, conservative (at that time) America's rural or small-town not-so-silent majority.

Because both Democratic and Republican politicians demonstrated their shifty venality, purists in both parties decided salvation lay elsewhere. The Prohibition party, established in 1869, and active in some twenty states, was by no means confined to cranks and religious fanatics. Among its members were distinguished liberals of all types, including partisans of women's franchise and of prison reform. But despite considerable media interest, and its later role as the Prohibition issue gathered momentum, this "third party" never changed American voting patterns significantly. Its first presidential nominee, James Black — a distinguished former preacher who had in earlier days been a Democrat and then a Republican, running for the presidency against Ulysses S. Grant in 1872 — made an abysmally poor showing in the election: the brewers, distillers, and saloon keepers all brought out the vote for the popular general, who was also a notorious drunkard. And though Grant's successor, Rutherford B. Hayes, was a Temperance sympathizer with a WCTU activist wife (a wit quipped that at White House state dinners, water flowed like champagne), the brewers' lobbying power made Prohibition not only unlikely but unthinkable. If Prohibition was — as the excesses of the nineteenth-century preachers showed — a confused, inchoate search for material as well as spiritual order in American life, the massive influx first of beer-drinking

Germans, then of beer- and whiskey-swilling Irish, and finally of wine-drinking Italians made it at the turn of the century look like a hopeless, long-lost cause.

But the Prohibition movement would soon develop a new, and formidable, weapon. The broad-based Anti-Saloon League (ASL), established in 1893, was dependent neither on women (though it welcomed their participation) nor on political parties. Although its board of directors consisted of leading representatives of the Protestant Church, which raised considerable funds for the ASL, church control was nominal. Decision-making was in the hands of a new breed of Americans — business-oriented, sophisticated, and almost self-consciously "modern." Religious fanatics were kept at arm's length.

The ASL's slow but inexorable Prohibition campaign, one of the most exemplary lobbying feats the world has ever seen, was enormously helped by the turn-of-the-century industrial revolution boom and its attendant communications revolution, bringing railroads to the remotest parts of the Northwest, then street-cars and electricity to the cities. With this revolutionary urban change came the predatory monopolies, and increasingly profit-oriented manufacturers. These in turn gave new strength to all those campaigning against child-labor abuses and for shorter working hours. The new breed of do-gooders also included socially conscious drys, intent on preserving both the physical and moral health of workers.

The "whiskey tents" of railroad workers; the rapid, nationwide industrial growth, especially in "new" territories, such as the Northwest, that had earlier been remote, rural settlements; and the influx of new Americans all contributed to a climate of fear caused by a sharp increase in crime of all types. America became increasingly aware in the nineteenth century of the havoc brought about by social and economic change: delinquency, poverty, prostitution, and excessive political corruption. It had long been a cliché that "liquor releases the brute nature in man." It was only too easy for the new generation of Prohibitionist activists to argue that liquor provoked and exacerbated all of these scourges. In their eagerness to put an end to them, the drys demonized not only all drinkers but all saloons that dispensed liquor.

In the pre-Prohibition era, there was a saloon for every three hundred Americans, but by no means all of them corresponded to the grim picture painted by the ASL and the WCTU. Jack London described the saloon as "a terribly wonderful place where life was different." Coming from an underprivileged background himself, and a born outsider, he saw it as a place "where men come together to exchange ideas, to laugh and boast and dare, to relax, to forget the dull toil of tiresome nights and days." More prosaically, a Washington State committee of prominent citizens in the 1890s wrote that the saloon "met the thirst for fellowship, or amusement and recreation."

In the nineteenth and early twentieth centuries, the saloon was not only the one place working-class men (the presence of women was not encouraged) got together and socialized, but it also served as their only available employment agency and club. There were newspapers, mailboxes, pencils, paper, bulletin boards advertising jobs, card tables, and sometimes bowling alleys and billiard tables. The saloons also served the much decried "free lunch," which although invariably salty to stimulate thirst was often of reasonable quality. Not all saloon keepers were ogres, throwing out those who cost more in food than they paid back in drink. And although prostitutes used some saloons to ply their trade, most saloons did not countenance their presence, and on weekends perfectly innocent social gatherings involving singing, dancing, and recitations took place. In short, the saloon was, except for the free lunch, not much different from the average English pub — except that until local "dry" restrictions started taking their toll, saloons were open seven days a week, twenty-four hours a day. This was because the saloon keepers were under considerable pressure from the brewery owners, eager to maximize their profits and recuperate their loans. Saloon keepers were also heavily taxed: just before Prohibition was introduced, they paid a yearly $1,000 fee.

The war for Prohibition was also a struggle for racial purity.

In the North-West, local legislators knew they were moving from a frontier to an industrial society, with the construction of the Pacific Highway, the growth of the railroads. They were determined that the laborers should not be a prey to the "hell on wheels" that accompanied the workers elsewhere. . . . the feeling was strong that workers must be protected from the saloon keepers.[2]

William Newell, Governor of Washington Territory (it only became a state in 1889) denounced "the fearful destruction of property

and happiness which [liquor] occasions in its march of desola-
tion, disease and death. . . . The vice, degeneration and crime which
it engenders . . . with no redeeming influence for the good, may well
cause it to be a subject of the greatest solicitude to our race." One of
the many nineteenth-century Temperance movements that prospered
from the Civil War days, the International Order of the Grand Templars,
also tirelessly equated Prohibition with family morality. Its message,
published in the Seattle *Mirror*,[3] was also a call to war: "The temperance war! It is coming! It is here! The issue involves the sanctity
of the home, the chastity of youth, the moral and political purity of
voters."

Class lines were increasingly drawn up. In 1890, an editorial in a
Prohibitionist paper asked: "Where else shall we look but to the farmer
to counteract the venality and corruption of the slums of our cities'
population, that seems to be so rapidly increasing by the aggregation
of alien voters, anarchists and saloon influences?" It was all part of
that constantly recurring element in American social and political life:
the "politics of virtue." But as various states, under pressure from increasingly assertive dry groups and opportunistic politicians, began to
introduce their own local laws, the battle remained fairly even-handed.

In the small town of Everett, in Washington State, where there
were forty saloons, the churches energetically campaigned for local prohibition in a 1910 election, though not all religious groups were dry.
Some Catholics, Lutherans, and Jews were in favor of "good" saloons,
and raised the issue of personal liberty and choice. The local *Labor
Journal*, a militant unionist newspaper, argued that the dramatically
lower life expectancy of working men (60 percent that of the rich) was
due not to drink but to the disastrous consequences of low wages and
working conditions generally. "Wets and drys boycotted each other's
businesses. There were street brawls, a frenzy of meetings, parades,
prayers."[4] In the event, Everett voted dry, but a subsequent state-level
vote rejected Prohibition entirely.

Thanks to men such as Newell, the Alcohol Education Act (AEA),
passed in Seattle in 1885–86, taught the evils of drink as a mandatory course in all schools. "The AEA was the compost heap that
brought the Volstead Act into being after three generations of indoctrination." But, as Norman Clark points out, "unlike the Indians, the
manual laborers who built the railroads had a common culture and

potential political clout." The short-lived Progressive party — which included among its "populists" beer-drinking first-generation German immigrants, whiskey-drinking Irish Catholics, and wine-drinking Italians — was powerful enough as the nineteenth century came to an end to equate Prohibitionists with cranks.

It was the Anti-Saloon League's sophisticated understanding of the confused, often contradictory, nature both of Prohibitionist activists and of the anti-Prohibitionist forces arrayed against them that made the ASL into the driving force that would eventually lead to the passing of the Volstead Act. Between 1893 and 1918, a handful of its leaders would bring about nothing less than a social, moral, and political revolution.

Whereas moral propagandists such as Ernest H. Cherrington brought the Prohibition message to the masses, it was Wayne Wheeler — the ASL's behind-the-scenes political manipulator ("controlling six Congresses, dictating to two Presidents" and "becoming the most masterful and powerful single individual in the United States")[5] — who, more than any other Prohibitionist activist, engineered the political change.

By all accounts, including those of his subordinates and fellow ASL executives, Wheeler was in many ways a deeply flawed, utterly ruthless manipulator of singularly limited vision. His conversion to Prohibition was not religious in origin, nor did he come from an alcoholic family. His later reminiscences about the evils of drink are curiously undramatic, though he did his best to sensationalize them: in one instance, he was forced to listen to the divagations of an " 'Old Soak' . . . acting out the story of *Ten Nights in a Bar Room* while mother and we children gasped in alarm. . . . My dreams were long colored by that scene." On another occasion, a farm laborer "stuck the tine of his fork into my bare leg while I was packing down the hay he pitched on the wagon. He had been drinking but did not believe his condition required any excuse." Wheeler's career suggests that he chose to make his mark as a Prohibitionist because he realized that with his natural talent for manipulation and intrigue this was the surest means of acquiring the behind-the-scenes power he craved.

His credentials were impeccable. The fourth of nine children of an Ohioan cattle dealer and farmer, young Wayne displayed from childhood onward the entrepreneurial skills so admired in nineteenth-century puritan society. As a schoolboy, he earned pocket money operating a sausage-making machine in a local butcher's shop. No sooner did he move to Oberlin College than he took a job as a dormitory janitor. "Wherever he saw a remunerative position open, he entered the gap," whether this meant waiting on tables, deputizing for the college chaplain, publishing scorecards, or dealing in books, rugs, or blackboard-desks. With this background and his trading skills, he might well have joined the ranks of the robber barons who were already changing the face of America.

But Wheeler also fancied himself a poet, orator, and debater, and it was this need to thrust himself into the limelight that first attracted him to the Prohibitionist cause. Oberlin college had been, since its early establishment as Oberlin Collegiate Institute in 1832, at the forefront of the abolitionist battle — and abolitionists were also, overwhelmingly, Prohibitionists. This deeply Calvinist college was a nurturing-ground for fledgling missionaries, and Wheeler quickly started mining a rich seam. In debates at religious meetings he began speaking out on the plight of the African Negro — whose wretchedness, at least according to American missionaries there, was not due to colonial abuses (about which Wheeler was curiously silent) but to overindulgence in alcohol.

As a freshman, Wheeler's speech to the college debating society, "Rum on the Congo," made considerable impact, and has been preserved. Based on letters to a fellow student of a missionary father, it was a typical example of the hyperbole that passed for eloquence at the time (1890).

Today, the eyes of the Christian world are turned to the "Free State" of the Congo. Its present condition and its future is the burden of every philanthropist's soul!

But let us for a moment turn to Germany. The representatives of the fourteen leading powers of the world have met in Berlin. They are considering the future relations of the Congo with the outside world.

The earnest petition to keep rum from the savages is scarcely noticed. The rum dealer who represents Germany urges absolute free commerce on the Congo. Holland heartily approves and in spite of the slight objection of the U.S. and England, the resolution is carried. Their object is accomplished. Henceforth the Congo will be prey to the ravenous trader! . . . Its only purpose is to increase commerce, no matter at what expense, even of innocent life.

Wheeler went on to paint an idyllic picture of the Congo "before the liquor traffic was legalized," with lucrative trade in ivory palm oil and coffee. "A commerce was fast developing which might have been the richest in the world, had it not been for the iniquitous rum dealer." Richest for whom? Wheeler did not pursue this line of thought. Given the brutal aspects of Belgian rule in the Congo, later stigmatized obliquely by Joseph Conrad in *Heart of Darkness* and more openly by André Gide, the beneficiaries would certainly not have been the native Congolese.

Be this as it may, the Congo was paradise no longer, for "The stupefying climate of the Congo renders men an easy prey to this evil of drink. . . . The Caffirs and the Hottentots have been reduced by this poison, until they are no longer distinct tribes." Wheeler cited missionary reports of

> four hundred blacks lying drunk in the streets. . . . Thirty girls under sixteen lay drunk, even parts of their clothing bartered for drink. . . . Germany and America export eight million gallons of rum to the Congo yearly, with the result that the Negro has degenerated morally and mentally. . . . remember as you go next Sunday morn to church that the Congo native, his wife and children lie in their hovels drunk.

There were no references to heavy-drinking Belgian colonial settlers.

When the ASL turned to Oberlin College to recruit a full-time worker to help bring about "an era of clear thinking and clean living," Wheeler was an obvious choice. At first, he demurred: the pay was low, and he had "another business proposition." But the ASL's Ohio League was headed by the Reverend Howard Hyde Russell, himself an Oberlin alumnus and a powerful, persuasive preacher. "When I pointed out to him," Russell later wrote, "that a man to fill the other position could be much more easily found than one for this complex and strenuous service, he agreed to treat the matter carefully and prayerfully. We bowed together — Oberlin's training had made it easy for us to do this — and we asked God to be the guide as to the duty involved and to inspire the right conclusion."

Russell got his way. Wheeler, however, committed himself to ASL work for "one year only." His duties as a full-time "dry worker" were twofold: as a church preacher on Sundays (he was already a regular speaker, his passionate delivery much appreciated by congregations of all types) and as an "Organizer of legislative districts." The issue was the Haskell Local Option Bill, allowing counties to become dry if a majority of voters so decided. There had been 200,000 dry petitioners in favor of the bill, but only 36 state legislators had voted for it. Whether the idea came from Wheeler or from Russell is not known, but the Ohio ASL took a step that would establish the pattern for Wheeler's later lobbying tactics: it informed the legislators who had voted for the bill that the ASL would throw its weight behind them, and at the same time do its best to discredit the bill's most vocal opponents.

Wheeler was assigned the task of ensuring the political demise of John Locke of London, Madison County, a virulent anti-Prohibitionist who had told the House: "If you want to dig your political grave, vote for the Haskell [dry] bill." Locke was a candidate for the State Senate, and seemed unbeatable. But Wheeler's tactics proved dazzling. He persuaded the ASL to buy him a bicycle, to give him the required mobility. He then tirelessly lobbied clergymen and leading citizens in the three counties casting their votes in the election. His next step was to persuade a prominent dry Methodist businessman, W. N. Jones, to stand against Locke, becoming, in effect, his campaign manager. The turning point was Wheeler's use of volunteers to bring the voters to the polling booths. Jones was elected, and offered to pay Wheeler a substantial fee for his invaluable services. Wheeler refused. The League, he said, was not out to make money but to "make it safe for men to vote right."

He had found his vocation, as a brilliant, behind-the-scenes operator. There was no further talk of leaving to go into a more profitable business. Instead, Wheeler realized that the ASL badly needed a fully trained lawyer in its ranks. Studying in his spare time, he graduated from the Western Reserve University in Cleveland in 1898 and became the ASL's first full-time attorney. In his defense of local liquor laws (dry counties had made their appearance all over Ohio) he appeared in over 3,000 cases — later claiming that he won all but ten of them.

Wheeler remained poorly paid. The ASL was not yet the recipient of huge endowments, and even had difficulty raising enough money to pay Wheeler's minimal expenses. In 1901, he married Ella Bell Candy, the daughter of a leading Columbus Prohibitionist, and they soon had three sons, but his financial prospects remained grim. The ASL did not pay enough to live on, and he depended on the generosity of his wealthy father-in-law.

He continued to hone his talent for manipulation. His language in court, deliberately intemperate, infuriated those judges unsympathetic to the cause, and Wheeler in turn pursued a ceaseless campaign against those he believed to be on the side of the wets. He was sensitive to any type of anti-ASL behavior, to the point of paranoia. He turned against the mayor of Cleveland for allowing a National Retail Liquor Dealers' convention to be held there, and supported his opponent, John H. Farley, for reelection despite the fact that Farley owned two saloons. "Owning a saloon doesn't have anything to do with his official actions," Wheeler told the press with a straight face. But political expediency mattered to him more than personal convictions: His endorsement of "personal wets" who were "politically dry" (because they knew the dry issue would get them votes) was criticized in some ASL circles, as was his habit of gaining the apparent friendship of known wets solely for tactical reasons.

Wheeler claimed, with reason, that such tactics worked. From his growing web of contacts, including staunch opponents of the ASL, he was obtaining valuable information about *their* tactics. He was not the only ASL worker to use such techniques. William ("Pussyfoot") E. Johnson became an even more astute political manipulator for the ASL, specializing in "publicity and underground activities" in several states, infiltrating wet lobbies of brewers and distillers, later reaping his reward as a leading executive of the World League Against Alcoholism.

But no other ASL official achieved national prominence comparable to Wheeler's, though he was never the official leader of the ASL. Despite his meteoric rise, becoming in the space of a few years its senior attorney as well as its Ohio superintendent, he always preferred working behind the scenes, an incomparable wheeler-dealer.

In Ohio, in his early days with the ASL, he used the methods that would later prove so effective in Washington. With a complete disregard for partisan labels, the ASL systematically supported the candidate who expressed a willingness to endorse dry policies — even if it was well known that he was both a hypocrite and a toper. The ASL's refusal to enter into a political alliance with either party turned out to be one of its key assets; it was well aware of the failure of the Prohibition party to make its mark on voters, even those highly sympathetic to the cause. One of the ASL's pamphlets was its "Church in Action Against the Saloon," a question-and-answer document modeled on the catechism and devised for the guidance of ASL instructors addressing schools and meetings. One of its questions was: "May the League, at any time, be identified with any one political party for the accomplishment of its purpose?" The answer was: "No. The League is under solemn promise not to form affiliations with any political party, nor to place in nomination a ticket of its own."

This crucial ideological plank was bitterly opposed by William Jennings Bryan, the perennial Democratic presidential candidate, later President Woodrow Wilson's Secretary of State, a fanatical dry — and, in his public utterances, an unspeakably boring, flatulent windbag, who early on in his political career had made the fatal mistake of arguing that the Democratic party should become the official dry party.

Myron T. Herrick, governor of Ohio, was among the prominent politicians whose careers Wheeler destroyed virtually single-handedly. Herrick, the Republican governor of a staunchly Republican state, seemed unbeatable when he ran for reelection. But Wheeler first got the ASL to endorse the Democratic candidate, John M. Pattison, from Cincinnati, a strict churchman and dry. "We had a hard job making the people see that they were not giving up their religion when they voted Democratic," Wheeler said later.[6] "That was especially true in the rural sections, where they always voted a straight Republican ticket. I used to tell them that Lincoln wasn't running that year." Pattison won. Herrick did, subsequently, reap his reward for lifelong service to the Republican party: he was appointed U.S. ambassador in Paris, and was on hand to greet Lindbergh after his historic flight across the Atlantic (1927). Prohibition was in full swing by this time, and Wheeler wondered what Herrick and Lindbergh, a staunch Prohibitionist, had had to say to each other in private.

Soon, under Wheeler's effective direction, Ohio became — long before Prohibition — one of the driest states in the Union. As he proudly noted in 1908, 57 of its counties had gone dry under County Local Option laws. Various other dry measures instituted since he had begun working full-time for the ASL affected most of the other counties as well, so that by 1908, 60 percent of Ohio's population, and 85 percent of its territory, was under "dry legislation," though its large towns, especially Cincinnati, remained almost aggressively wet. The Ohio legislators, for all their "prohibition correctness," were well aware of the revenues liquor brought into the state coffers. Saloon licenses, introduced in 1896, first cost $350 a year, then — in 1906 — $1,000. In 1908, there were 7,050 saloons in Ohio, and 690 more opened in 1911. The ASL's position was that licensing saloons was immoral, but this challenge failed, and a licensing law gained a substantial majority. Wheeler's rearguard action was to make life more difficult for saloon keepers by prohibiting saloon operations within 300 feet of a school-house, forbidding "loitering by minors" there, compelling Sunday closings, and denying licenses to noncitizens and those of insufficiently good "moral conduct."

Wheeler was helped, indirectly, by the blatant political immorality of the times. License commissioners in Ohio and elsewhere were known to take bribes and favor friendly candidates, and many were in league with the major breweries, which in most cases were the saloons' real owners (they also maintained close relations with owners of the technically illegal speakeasies). In the course of his work, Wheeler — who in middle age bore a striking resemblance to France's elder statesman, the late Antoine Pinay — had met most of the influential figures in the business world. John D. Rockefeller, after hearing him preach, presented him with a paper vest against the cold — and $5,000 for the ASL, the first of many contributions. He was becoming an acknowledged behind-the-scenes political power in Ohio, but now he had further ambitions. Ohio was at the forefront of the war on liquor, and, in many respects, a microcosm of still overwhelmingly rural America. Wheeler was sufficiently sensitive to the public mood to know that nationwide Prohibition was becoming a distinct possibility. As a first step, he persuaded the ASL to announce that statewide Prohibition was "imminent and inevitable," introducing for the first time the notion of "a national constitutional amendment prohibiting the manufacture and sale of intoxicating liquors for beverage purposes" in the ASL's organ *The American Patriot*.

In 1913, the ASL's National Board of Trustees met in Columbus to celebrate their Jubilee Convention. Wheeler, in the wings as usual, let J. Frank Hanly, a former Governor of Indiana, make the actual call for national Prohibition, to be brought about by constitutional amendment. "For a moment there was silence, deep and tense," Wheeler recalled. "Then the convention cut loose. With a roar as wild as the raging storm outside it jumped to its feet and yelled approval. The first shot in the Eighteenth Amendment had been fired." The proposal was unanimously carried, and on December 10, 1913, a 1,000-member ASL delegation met in Washington on the steps of the Capitol, demonstrating its power and nationwide impact.

About this time, the drys were also provided with further "scientific" evidence — this time from Europe — of the ill effects of alcohol, even taken in small quantities. August Forel, a noted Swiss brain specialist, had investigated its effect on mental processes, and professed they were terrifying. So too did Emil Kraeplin, a German psychiatrist. This boosted the campaign for sobriety that was a growing feature in factories. As Norman Clark wrote, "probably even more than religion, science had prepared the public mind for complete prohibition." Ever since he began making automobiles, Henry Ford had insisted that his workers be teetotalers, and used a private police force to spy on them; anyone caught buying hard liquor in a store a second time was fired.

Throughout his subsequent dry campaign, Wheeler had systematically favored the rural dry vote. "God made the country, but man made the town" was his *leitmotif,* and, as his personal secretary noted, he viewed the cities as "un-American, lawless and wet," reserving special scorn for the "Irish, the continentals with their beer and wine, and the guzzling wet Democrats in the North and East."[7]

Even in Ohio, a model for other states, the dry vote, though effective (for the towns were underrepresented), was always a minority. He himself noted that there were only 400,000 dry voters out of a total Ohio voting population of 1,250,000. The success of ASL tactics depended to a large extent on overrepresentation in the rural areas and underrepresentation in the towns.

This led the Ohio ASL to gravely miscalculate its chances. In 1914, constitutional amendments to declare the whole of Ohio dry were defeated, and many previously dry counties returned to their wet state.

The 1914 congressional elections did, however, provide the ASL with a heaven-sent opportunity to bring the Prohibition issue to the public. In the *New York Times,*[8] Wheeler reminisced that it "mobilized 50,000 trained speakers, volunteers and regulars directing their fire

upon the wets in every village, town, city, county and state." Its literature, he wrote, "found its way to every spot in the United States. . . .
While we were fighting back in the districts, we were also bombarding
the House and Senate in Washington. . . . We kept the field workers
advised of the attitude of every individual member of Congress and
suggested ways to the local workers of winning converts."

The result, Wheeler noted, was a triumph "beyond our hopes."
The ASL knew it lacked — for the time being, at least — the votes to
push for a constitutional amendment that would make Prohibition a
reality nationwide. But it was soon to use another formidable weapon.
In March of 1917, President Woodrow Wilson called the Sixty-fifth
Congress (elected in 1916) into special session to declare war on Germany. America's entry into the war would provide a new weapon —
patriotism — to undermine the anti-Prohibitionist campaign carried
out by the saloon, liquor, and brewery vested interests.

At first the anti-Prohibitionists did not realize how effective the
jingoist campaign of the ASL would be. When they did retaliate, theirs
was a costly, bumbling, piecemeal, ineffective campaign. The brewers
and the hard liquor interests never did manage to coordinate their
efforts, for in the last resort the brewers were ready to abandon the
distillers to their fate. The brewers felt that although there was a possible case for banning hard liquor outright, beer — a benign, natural
substance — would never be banned.

The war drastically altered the picture and advanced the dry cause
beyond Wheeler's wildest hopes. After Britain and France went to war
with Germany in 1914, Wheeler, accurately gauging the feelings of his
fellow Americans, was aware that the increasingly anti-German mood,
rapidly amounting to hysteria, would be a godsend to the dry cause.
He would exploit this cynically and crudely, but with enormous effectiveness. As, in state after state, the strength of the dry vote became
increasingly apparent, it was clear to him that the Great War would
administer the final coup de grace to the opponents of Prohibition.

This was also becoming apparent to politicians all over America,
especially the most opportunistic, unscrupulous ones. In 1917, Harry
Micajah Daugherty — later to become attorney general during the
first Prohibition years and one of the most corrupt members of any
American administration — conferred with Warren Harding, then an
Ohio senator, and decided to climb on the Prohibition wagon as a

means of strengthening Republican fortunes in the state. "Prohibition," Daugherty wrote to Harding, "is going to be a movement that has come to stay and it will be joined by the strong men of the party."[9]

In fact, Wheeler's victory was assured the day America itself entered the war (April 6, 1917). In the last resort, it was a misguided form of patriotism, amounting to jingoism, that would ensure the prompt passing of the Eighteenth Amendment.

5

PROHIBITION'S
FIRST VICTIMS

Although many Americans were unaware of it, a massive transformation in the ethnic mix of the United States occurred in the half-century that preceded America's entry into the First World War. Millions of Europeans, taking advantage of its ultraliberal immigration policy, settled in America, changing the country's ways.

To some Americans, steeped in the puritan culture that still centered around the farm, the family, and the church, these newly emerging ethnic patterns were deeply disturbing. As historian Dennis Brogan has noted, in New York a great and increasing part of the population was now composed of recent immigrants, usually indifferent to American issues, "having nothing to lose but their chains and little to sell but their votes."

Arguably, the single most influential group of immigrants — over eight million in the second half of the nineteenth century — came from Germany. Their culture and industriousness put an indelible stamp on the areas they settled into — and transformed American drinking habits.

The Germans had been among the earliest of America's immigrants. Germantown, Pennsylvania (now part of Philadelphia), was founded in 1683. From 1832 onward, the trickle of German immigrants to America turned into a flood. Political unrest in Germany accelerated their departure: socialists and liberals hostile to Metternich's policies began fleeing in large numbers after a brutally suppressed protest movement in 1832; then came the failed revolution of 1848, provoking a further flood of departures, to such an extent that by the time the Civil War broke out there were German-speaking regiments fighting in Lincoln's army. Bismarck's authoritarianism, especially after 1870, led to another influx. Although some of the German immigrants were motivated by the classic hope of a better life, what set them apart from other categories was the large proportion of highly educated, politically sophisticated liberal intellectuals in their midst.

By 1914, they were all over America, concentrating in places where German-Americans had already made good, such as Chicago and Milwaukee, but nowhere was their impact greater than in Cincinnati, which became, in many ways, from the 1850s onward, almost a German city.[1] German-American historian Friedrich Gerstacker described Cincinnati as "the Queen of the West, the Eldorado of the German immigrant." For many years, he wrote, Cincinnati did not even try to assimilate its German immigrants — "instead, they assimilated Cincinnati." In 1820, they had been 5 percent of the population. In 1917, 35 percent of Cincinnati was German, and almost half its inhabitants were German-speaking. German was taught in schools not as a foreign language but as a mother tongue. Many of Cincinnati's inhabitants spoke nothing but German, and found it unnecessary to learn English. There were German orchestras, theater groups, gymnasiums, libraries, credit unions, and trade associations and "Vereine" (associations) of all types. In many Methodist and Lutheran churches, services were in German. In the years 1870–1917, when the German cultural influence was at its peak, there were twenty-seven German newspapers and magazines in the Cincinnati area.

Cincinnati benefited enormously from the German-American presence: they were energetic, industrious, entrepreneurial, and, above all, civic-minded. Cincinnati's red-brick "Theatrum," said to have the finest acoustics in the world, and now the site of the town's opera company, is but one of their still extant landmarks. German-Americans funded hospitals, old people's homes, cultural centers, gymnasiums, and charities of all types. In that successive immigration, waves were triggered not only by poverty and the hope of a better life but by political opposition. The town's rich cultural life reflected the diversity and intellectualism of its German-American element, including teachers, lawyers, artists, soldiers, artisans, and laborers. Tolerance prevailed: there was little or no anti-Semitism in Cincinnati — at least among its German-American element. In 1914–1915, the Mayor of Cincinnati was Frederick S. Spiegel, a Prussian-born Jew.

The German influx after 1832 made America beer-conscious. In Cincinnati especially (where beer consumption was four times the national average), beer drinking was part of the German-American way of life. There was little drunkenness; it was a social phenomenon, part of the cultural scene, on a par with oom-pah-pah brass bands, Strauss music, and choir-singing. Parties, birthdays, and commemorations of all types would have been unthinkable without the true natural tonic, the "teutonic" stein of beer. There were German-Americans all over the city, but part of Cincinnati was so German it was known as "Across the Rhine" — the "Rhine" being the old Florida-Erie Canal, since filled in. "Across the Rhine" had over a hundred cafés, *Bierstuben*, restaurants, and beer gardens with German brass bands and string orchestras. It was famous all over America: in the early 1900s, Cincinnati rivaled Niagara Falls as America's favorite honeymoon destination.

Beer-making was still a relatively small-scale business then, but in the Cincinnati area alone, in the early 1900s, there were as many breweries — all of them German-American owned — as there were German newspapers. All thrived, and all were major contributors to the local German-American League, which supported schools and charities of all kinds. They also funded their own causes. John Caspar Bruckmann had been a carpenter in his native Thuringen before coming to America in 1847, where he worked for a time as a barrel maker before establishing Bruck's, a well-known local brewery. Even as a successful entrepreneur, Bruckmann remained a farmer, growing hops in a field adjoining the Ohio-Erie Canal. On their farm, his wife Maria, herself the daughter of an inn-keeping family in Thuringen, sold homemade beer to tourists on Sundays from their front porch. Kristian Moerlein had been a blacksmith before founding Moerlein's Brewery, soon to become the biggest in Ohio. Some German-Americans also branched out into the hard liquor business: the founder of Jim Beame whiskey was Jacob Boehm.

With its beer-drinking German-Americans and its profusion of brewers on one hand, and its Prohibitionist militants on the other, Ohio became a microcosm of America as a whole: nowhere was the struggle for and against Prohibition more dramatic, and nowhere would the consequences be more tragic. Until 1914, Cincinnati's inhabitants had been a perfect illustration of melting pot virtues: though "Across the Rhine" was almost all German, there were other parts of the town in which German-Americans and Irish-Americans lived cheek-by-jowl, and if mixed marriages were rare and frowned on by both communities, altercations were even rarer. The First World War — and the growing pressures of the Prohibitionists — put an end to this halcyon period of prosperity, mutual esteem, and tolerance.

The German-American community cannot be entirely absolved from blame for what happened from 1914 onward. For all its admirable civic-mindedness, it was also deeply imbued with the notion that German cultural traditions had to be carefully preserved, that "language saves faith," and its leaders sometimes went too far, provoking charges of nationalism. Some of the decisions of the Ohio section of the German-American League, or Stadtsverband — such as choosing the twenty-fifth anniversary of the Battle of Sedan (1871) to commemorate Germany Day in 1896 — were injudicious, to say the least. It was a prickly, conservative community, highly conscious of what it regarded as particular German virtues — thrift, hard work, and godliness. It voted heavily Republican. From the moment Britain and France went to war against Germany, it also became a beleaguered minority group, preoccupied by the fate of its former compatriots (German-Americans from Cincinnati raised over $140,000 in 1914–1915 for German war victims), its loyalties to the homeland reinforced or resurrected. Early German victories were openly celebrated, both in private homes and in the columns of Cincinnati's German-language papers, the *Volksblatt* and *Freie Presse*. Ohio's German-language press constantly berated the "pro-English bias" of the *New York Times* and the Cincinnati *Times-Star* published by Charles P. Taft, a member of Ohio's most prominent family (and son of President Taft) and called for more "objective" reporting of the war. There were huge "peace demonstrations" in August of 1914 attended by Cincinnati's mayor,

Frederick Spiegel. Although he did not speak at these meetings, he had no quarrel with the *Cincinnati Enquirer*'s description of him as a "loyal German" or with gatherings of this type [the language used, of course, was German, and often ended with the singing of "Die Wacht am Rhein" ("The Watch on the Rhine") to the fury of Cincinnatians of English descent]. "A war with Germany," *Volksblatt* wrote in 1916, would be "a crime against civilization and be condemned by all fair-minded people in America." So sure were its readers of an eventual German victory that the newspaper suggested a debate on the spoils of war, also proposing both the formation of a corps of German-American volunteers to fight alongside Germany and the conquest of Canada.

Needless to say, this gave not only the xenophobic "nativists" but the drys ample anti-German ammunition. The ASL by 1914 had a hugely powerful public relations operation going (with millions of brochures distributed all over America every week), and Wheeler and his assistants lost no time reminding Americans that the brewing interests were almost all in German hands, and that at some brewers' meetings the very language used was German.

The malaise worsened with the increasing likelihood of American entry into the war. Overwhelmingly, the German-American community voted against Woodrow Wilson in the 1916 presidential election, and in turn the newly elected president stigmatized "hyphenism" — an oblique way of attacking German-Americans for their disloyalty. The German-Americans, overwhelmingly anti-Prohibitionist (though some German Methodist churches were not), also entered the fray. As early as 1914, Judge John Schwaab, president of the Ohio section of the German-American Alliance (Stadtsverband), had expressed the feelings of his community with rage bordering on paranoia: "The drink question," he thundered, "is forced upon us by the same hypocritical puritans as over there (i.e., in Europe) are endeavoring to exterminate the German nation." He was ready to fight the ASL "and the equally obnoxious advocates of female suffrage."

To their credit, when America actually entered the war (April 6, 1917) German-Americans, with very few exceptions, rallied behind the flag (Schwaab pledged his loyalty to Wilson), though there were demands (not confined to German-Americans) that conscription and the deployment of troops overseas should be determined by referendum. "Henceforth all discussion of the war and its justification must stop," said *Christliche Apologete,* the organ of the German Methodist Church in America. "Every American owes his government loyalty and obedience." A few irrepressibly vocal German-Americans who had not yet taken out U.S. citizenship returned to Germany (including the conductor of Cincinnati's symphonic orchestra); others were interned.

In Cincinnati itself, immediately after America's 1917 entry into the war, the statue of Germania, with a few minor alterations, became the statue of Columbia; Bismarck Street became Montreal Street; Frankfurt Avenue, Connecticut Avenue; Schumann Street, Meredith Street; and, significantly, German Street was changed to English Street. German was banned from schools ("Dropped! Hun language barred!" headlined the *Cincinnati Enquirer* on December 12, 1918), and books considered pro-German were removed from libraries. Vicious anti-German rumors — such as the canard that German-American meat-packing companies were deliberately putting ground glass in their hamburger — were current. The German-American Alliance was dissolved by Congress.

The German-American brewers had naively believed that even if the Prohibitionists succeeded in banning hard liquor, they themselves would remain in business. As state after state passed dry legislation, they realized they had been overly optimistic and belatedly increased their lobbying in Washington. Wheeler was quick to ride the wave of anti-German hysteria by calling attention to such "unpatriotic" practices. The United States Brewers Association, a year before America's entry into the war, came under heavy judicial scrutiny all over the country.

In Pittsburgh, a federal grand jury began investigating their political activity, and as a result scores of brewers were fined. Texas brewers were fined $281,000. Rather than have their files scrutinized and revealed to the press, the Brewers Association in New York pleaded guilty and was fined $100,000.

Without any evidence to back his charges, Wheeler claimed that not only the brewers' money but German government funds had been used to "subvert" the administration. It was Wheeler again, behind the scenes, who initiated the setting up of a Senate investigative committee, which began examining the activities of the German-American Alliance in February of 1918. In a note to the ASL, he cynically admitted that "we could not have bought for $50,000 what we have gotten on this investigation thus far, and it will continue. . . . We are not willing it to be known at present that we started the investigation." Later he wrote:

> It is a conservative statement to say that we have secured more than a million dollars worth of free advertising against the liquor traffic, through the investigation and the material that we have secured and used. There is not a week passes now but that some magazine or paper has in it a special article relating to the Alliance.

The German Alliance and its financial backers, the Brewers Association, were the "enemy in the home camp." Shortly afterward, the Alliance decided to disband, its charter was revoked, and Wayne Wheeler announced that "an active, organized opposition to Prohibition was silenced."

But as far as Wheeler was concerned, this was not sufficient. He wrote to A. Mitchell Palmer, who had been appointed Custodian of Alien Property.

> I am informed that there are a number of breweries around the country which are owned in part by alien enemies. It is reported to me that the Anheuser-Busch Company and some of the Milwaukee companies are largely controlled by alien Germans. . . . Have you made an investigation?

Palmer subsequently attacked the United States Brewers publicly for "subsidizing the press, dominating politics, being unpatriotic and preventing youth of German descent from becoming Americanized." There were "sensational" disclosures in the media. Like all good lobbyists, Wheeler never forgot a favor. In due course, he would use his influence with the Wilson Administration to get Palmer appointed attorney general.

Palmer's disclosures also enabled Wheeler to press for the first Senate investigation of the Brewers Association, and the findings, though lacking the sensational quality Wheeler had hoped for, further exacerbated ill public opinion. The fact that Arthur Brisbane — owner-publisher of the *Washington Times,* which mildly opposed total Prohibition and argued that beer should be exempt — had been loaned

$500,000 by the brewers to take control of the paper was a further triumph for the extreme drys. It was all grist to the ASL's propaganda department, by now working overtime — its printing operations working in shifts around the clock.

Wheeler also made headlines on his own. As the *éminence grise* of the Senate committee investigating the German-American Alliance, he had access to seized confidential papers. While he was on a train to Chicago to make one of his innumerable speeches to a church audience, a page fell to the floor. It was part of a compromising German-Alliance document, inciting some Germans in America to stick together and aid the Kaiser in winning the war. The alert train attendant who picked it up believed he had laid hands on an important German spy, and alerted the police. On arrival at Elizabeth, the next stop, Wheeler was arrested. As his biographer noted, "he made capital at once of the arrest by citing it as evidence of the alertness of America and the popular hatred of the Germans, especially those connected with the brewing industry."

Wheeler also used America's entry into the war to push through dry measures for the armed forces. The passing of the agricultural appropriations bill banning the sale of grain to distillers was largely his doing (to their consternation, it would remain in force after the end of the war). The measure did not, however, extend to either beer or wine, and the ASL, in a letter to President Woodrow Wilson, made its disappointment clear — adding, with surprising arrogance, that "It will be our purpose to urge the passage of the legislation prohibiting the waste of foodstuffs in the manufacture of beer and wines at the earliest date." This in turn provoked an angry editorial in the *Cincinnati Enquirer:* "for brazen effrontery, unmitigated gall, superegoism, transcendent authority, supreme impudence, commend us to the legislative committee of the Prohibition lobby. . . . Here we have the President of the United States under orders to an officious and offensive lobby."

Wheeler was delighted by attacks of this type, and pressed on. He wrote Newton D. Baker, Wilson's secretary of war, reminding him that 65 percent of the country was already dry.

> I hope you will use the weight of your influence to protect the boys in the army from the ruinous effect of liquor during the war. . . . The

parents and friends of the boys from these places especially are vitally interested in having a safe environment for them at a time when they are homesick and lonesome in the training camps. Why would it not be a good thing to establish the mobilization camps in the dry states? Several measures have already been taken in Congress to prevent the sale of liquor in or near the training camps and also the sale of liquor to persons in uniform. A bill has been introduced also to prohibit anyone from using grain in making the liquor during the war. I am sure that the people of the nation would sustain you in any effort you may make along the lines of protecting the soldiers and the resources of our nation in this hour of peril.

He even tried, but without success, to "protect the soldiers from the evils of the liquor traffic in France." In a further letter to Baker, he urged him "inasmuch as this government cannot prohibit the sale of liquor to the soldiers in France as they do in this country" to promulgate an Army order to that effect, reminding him that "this has already been done with reference to spirituous liquors." But the Army proved uncooperative, the Navy even more so. The monitoring vigilance of the ASL was such that it quickly reacted to an anti-Prohibition remark made in England by a senior U.S. Navy admiral, who had publicly referred to England's "traditions of personal liberty, where I know I could get a drink of any kind I wanted if I came to England fifty years from now." There were limits to Baker's docility, as far as the ASL was concerned: he told Wheeler that "the department is not responsible for the individual utterances of the men in the Navy."

Wheeler had discovered a rich propaganda lode and was intent on exploiting it to fullest advantage. During the war, the Prohibition cause advanced hand-in-hand with the growing wave of anti-German sentiment, and largely because of the ASL propaganda machine, anti-German hysteria did not come to an end with the Armistice but persisted in one form or another until the very end of Prohibition. In 1923, five years after the end of the war, an ASL-inspired Senate Judiciary Committee would begin hearings on "brewing and liquor interests and German and Bolshevik propaganda." It prefigured McCarthyism in action: nothing in its findings justified its title, for the only evidence Senate investigators could produce was that most breweries had contributed to various German-American associations throughout the country. There was absolutely no evidence they

had financed anti-American propaganda in wartime, and the very idea
that the overwhelmingly Protestant, conservative German-American
brewery-owning families might be Bolshevik dupes or stalking-horses
was so ridiculous that the subject was not even brought up during the
proceedings.

The ASL's finest hour, in the pre-Prohibition period, came with
the Worldwide Prohibition Congress, held in Columbus, Ohio, in November of 1918, only a few days after the Armistice. By this time it
was clear to all that nationwide Prohibition was unstoppable. The only
point at issue was when it would finally be voted in by a three-fourths
majority of state votes — some observers convinced that this would
happen within a year and others that the states' response would be
unanimously favorable.

Representatives from all over the world attended, though,
reflecting the moral as well as imperial colonialism of the times, the
Indian and Chinese delegations to the Congress supposed to represent
their countries consisted exclusively of American missionaries. The
ASL literature distributed to delegates made somewhat inflated claims:
among countries "with Prohibition" figured "300 million people, or
one sixth of the world's population." These included not only Canada
and Iceland, Greenland and the Faroes (the latter not really sovereign
countries), but Rumania and even Russia (with the cautionary aster-
isk: prior to 1914). "It is significant," the ASL report added, "that
they are all Christian nations." Countries with "partial prohibition" included Denmark, Sweden, Australia, New Zealand, and Scotland, and
a special mention was made of France, Belgium, Switzerland, and Italy,
"which outlawed absinthe." Despite the bias in favor of Christianity,
countries "under the influence of so-called Prohibition religions" were
China, Manchuria, Japan, India, Persia, Afghanistan, Turkey, Arabia,
and some parts of North Africa and Asia, whereas there was "nominal
prohibition" in Africa. Liquor was "regulated" (and taxed) "in Britain, France, Germany, Austria, Hungary, Italy, Switzerland, Belgium,
Holland, Spain, Portugal and their colonial possessions."

Delegate after delegate rejoiced in (usually mercifully short) emotional addresses. The tone was set by James A. White, superintendent
of the Ohio ASL (the state that witnessed the initial Oberlin College
conferences that brought it into being in the first place): "God has
wrought wonders in Ohio!" he proclaimed. The Reverend Sam Small,

D.D., a favorite keynote speaker, indulged in the type of oratory that had been popular in the past, but was largely irrelevant now that the United States was on the verge of nationwide Prohibition: "From the Great Lakes to the Gulf a militant majority of American people are crucifying that beastly, bloated bastard of Beelzebub, the liquor traffic. . . . Yet a few months more, and we will bury the putrid corpse of John Barleycorn."

William Jennings Bryan, the former Secretary of State and Democratic veteran — who a year later would suffer considerable embarrassment with the press revelation that he had long been on the ASL payroll (at a stipend of $11,000 a year) — intervened twice, at considerable length. By now a somewhat passé figurehead who had never recovered from his policy differences with the ASL (until he was overruled by Wheeler and the majority of his party, he had systematically opposed the ASL's "nonpolitical" policy and insisted that Prohibition should remain an exclusively Democratic issue), Bryan could not resist a sly dig at Republicans. He told the conference:

> I have a joy as a citizen and I have a joy the Democrat has, which is more than any Republican can possibly have. Now the fight is almost over, a prediction: we will have prohibition by universal assent! [He was as wrong about that, as he was about ASL nonpartisan strategy.] Is the fight ended? No. We must give the people an understanding of what alcohol means, so that back of these laws we will have a total abstinence nation and boys and girls will be taught that alcohol is a poison, for after we have won this victory, it will have to be guarded by eternal vigilance.

He did, however, accurately reflect the ASL's new internationalist militancy: in the light of its amazing successes of the last few years, it was now imperative "to export the gift of Prohibition to other countries, turning the whole world dry." In a tub-thumping speech (that fully endorsed H. L. Mencken's comment about him that "He was born with a roaring voice, and it had the trick of inflaming half-wits") he urged his fellow Prohibitionists to conquer even more distant goals.

> We must turn our energies to other countries until the whole world is brought to understand that alcohol is man's greatest enemy. Thus it is a fortunate thing that the abdication of the Kaiser and the fall of

arbitrary power came in the same year as does the fall of the brewery autocracy and that these two evils came down together. . . . Now
we can go out for the evangelization of the world on the subject of
intoxicating liquor.

His call was taken up by Ernest Cherrington, the ASL's president,
who stigmatized "the power of the French Bourse" as an "important
factor in the propagation and protection of the wine industry and traffic." He continued: "Our imperative demands are not limited to the
[Versailles] Peace Conference. The important need for temperance reform must be recognized in the reconstruction program of the several
nations of Europe."

What he then outlined was no less than a blueprint "for universal, world-wide prohibition . . . for now is the psychological time
to strike." With considerable naiveté, the final resolutions of the
conference reflected this missionary zeal.

"The time has come," they read, "for the formation of an international league for the extermination of the beverage traffic throughout the world." ASL field agents were to be stationed abroad and
there was to be an international Prohibition press association, "with
the launching of a prohibition periodical with a worldwide editorial
policy."

The ASL was also mandated to "get in touch with American Consulates to bring directly to the attention of official foreign representatives of the U.S. government the facts as to the success and benefits
of prohibition in the U.S." The ASL also pledged financial assistance
to foreign temperance movements and announced that ASL lobbyists
would attend the forthcoming Versailles Peace Conference.

It all reflected a new arrogance. American entry into the war had
made it a world power, and the ASL delegates naively assumed that
their all-powerful lobby could impose their views not only on vote-
hungry American politicians but on the rest of the world. The Conference unanimously called on the governments of Great Britain and
France to "issue an order prohibiting the sale of intoxicants to American soldiers and sailors in uniform. . . . We insist there should be no
hesitation and no delay in issuing this order, for prompt action will
prevent the formation of the wine drinking habit by our soldiers and
sailors." Wheeler himself, always a political realist, doubtless knew what

the Allies' answer would be, and there is no trace of an official follow-up. But with Prohibition a virtual certainty in the near future, the ASL showed it really believed — in the words of the communist hymn, the "Internationale" — that in a short space of time, Prohibition was fated to be the destiny of mankind, "Sera le genre humain."

6

AMERICA GOES DRY

Prohibition turned Andrew J. Volstead, an otherwise obscure Republican congressman from Minnesota, into a household name. It was commonly assumed that because the Eighteenth Amendment to the Constitution introducing nationwide Prohibition bore his name it was largely his doing. In fact, Volstead was its facilitator rather than its architect. Wheeler himself, as he would later boast, conceived, drafted, and copiously rewrote it. Its many weaknesses, and omissions, are largely attributable to him.

Volstead, a dour Lutheran of Norwegian origin, with a huge bristling mustache, was not even part of the hard core of dry advocates in Congress and, in his long political career, had never used the Prohibition platform as part of his election campaign strategy. On two occasions, his unsuccessful challengers to his House of Representatives seat had even been Prohibition candidates. As county prosecutor in his earlier days, he had prosecuted many cases involving illicit liquor because Minnesota had been a dry state long before 1917, but he had done so routinely, with no dogmatic belief in Prohibition's inherent virtues. It was in this same spirit, as chairman of the Senate Judiciary Committee, that he oversaw its passage, after the Supreme Court had narrowly (by five votes to four) validated its constitutionality.

Introduced on May 27, 1919, the bill was passed (255 to 166) after a three-month debate. The Senate vote followed on September 5, and, as part of routine procedure, it then went back to the House, to be adopted on October 10 by 321 to 70 votes. An already desperately ill President Wilson, further weakened by his losing fight to keep America within the League of Nations, vetoed it, on both constitutional and ethical grounds. "In all matters having to do with personal habits and customs of large numbers of our people," he wrote, "we must be certain that the established processes of legal change are followed." But that same day, the veto was overridden in Congress, and the act became law. Henceforth, the act determined, "No person shall manufacture, sell, barter, transport, import, export, deliver, furnish or possess any intoxicating liquor except as authorized in this act." The act replaced all previous dry legislation measures in force in the various states.

On the face of it, the Volstead Act was both all-encompassing and foolproof, though it did contain specific exemptions — regarding industrial alcohol, sacramental wine, certain patent medicines, doctors' prescriptions (but no more than a pint at a time per patient within a ten-day period), toilet preparations, flavoring extracts, syrups, vinegar, and cider. Brewers could remain in business provided they confined themselves to making "near-beer," with a maximum 0.5 percent alcohol content. Penalties for improper use were to be fines and prison terms — $1,000 or 30 days for the first offense, rising to $10,000 and a year for further convictions.

The act also banned liquor advertising, and the use or sale of anything that might lead to its manufacture. "Any room, house, building, boat, vehicle, structure or place where intoxicating liquor is manufactured, sold, kept or bartered in violation of this title . . . is hereby declared a common nuisance," it said, outlining the scale of fines and jail sentences for transgressors. Liquor stored for sale or vehicles used for transport were to be seized and destroyed. But the act was mute concerning the actual consumption of liquor in private homes — the one concession to individual liberty. The day before Prohibition came into effect, the New York *Daily News* gave its readers the following invaluable advice:

You may drink intoxicating liquor in your own home or in the home of a friend when you are a bona fide guest.

You may buy intoxicating liquor on a bona fide medical prescription of a doctor. A pint can be bought every ten days.

You may consider any place you live permanently as your home. If you have more than one home, you may keep a stock of liquor in each.

You may keep liquor in any storage room or club locker, provided the storage place is for the exclusive use of yourself, family or bona fide friends.

You may get a permit to move liquor when you change your residence.

You may manufacture, sell or transport liquor for non-beverage or sacramental purposes provided you obtain a Government permit.

You cannot carry a hip flask.

You cannot give away or receive a bottle of liquor as a gift.

You cannot take liquor to hotels or restaurants and drink it in the public dining rooms.

You cannot buy or sell formulas or recipes for homemade liquors.

You cannot ship liquor for beverage use.

You cannot manufacture anything above one half of one percent (liquor strength) in your home.

You cannot store liquor in any place except your own home.

You cannot display liquor signs or advertisements on your premises.

You cannot remove reserve stocks from storage.

In retrospect, the Volstead Act was hopelessly inadequate, because it grossly underestimated the willingness of the lawbreakers to risk conviction, the degree of human ingenuity displayed to get around its provisions, and the ease with which the lawbreakers would be able to subvert all those whose job was to enforce it. Above all, its failure resulted from a naive American belief in the effectiveness of law: the drys, whether ASL or church activists, politicians, law enforcers, or simply individuals of strong moral convictions, were convinced that Americans, as law-abiding citizens intensely respectful of established authority, would obey the provisions of the Volstead Act, even if, as drinkers and as advocates of personal, individual liberty, they deeply resented it.

One of the few hard-headed realists who felt otherwise, immediately after the passage of the Volstead Act, was ex-President William Howard Taft. Those who thought that "an era of clear thinking and clean living" was at hand were living in a fool's paradise, he wrote. The law had been passed ". . . against the views and practices of a majority of people in many of the large cities. . . . The business of manufacturing alcohol, liquor and beer will go out of the hands of law-abiding members of the community and will be transferred to the quasi-criminal classes."

The "bond of national union" would come under severe strain, and he warned against "variations in the enforcement of the law." But even Taft scarcely foresaw the extent of the damage Prohibition would inflict on the American body politic.

To become effective, the Eighteenth Amendment required ratification by a two-thirds majority of states. The result was a foregone conclusion. Many of them were already wholly or partially dry, and Prohibition was clearly a vote-winning issue. For all that, the ASL propaganda machine moved into high gear, and a spate of songs, based on popular tunes such as "Annie Laurie" and "The Battle Hymn of the Republic," were sung in churches and Sunday schools all over America.[1] Mississippi became the first to vote for the measure. A year later, Nebraska became the thirty-sixth — and last — state whose voice was needed to make it part of the Constitution. The act prescribed a year's grace between final ratification and implementation. Twelve months later, on January 17, 1920, at the stroke of midnight, the whole of America officially went dry.

Along with the war, Prohibition had been the most talked-about issue in American homes and editorial columns. Since 1917, the debate had been so acrimonious that everyone knew what to expect. In the months leading up to January of 1920, some distillers moved large quantities of liquor abroad — the Bahamas becoming a huge storage area, which would make it, after 1920, a bootlegger's paradise. Other, less far-seeing distillers had accumulated huge stocks, for sale while purchases were still legal. But these were not as lucrative as they had expected, for prices had risen steeply, and they decided to advertise. Posters bearing the effigy of Uncle Sam appeared all over America, urging consumers to "Buy now. Uncle Sam will ENFORCE prohibition!"

Most distillers believed Prohibition would prove so unpopular and unworkable it would quickly be repealed. Hardest hit were private investors in distilleries, who held "whiskey certificates," shares measured in multigallon cases (not much different from today's coffee futures). There had been some talk of compensation, the government buying up all certificates, for eventual legal use. This was quickly dropped. By 1920, the value of whiskey certificates had plummeted to nearly nothing, their holders almost as penalized as investors holding Russian loan bonds. Failure to compensate the whiskey investors would have huge repercussions.

In the final few weeks before January 17, 1920, Americans did stock up, to the limit of their financial restrictions. Those who could afford it rented space for storage in warehouses and even in safe deposit boxes. But on January 15, 1920, two days before the act came into force, New York judge John C. Knox decreed that all liquor stocks outside the home broke the law and were liable to seizure. All across America, there was a huge panic as millions of Americans carted their liquor stocks back to their homes. The New York *Evening Post* reported a rush to "hire trucks or baby carriages or anything else on wheels." "Fair ladies sat in limousines behind alluring barricades of cases," wrote a San Francisco *Chronicle* reporter.

Surprisingly, though a phenomenal amount of drinking took place all over America on the night of January 16, the occasion failed to live up to reporters' (and saloon keepers') expectations. Whiskey had become expensive (only in one bar, the Della Robbia Room in the Hotel Vanderbilt, was it given away free), revelry was muted, and there were no great crowds on the Manhattan streets, perhaps because it was a bitterly cold night. Although mock wakes were a favorite theme (in Healey's restaurant customers were given small wooden coffins as mementos), the New York *Tribune* reported "sad scenes" on Broadway, and the *Evening Post* noted that "the big farewell failed to materialize." In somewhat hyphenated prose, the *New York Times* wrote that "the spontaneous orgies of drink that were predicted failed in large part to occur on schedule. . . . Instead of passing from us in violent paroxysms, the rum demon lay down to a painless, peaceful, though lamented, by some, death." A walk through Broadway at midnight, a *Sun* reporter observed, "revealed an almost empty thoroughfare."

There were a few exceptions: a wealthy client took over the Park Avenue Hotel for a large private party. Black cloth draped the walls; tables were covered with black crepe; waiters, musicians, and guests were dressed uniformly in black; black caviar was served; and drink came in black glasses specially ordered for the occasion. In the center of the dining room, in the place of honor, stood a black coffin filled with black bottles. The orchestra played funeral dirges, and at midnight the guests filed past the coffin as though mourning a dead person. "Lights were extinguished, and the orchestra played a few bars of dirge. Then a spotlight picked up the final spectacle — two young men and two girls, all in black, sitting at a black table and pouring the last drops from four black bottles, while they held their pocket handkerchiefs before their streaming eyes. A newspaperman who wandered into this party for a few minutes reported that it was 'the damndest thing I ever saw.' "[2] In Cincinnati, more decorously, a melancholy beerfest took place under the auspices of the old German-American Alliance, now renamed the Citizens' League.

In contrast, the following day, the Prohibitionists' self-congratulatory celebrations were awesome, their oratorical hyperbole more extravagant than ever. "They are dead, that sought the child's life," thundered the inevitable William Jennings Bryan at a huge rally in Washington attended by hundreds of Congressmen, the entire ASL establishment, and thousands of well-wishers. "They are dead! They are dead! King Alcohol has slain more children than Herod ever did. The revolution that rocked the foundation of the Republic will be felt all over the earth. As we grow better and stronger through the good influence of Prohibition, we will be in a position to give greater aid to the world."

In Norfolk, Virginia, Billy Sunday, the most famous evangelist of his day and a lifelong campaigner since his "conversion" (in earlier days he had been a noted song writer, baseball player, and an even more noted drunk), staged a mock funeral service for John Barleycorn. With his usual showmanship, he had a troupe of mimes, impersonating drunkards and devils, accompany the 20-foot-long coffin to its final resting place. "The reign of tears is over," he told a huge crowd. "The slums will soon only be a memory. We will turn our prisons into factories and our jails into storehouses and corn-cribs. Men will walk upright now, women will smile, and children will laugh. Hell will be forever for rent." Ominously, in Chicago, within an hour of the Volstead Act taking effect, six armed, masked men made away with whiskey earmarked for "medicinal use," worth $100,000.

The delay between the passing of the act and its implementation was no humane measure that let Americans enjoy one last year of legal drinking. The intervening year had been spent setting up some of the new law enforcement machinery, for which Congress had earmarked a meager $3 million. Some 1,500 agents of the new Prohibition Unit (soon to be called the Prohibition Bureau) were recruited, and the Coast Guard, the Customs Service, and the Internal Revenue Service trained in their new duties.

The decision to put the Prohibition Bureau under the authority of the Treasury Department — instead of the Justice Department — was Wheeler's idea, and he had personally lobbied (then) Senator Warren Harding, soon to succeed Wilson as president, to that effect. Very early on, it proved to be a disastrous decision, but not nearly as disastrous as the other decision, made concurrently, to exclude the new Prohibition agents from the Civil Service and to exempt them from its rules. In every state, their recruitment was political, an integral part of the spoils system, in the hands of local politicians whose careers depended on patronage. All that was required on the part of an aspiring Prohibition agent was the endorsement of the ASL, a congressman, or other prominent local politician. No other qualifications or character references were needed; some of the new recruits even had criminal records. The job paid a maximum salary of $2,300 a year, barely enough to live on — almost inviting corruption. The ASL later justified this decision on the grounds that had it insisted on Civil Service status for the new recruits, "to have forced the issue would have been to jeopardize the passage of the bill." But in a reply to the ASL, a National Civil Service Reform League spokesman wrote that "the plain fact is that the congressmen wanted the plunder and you let them have it." In the first few months of Prohibition, the agents were mostly Democratic appointees. When the Harding administration took over, almost all were dismissed and replaced by Republicans. The turnover was huge: in any one year, there were 10,000 applicants for 2,000 jobs, and the average length of service was only a few months — most agents being "let go" for corrupt practices that could not be satisfactorily proved or prosecuted.

Although Prohibition had been in the cards for several years, many Americans simply did not know what to expect. Whereas Colonel Daniel Porter, a New York supervising revenue agent, announced that he was confident "there will not be any violations to speak of," New Jersey Governor Edward I. Edwards said he hoped to keep New Jersey "as wet as the Atlantic ocean." In truth, the Volstead Act was flagrantly broken from the moment it became law, and continued to be flouted for the next thirteen years.

The nation's legislators and law enforcers professed to be completely taken aback, after 1920, by the extent of Prohibition-related lawbreaking — and the concomitant, almost immediate proliferation of speakeasies, bootleggers, rumrunners, moonshiners, and hijackers, all bringing violence in their wake. They need not have been so surprised. Had they bothered to look at those towns and states where Prohibition had already become law *before* 1920, they would have realized what was in store. In 1916, for instance, Prohibition had finally become a reality in Washington State, and immediately the new law there (very similar in content to the Volstead Act) had been totally ignored or subverted. A month after Spokane, then a town of 44,000 registered voters, became dry, 34,000 liquor permits had been issued, and soft-drink shops selling under-the-counter liquor were doing a roaring trade, with sixty-five brand-new drugstores — all selling liquor — competing for business. Moonshine liquor was freely available, there was a constant stream of smuggled liquor from across the nearby Canadian border, and a drugstore-owning couple whose establishment was, Carry Nation style, "hatchetized" by Prohibition vigilantes, promptly went into another line of business, running a company shipping rum from Cuba to Canada, but in fact smuggling it back into the twenty-eight dry states.

What had happened in Spokane four years before national Prohibition became law was to become the norm all over America. "A staggering increase in liquor prescribed as medicine occurred during the first five months throughout the country."[3] In Chicago alone, as soon as the Volstead Act became law, over 15,000 doctors and 57,000 retail druggists applied for licenses to sell "medicinal" liquor, and in the next three years there would be 7,000 (mostly new) "soft-drinking" parlors, actually dispensing liquor. Scores of clandestine breweries also set up shop, and small fortunes were made by printers supplying fake whiskey labels, carpenters making fake wooden crates for brand-name whiskey, and pharmacists selling ingredients for homemade stills (yeast, juniper oil, fusel oil, iodine, and caramel). Americans bought huge quantities of malt syrup, essential for turning "near-beer" into the real thing, and the Prohibition Bureau estimated that several hundred million gallons of homemade 2.5-degree beer were consumed every year. There was a run on anything containing alcohol that could be used as a basis for homemade liquor — embalming fluid, antifreeze solution, solidified and rubbing alcohol, bay rum — often with horrendous consequences, for, inexplicably, old rules requiring denatured alcohol to bear the POISON warning were discontinued.

The ingenuity of clandestine liquor manufacturers was considerable. In the Midwest, the liquid residue of silos was collected and turned into liquor. New brands sprang up: Panther Whiskey, Red Eye, Cherry Dynamite, Old Stingo, Old Horsey, Scat Whiskey, Happy Sally, Jump Steady, Soda Pop Moon, Sugar Moon, and Jackass Brandy, supposedly made of peaches. In the South, a brand called Squirrel Whiskey got its name because it was so strong it was supposed to make consumers climb trees. In the ghettos, a popular drink was known simply as nigger gin. "Sweet whiskey" was made with nitrous ether — alcohol mixed with nitric and sulfuric acid. Yack-yack Bourbon, a popular Chicago drink, was made with iodine and burnt sugar. From Mexico came "American" whiskey, made from potatoes and cactus, and from Jamaica a 90-proof alcohol concoction known as Jamaica ginger, or Jake. *Colliers* reported that victims of Jake paralysis lost control of their extremities: ". . . the victim has no control over the muscles that normally point the toes upward."

Although some Californian vineyards were ruined by Prohibition, certain Napa Valley wine-making families became exceedingly wealthy. In fact, grape production, far from declining, increased tenfold between 1920 and 1933, the main reason being the manufacture of dried grape and "raisin cakes." These were allowed, under a provision of the Volstead Act, to prevent farmers from going under entirely. The aim was, officially, to allow householders to make "nonintoxicating cider and fruit juices for home consumption to the extent of 200 gallons annually."

The raisin cakes were easily turned into something else. Wholesalers used demonstrators (often attractive, well-spoken young women) in large stores to draw attention to the wine-making possibilities of their cakes (or "bricks") while ostensibly warning against fermentation — their straight-faced cautionary patter urging buyers "not to place the liquid in a jug and put it aside for twenty-one days because it would turn into wine . . . and not to stop the bottle with a cork because this is necessary only if fermentation occurs." The bricks were sold with a label that read "Caution: will ferment and turn into wine." The biggest beneficiary of all was Beringer Vineyards in Napa Valley, whose owners, Charles and Bertha Beringer, were the first to take advantage of the obscure Volstead Act loophole. Bertha Beringer, only 32 when Prohibition began, and recently wedded to Charles, was the real brains behind the scheme, saving the family business — and inspiring countless later competitors.

The year 1917 was a record vintage year for California wines, in terms of both quality and quantity. For the first time, owing to a wartime manpower shortage, Mexican workers were recruited for the harvest. The threat of Prohibition was already very real — thanks to Wheeler, servicemen in uniform were not allowed into bars or saloons — and Bertha saw the writing on the wall. But unlike many Napa Valley owners, who ploughed up their vineyards to plant fruit trees rather than be caught with large stocks of unsellable wine, she devised the "raisin cake" *in advance of* the Volstead Act. "Instead of converting their grapes into either grape juice or sacramental wines, Beringer Brothers will dry most of them," the Saint Helena *Star* reported in September of 1919. The Charles Krug winery also beat the Volstead Act, investing in nonalcoholic grape juice and extract-making plants.

Other, less innovative vineyards went to the wall, in the first few years of Prohibition, after an initial selling spree — for in the first three months of Prohibition, the wineries were allowed to liquidate their stocks to private buyers, which they did at hugely inflated prices. But one famous Napa Valley vineyard, established in the nineteenth century by a French farmer from the Perigord, Georges de Latour (whose French vineyard had been wiped out by phylloxera), prospered for a wholly different reason.

Georges de Latour was a practicing Catholic, and an intimate friend of the archbishop of San Francisco, who instructed all the priests in his diocese to buy their sacramental wine only from him. The amounts were so huge that it is clear that most of the priests must have been bootleggers as well, for the de Latour books show that all sorts of table wines were sold to the churches. Other famous vineyards established equally lucrative contracts with Californian rabbis, many of whom became, in effect, bootleggers for their flocks — the title of rabbi guaranteeing virtual immunity from prosecution. The Prohibition Bureau's estimate was that 678 million gallons of homemade wine alone were consumed between 1925 and 1929.

In New York, whereas many great restaurants simply closed down (their owners reluctant to break the law and unwilling to provide meals without vintage wines), speakeasies proliferated on a truly startling scale. By 1922, there would be at least 5,000, and by 1927, over 30,000 — twice as many as all legal bars, restaurants, and nightclubs *before* Prohibition. Some of them — such as the Twenty-One and the Stork Club — would survive repeated closures to become fashionable post-Prohibition restaurants, just as prominent bootlegging personalities such as William "Big Bill" Dwyer and "impresario" Larry Fay would eventually become respected, adulated "café society" figures.

The career of Sherman Billingsley, the owner-founder of the Stork Club — in its day the most famous speakeasy in America — revealed the extent of Prohibition's "window of opportunity" — and how pre-1920 dry legislation provided bold entrepreneurs with valuable experience in skirting the Volstead Act's laws. Oklahoma-born Billingsley began selling bootleg liquor in a drugstore when he was twelve. He was sixteen when he was first arrested, in Seattle, for contravening the local liquor laws. Soon afterward, he was running bootleg liquor from Canada and managing three speakeasies in Detroit; at nineteen, in New York, he was running a Bronx drugstore selling medicinal whiskey.

Billingsley opened the Stork Club, with money from Frank Costello, New York's leading gangster, in 1927, and the nightly presence there of Walter Winchell, America's most famous syndicated gossip columnist (his drinks, and meals, were on the house), made it *the* place to be seen. A raid in 1931 led to its temporary closure, but the "right people" soon flocked to the new address on Fifty-third Street, undeterred by sky-high prices (a $20 cover charge, $2 for a carafe of plain water).

There were hundreds of lesser-known private drinking clubs, where affluent members could store their own liquor. According to humorist Robert Benchley (himself a serious drinker), there were thirty-eight speakeasies on East Fifty-second Street alone, and potential buyers were so convinced that every house there was a speakeasy that one householder — rather in the manner of today's New York car owners, notifying potential burglars of "no radio" — put up a notice on her front door: "This is a private residence. Do not ring." McSorley's saloon in Greenwich Village never bothered to reduce its potent beer to near beer — its popularity with the police and local politicians such that it was never raided once. A new type of nightclub became fashionable: the expensive, barely clandestine night spot run by socialites (Sherman Billingsley's Stork Club) and showbiz veterans (Belle Livingstone's Country Club on East Fifty-eighth Street and "Texas" Guinan's El Fay Club on West Forty-fifth Street). These typically included cabaret shows, dancing girls, and exotic acts. Prohibition encouraged the emergence of uniquely colorful women, whose wit and toughness attracted huge numbers of admiring customers. Belle Livingstone, a much-married ex-Broadway showgirl (her husbands included a paint salesman, an Italian count, a Cleveland millionaire, and an English engineer), charged a $5 entrance fee and $40 for a bottle of champagne. Mary Louise "Texas" Guinan was a former star of silent westerns, ex-circus rider, and vaudeville singer whose generous disposition was legendary. She even urged Walter Winchell, one of her devoted admirers, to promote, in his columns, speakeasies owned by less fortunate competitors.

The trashing of the Times Square area of New York, once the site of large numbers of respectable bars and restaurants, began with Prohibition, for not all speakeasies were furnished in the Louis XV style like the luxurious five-story Country Club. Most were dark, sordid clip joints haunted by bar girls pushing foul drinks in exchange for the promise of spurious sex to come. In Cincinnati, the attractive Across the Rhine beer gardens soon became a distant memory.

Some Prohibition advocates felt that "wide-open" towns such as New York and Chicago should be brought to heel, and called for more Prohibition agents and harsher laws (which were in fact introduced in 1925). Others became disenchanted for different reasons. Senator Thomas B. Watson (Democrat, Georgia), a lifelong dry, shocked the

Senate by drawing attention to "murder and other outrages carried out by Prohibition agents" in his state.

There was an almost immediate, nationwide change in drinking habits. It became the thing to do, among students, flappers, and respectable middle-class Americans all over the country, to defy the law — as much a manifestation of personal liberty as a thirst for alcohol.

Other changes manifested themselves. The saloon had been an almost exclusively male preserve, but the new speakeasies welcomed women. The cocktail was largely born as a result of Prohibition, because this was the only way of disguising the often horrible taste of homemade gin or flavored wood alcohol. And tens of thousands of people would die before Prohibition was over, poisoned by wood alcohol and moonshine.

7

THE PROVIDERS

With Prohibition, America was all set for a wild drinking spree that would last thirteen years, five months, and nine days. It would transform the country's morals; alter American attitudes toward law enforcers, politicians, and all those in authority; and herald a new mood of cynicism, along with an often justified conviction that the courts dispensed a form of two-tier justice based on class, wealth, and rank. And even if the Prohibition phenomenon itself, which was largely responsible for this general, unfocused resentment, was soon forgotten, for other reasons the mood of distrust has persisted to this day.

The Prohibition era has been chronicled in hundreds of films and classics, such as F. Scott Fitzgerald's *The Great Gatsby*. Underworld figures such as Al Capone, catapulted onto the world scene by Prohibition, became in time mythic heroes, as did the bootleggers' nemesis, Eliot Ness.

But the political immorality in high places that allowed the law-breakers to flourish — and that marked the 1920s in other ways — has been largely ignored or forgotten. It is as if those Americans who experienced the Prohibition years were determined to put them out of their minds as soon as it was repealed. Their reaction was understandable. Compared to the years of the Harding presidency, at the beginning of Prohibition (1920–1923), major scandals such as those that brought about the collapse of the Italian Christian Democratic hegemony looked like trifling peccadilloes.

For gangsters, bootleggers, and speakeasies to flourish, the liquor had to come from somewhere. The story of George Remus, the German-born American who became the richest bootlegger of all, shows how simple it was to lay one's hands on almost limitless quantities of whiskey without resorting to rumrunners or homemade stills — and often without even formally breaking the law.

Remus exemplified the new breed of American. His father, Franck Remus (who dropped the Germanic spelling of his first name after immigrating to America), came from Friedeberg, near Berlin. The history of the Remus family is a textbook illustration of the appalling health hazards prevalent in the nineteenth century. Franck's parents both died a few weeks after his birth, probably from cholera, and he subsequently became an apprentice in a woolen mill. There, he did well, marrying Maria Karg, the mill owner's daughter, in 1871. They had three girls, but all died in infancy. Their fourth child, George Remus, lived, and when he was four and a half years old, the three of them left for Milwaukee, then almost a German enclave, where several members of the Karg family had already settled.

In Milwaukee, tragedy continued to dog the Remus family. Maria gave birth to two more sons, who also died in infancy. She then had three more children, all girls, who lived, followed by a third son, Herman, who, as a child, was hit on the back of the head by a flying brick, and as a result became mentally unstable. He died in 1918.

Try as they might, the panel of psychiatrists who, at the request of the court, examined George Remus before his trial, and spent hours debriefing him on his antecedents, found "no record of suicidal or criminal tendencies upon the part of any member of this family." "None of the family could be called 'alcoholic,' " the panel wrote, "although many of them, as is common with their countrymen, drank considerable beer. George Remus's father drank only moderately, usually on Saturdays."

George was a good child in every way, an older sister, Mrs. Gabriel Ryerson, told the panel, "talkative, energetic, a book lover, careful in his appearance, and very seldom had to be scolded. He always looked on the bright side of things and had a sense of humor." Although Remus himself remained a lifelong teetotaler and nonsmoker, he was "fond of parties, always celebrating good news or success, dismissing discomforts of all kinds with feelings of lightheartedness. Irritations were never of long duration." Although he was quick-tempered, his sister recalled, he was affectionate, made friends easily, and had a natural sense of responsibility, even as a child. He had been confirmed in the Lutheran Church (though neither George Remus nor his family were particularly religious), but was sufficiently intrigued by the dogma of various churches to attend Catholic, Presbyterian, and occasionally Christian Science church services. Apparently, none fully satisfied him. "My religion," he told the panel, "is to pay my obligations and keep my word." He was "dubious about the hereafter and did not worry much about it." Despite his short, stocky build (in his early photographs he resembles Danny de Vito; in his later ones, Mussolini) and his one indulgence — good food — he became a strong swimmer and a much-sought-after member of the Illinois Athletic Club's water polo team. The examining psychiatrists found him "alert, friendly, courteous and perfectly willing to cooperate in every way."

As Remus told the panel, despite his mother's relatively prosperous background, his family fell on hard times shortly after settling in Milwaukee. Frank, no longer a weaver but a lumber scorer, became crippled with articular rheumatism, a virtual invalid no longer able to work.

They left for Chicago, and soon young George Remus, still in his early teens, became the family's mainstay. An uncle, George Karg, had a drugstore there, and George left school to work as his assistant. When his uncle decided to sell his shop, George obtained a bank loan and bought and ran the store himself, with a much increased profit. He was only nineteen, but had by this time become a licensed pharmacologist (by making himself out to be older than he was). He never graduated, displaying, as a student, the same headstrong qualities that were to plague him in later life. Just before his final examination, he led a student walkout to protest the behavior of an unpopular teacher, and when the teacher took his revenge, handing out punitive low grades, Remus never returned to school.

This in no way, however, prevented him from prospering. From the profits of his first shop, he bought a second drugstore near Milwaukee Avenue. He also became a certified optometrist, and his examining panel also noted that he "indulged in the practice of medicine in connection with his drug store among the people of his neighborhood." The practice was common among pharmacists; doctors were expensive, and there was no social security. Among his clients was a neighbor, Lillian Kraus. They fell in love, married, and had a daughter, Romola. In the somewhat dated jargon of the times, the panel noted that "his sexual life showed no perversities."

George Remus, in his twenties, found time not only to run two drugstores, write out prescriptions for glasses, act as an unlicensed doctor, and raise a family, but to study law at night school. At age 24 he was admitted to the Illinois Bar, and started his own practice. From the very start, he was successful. He specialized in criminal law, but also actively represented several Chicago labor unions, and made quite a name for himself as a divorce lawyer. A well-known local figure, with many Democratic connections, Remus was several times approached and asked to stand for local political office. "I could easily have become a District Attorney," he told the panel. "I was prominent enough politically to secure public office, but have never wanted to take the prosecutor's side in my life." In light of his many achievements, it is somewhat surprising that at the time of his murder trial, when they submitted him to various tests, including those standard 1920s examinations the Stanford Revision of the Binet-Simon Scale and the Otis Self-Administering Test of Mental Ability, the psychiatrists examining him found George Remus to be "of only average adult intelligence." They did add that "the possibility that this record may have been lowered by mental distraction at the time of the examination should not be overlooked."

Remus hired a legal secretary, Imogene Holmes, a young divorcée with a small daughter, Ruth. Imogene, a remarkably strong, graceful swimmer, was a voluptuous woman with somewhat extravagant tastes in clothes and unusual hats. Little is known of her family background, though she boasted to George Remus that she came "from the top drawer." Remus divorced Lillian in 1917, but continued to support her, remaining on good terms with her and their daughter, Romola, who adored him.

Chicago became dry in 1918. In this hugely corrupt city, where underworld characters immediately became bootleggers, Remus, the criminal lawyer they knew and trusted, was much in demand. Among his clients was Johnny Torrio, a nightclub and brothel owner, and one of the first Chicago bootleggers and speakeasy kings. Torrio, himself a straitlaced family man and practicing Catholic for all his many brothel ownerships, summoned one of his distant New York relatives, Alfonso Caponi, to assist him in his operations. Remus knew Capone, too, but only slightly. His acquaintanceship with the Chicago underworld was strictly professional: many of its minor members had visited his office at 167 North Clark Street, on the Chicago "Loop," some of them on murder charges. It was because as defense counsel he had been compelled to witness the capital executions of some of his clients (in the electric chair) that he came out strongly against the death penalty. Clarence Darrow, the best-known criminal lawyer in America, also a Chicago colleague, spoke highly of his abilities.

As a brilliant lawyer, and an ex-pharmacist, Remus was uniquely qualified to make a fortune out of the Volstead Act. In a series of articles about him in the St. Louis *Post-Dispatch* ("The Inside Story of the Amazing Career of George Remus, millionaire bootlegger and his band of rumrunners," St. Louis *Post-Dispatch*, January 3–20, 1926), Paul Y. Anderson wrote:

> If there has ever been a bigger bootlegger than Remus, the fact remains a secret. . . . Remus was to bootlegging what Rockefeller was to oil. In the sheer imagination of his plan, in the insolent sweep of his ambition and power with which he swept upward toward his goal, Remus can bear comparison with the captains of industry.

Remus told Anderson how the idea came to him. If gangsters of limited intelligence could make a fortune, "Remus could surely do better than they."[1]

His first step was to sell his law practice (though he remained a member of the Bar Association). He then moved, with Imogene, to Cincinnati, where they got married. It was a shrewd move: most of America's whiskey distilleries were within 300 miles of the town, and Remus knew that despite the wartime ban on grain supplies, the

distilleries operating in America and producing an annual out-
put of 286 million gallons had virtually limitless bonded stocks at
their disposal. He also knew it was a seller's market: in 1917, the last
"normal" year before Prohibition became law in several major states,
Americans had consumed two billion gallons of hard liquor. Although
some distillers sent their liquor stocks abroad before 1920, hundreds
of millions of gallons remained in distilleries and government-bonded
warehouses, most of them within easy reach of Cincinnati. In addition,
because of Prohibition, "whiskey certificates" were worth next to
nothing.

Entirely legally, using his life savings ($100,000), Remus started
buying up certificates. His operations became lucrative quickly, and he
was soon able to acquire entire distilleries, complete with offices, machinery, furniture, and even abandoned corner saloons, for which he
did not have the slightest use. In time, Remus became the largest owner
of distilleries in America, his properties including famous brand names:
Fleischmann, Old Lexington Club, Rugby, Greendale, and Squibb,
the largest in the country. The Fleischmann Distillery, which cost him
$197,000, came with 3,100 barrels of prime rye whiskey.

The next step was to get official permission to remove the whiskey and — again quite legally — sell it to drug companies licensed to
sell medicinal whiskey. "I started out buying a retail drug store in Cincinnati and converting it into a wholesale drug company," Remus told
the *Post-Dispatch*. "As soon as that company had withdrawn as much
liquor as possible without attracting undue attention, I organized another wholesale company, closed up the first one, and shipped the stock
of drugs off to the second one. We made that carload of drugs serve
as the stock for three or four wholesale companies." Surplus nonalcoholic stocks were "fired off into space" (Anderson's words) to fictitious
buyers, eventually sold off as unclaimed freight. In the first few months
of Prohibition, Remus set up over a dozen drug companies, closing
them down when they began attracting the curiosity of enforcement
agents and inventing new ones. When the regulations changed, as they
soon did, to limit liquor acquisitions on the part of drug companies to
10 percent of their business, Remus simply cooked the books, showing
a huge imaginary turnover.

Once in the hands of the drug companies, some of the whiskey duly ended up in pint bottles labeled "medicinal whiskey," but

most of it ended up elsewhere, in the hands of bootleggers, nightclub owners, middlemen, and in exceptional cases a carefully vetted private clientele. Only a small proportion ended up as "straight" medicinal whiskey — the bootleggers and private customers a far more lucrative market. Anderson wrote that "Once out from under the eye of the government, the disposal of whiskey at fabulous prices became a simple matter. The whiskey market is always a seller's market. The supply never equals the demand. Remus's associates already had made contacts with retail bootleggers who would snap up all the good liquor that could be furnished, and would pay $80 a case and upward. There are 12 quarts, or three gallons, to a case. Remus paid from 65 cents to $4 (per case) for the certificates."

"What was wrong with that?" George Conners, Remus's closest associate, asked Anderson. "If anything was wrong it was wrong for the Government to destroy the value of those people's property without compensating them for it. If the Government wanted to abolish whiskey drinking, why didn't it buy all this whiskey and dump it in the river?" Conners told Anderson he had not intended to get into the whiskey business, "but after several of these fellows came to me, I asked Remus what he would charge me for liquor in 15 or 20 case lots." Remus suggested he think big, and quoted a price for 250-case lots. This was the start of the Remus-Conners bootleg operation on a grand scale, with Conners handling sales on a commission basis and drumming up business all over America.

"We never poisoned anybody. We sold good liquor and didn't cut it," Remus told Anderson. This and his meticulously run operation — involving shippers, drivers, bodyguards, and accountants (at his peak there were 3,000 people on his payroll) — went far to explain Remus's meteoric career. Within a few months of Prohibition, he was depositing tens of thousands of dollars a day into various bank accounts both in his own name and under aliases.

Remus had one innocuous weakness: he wanted to become a respected member of Cincinnati society. He set about it with his usual thoroughness. First he bought a huge property on Price Hill, overlooking the town, at Eighth and Hermosa Avenue, in what was then its most desirable suburb. Then, regardless of expense (it cost him $750,000, or close to several million dollars today), he had the place remodeled, furnished in somewhat garish taste, and on its extensive grounds built a greenhouse, a racing stable (he soon owned a string of racing thoroughbreds), a landscaped garden, and a series of outhouses. All but one were for his many servants, chauffeurs, and their families, but the largest housed a specially built, Olympic-size indoor swimming pool. This alone cost him another $100,000 (1920).

Much later, when Remus's mansion was demolished, two tunnels were discovered. Remus had had these built to store whiskey for his parties and as a possible getaway. "We found many empty bottles there," said Jack Doll, who, as a child, and neighbor, had played in Remus's garden, used the pool, and later was present when the mansion was pulled down. Doll would remember Remus with affection: he was friendly, welcomed poor children on his premises, and, though the property was surrounded by a chain link fence to keep the racehorses from straying, instructed his gardener to leave a space so that the local kids could squeeze under it to come and play. Doll remembers Remus playfully pushing a ten-year-old into the pool fully clothed, and then giving him a $10 bill "to buy a new suit." "You could buy a whole boy's outfit for a dollar in those days," Doll noted.

As soon as the house was ready, Remus started giving lavish parties. While Cincinnati "old money" either stayed away or made snide remarks behind his back while enjoying his hospitality, almost all found his invitations irresistible. At formal dinners (the dining room table was big enough to seat twenty in comfort), Remus slipped $100 bills under his guests' plates. On March 21, 1921, at a party staged to celebrate the completion of his swimming pool, he presented all of his guests with gold-engraved Elgin watches, as well as photographs of the occasion, taken by a specially hired photographer.

Two years later, in July of 1923, Remus, though by this time in serious trouble with the Justice Department, staged what was even by his standards an extraordinarily elaborate dancing and swimming party. The hundred guests were entertained by a fifteen-piece orchestra and a water-ballet, with Imogene Remus, herself a talented swimmer, making a guest appearance in a daringly cut swimsuit. Remus had bought up the stock of a bankrupt Cincinnati jeweler for $25,000, and upon arrival, all of the female guests got rings, and the males diamond tieclasps. On leaving, in the early hours of the morning, there was another surprise waiting: each female guest (there were fifty in all) was presented with a brand-new 1923 Pontiac. The descendant of one of the assiduous party-goers recalled his parents saying that on these occasions Remus himself was a discreet, almost invisible host. Exploring the mansion during the 1923 extravaganza, they came across him in his library, alone, reading a book and reluctant to be disturbed.

This quest for social respectability at almost any cost was shared by many leading bootleggers elsewhere. "Lucky" Luciano (in his posthumous memoirs) recalled with obvious pride how he had mingled with Wall Street tycoons such as banker Julie Bach, attended lavish parties given on the estate of the famous Whitney family, and ingratiated himself with over a hundred top socialites, police officials, and politicians by providing them, at huge cost, with black market tickets to the 1923 Jack Dempsey–Luis Angel Firpo fight at the New York Polo Grounds.

Remus did not confine his parties to his home. There were elaborate lunch parties in his downtown Cincinnati office (on the corner of Race and Pearl Streets), with a butler and chef in constant attendance. Also in 1923, he gave a memorable birthday party for Imogene (also attended by hundreds of guests) in the ballroom of one of its most famous hotels, the Sinton.

Some of Remus's social activities were chronicled in the Cincinnati papers (though the 1923 swimming pool party was not), and he became a household name so quickly that F. Scott Fitzgerald may well have been inspired by him. In many respects, the real-life Remus and the fictional Gatsby were similar. Both were self-made men, both gave lavish parties, both despised their guests' venality, and both were low-key hosts, observing rather than dominating the party scene. There was, however, a major difference between them. Remus, in 1923, was happily married — an adoring husband and doting father who lavished every type of expensive gift on Imogene's daughter Ruth, including a gold-plated grand piano — whereas Gatsby was a loner, at heart an unrequited romantic.

It was while looking for a suitable house that Remus first met Conners, then a real-estate agent. Conners failed to sell Remus a house, but was hired by him — first as a gofer, then as a minor bootlegging partner before becoming Remus's fanatically loyal "number two." A compulsive horse-racing gambler, Conners was soon able to afford this expensive habit: working on a percentage basis, as he did from the beginning, he became a wealthy man.

Because only a small proportion of the cases removed from the distilleries ended up as medicinal whiskey, Remus needed a halfway house where the whiskey in the multigallon drums and barrels could be discreetly repackaged and bottled. Remus and Conners first went into partnership with "John Jew" Marcus, a member of the Cincinnati underworld, but this did not last. Remus wanted to preserve his respectable image, and suspected Marcus of cheating him. It was Conners who came across an isolated farmhouse in Westwood, a rural Cincinnati suburb, enabling Remus to move into the really big time, handling huge quantities of liquor while keeping everything under his personal control.

Death Valley Farm, as it was renamed, was off the beaten track, accessible by a single dirt road and virtually impossible to find unless one knew how to get there.[2] Its owner, George Dater, a bachelor, had tried his hand at making homemade wine, but nobody would buy it. Dater's assistant, hired by Remus as caretaker, was George Gehrum, "a little, rat-faced, shifty-eyed individual[3] who lived in perpetual fear of his wife, a young woman of vigorous propensities and a taste for strong drink." She had four unruly children and ran the farm.

At first Conners paid Gehrum $100 a week to store liquor there. But when the cases arrived, Gehrum panicked, and told him to clear out and take his whiskey with him. Eventually, Remus made him a rental offer he couldn't refuse. The farm was entirely remodeled. Several large cellars were built, housing storage rooms and an underground bottling plant. A block and tackle system was installed to lower barrels into the cellars. Two men were hired full-time, whose sole job was to break up the wooden cases containing the three-gallon jars that came from the distilleries.

Remus turned Death Valley Farm into a fortified enclave. He installed floodlights and hired a permanent contingent of armed men to guard it. Conners found a mobile polling booth on wheels and turned it into a sentry box at the gate entrance, staffed twenty-four hours a day by two armed men. They had a buzzer to activate a warning signal in the main building whenever anyone approached the farm. Another buzzer turned on the floodlights installed on the main building's second floor, illuminating the entire area.

These security precautions were essential. To bona fide bootleggers such as Remus and Conners, the real enemy was not the army of bureaucrats and Prohibition Bureau agents, but hijackers. Although a convoy of Remus's liquor did fall into their hands once, no "pirates" ever succeeded in breaking into Death Valley Farm, though they tried. One night in 1920, an armed gang did manage to creep up to the gate undetected. They fired volley after volley into the building, expecting its inhabitants to flee or surrender. Remus's men fired back, with devastating effect, and the gang left, taking their casualties with them. Although the battle went on for some time, no police ever showed up. There was a tacit understanding, on all sides, that encounters such as these were part of a private war between bootleggers and hijackers, not the responsibility of the police.

The sheer size of Remus's operations required him to expand in other directions. He hired a Cincinnati-based American Express employee, Harry Stratton, to act as his shipping manager, who began moonlighting for Remus while holding down what his American Express employers believed was a full-time job. It was a lucrative arrangement for all concerned: Stratton moved Remus's liquor, crated up and bearing innocuous labels, all over the United States by "American Express" for several months — until his official employers discovered what he was up to and fired him.

This compelled Remus to set up his own delivery system. He bought twenty trucks, and had them armor-plated and redesigned to carry crates securely, without risk of contents breakage. This alone cost him $20,000 — over $200,000 today. But once they left Death Valley Farm, the "pirate" predators were on the lookout for them, so he also purchased a fleet of fast cars: six armor-plated Marmots, and Packards, Locomobiles, Dodges, a Cadillac, and a Pierce-Arrow to carry squads of heavily armed men to accompany the trucks and fend off possible attacks. There were also "runners," whose fast cars were designed to carry whiskey, on a fixed-fee, per-case basis. Because Prohibition Bureau road patrols were on the lookout for sagging springs, their chassis were reinforced. At one stage, Remus even invested in some railroad cars.

Eventually, the traffic became two-way: carefully selected bootlegger middlemen from all over America (including faraway Texas, Florida, and California) were allowed to enter Death Valley Farm in their own vehicles, to carry away their merchandise themselves. The private customers even arranged for barter deals. Those driving in from the north, for instance, came with champagne and scotch whiskey smuggled in from Canada, departing with rye and bourbon. Remus's organizational talent turned Death Valley Farm into a huge liquor supermarket. Soon, he acquired five similar "halfway houses" in other parts of the country.

As a routine precaution (for he knew law enforcement patrols were watching out for suspicious-looking trucks and cars), the trucks were hosed down, washed, and waxed while the whiskey was being loaded and paid for, so that when they left the farm they looked brand new. Ever attentive to detail, and eager to keep his "respectable" bootlegger clientele, Remus provided the truck drivers with beds, meals (cooked by a reluctant Mrs. Gehrum, who complained that her employer was far too generous), and even free whiskey tots.

While at first Remus's modus operandi was so foolproof it attracted little attention, the scale of his operations was such that local and regional Prohibition directors rapidly became aware that only a fraction of the withdrawals from his newly acquired distilleries ended up as medicinal whiskey. In return for a fee — usually $3,000 per permit issue — they looked the other way. "I never handed over the money personally," Remus told the St. Louis *Post-Dispatch*.

> Usually the go-between was the politician who had got the official his job. In that case, he sometimes got more out of it than the official himself. . . . a greedier lot of parasites never existed. . . . A few men have tried to corner the wheat market only to find that there is too much wheat in the world. I tried to corner the graft market, but I learnt there isn't enough money in the world to buy up all the public officials who demand their share of it.

Among the "parasites" were many local politicians who attended his parties. Government store keepers, known as gaugers, were also systematically bribed. An unofficial "permit" market eventually sprang up all over America, with the high-level connivance of Washington-based politicians. Blank forms, already signed, made their appearance. A standard fee, Remus later reported, was $42,000, but for that money he could withdraw unlimited quantities of liquor from distilleries he did not even own, as well as government-run bonded warehouses. There was also a traffic in practically undetectable forged blank "B permits," as the authorizations were called.

The area around Death Valley Farm was regularly patrolled by mounted police, who were fully aware of its activities. "We never paid the police, there were simply too many of them," Conners told the St. Louis *Post-Dispatch*, but "a couple of mounted police came every day. We gave them a couple of quarts a week and $10 or $15 spending money. They also had a few customers of their own in town. We let them have the stuff at $80 a case."

Prohibition agents knew about Death Valley Farm, but the amount of protection paid turned it into an "off limits" area. One day, Conners later told the St. Louis *Post-Dispatch*'s Paul Anderson, two Prohibition agents blundered into the farm, apparently by mistake. They quickly realized they had made a spectacular catch. Conners immediately phoned their superior in Cincinnati, who apologized for the intrusion and asked to talk to them. "They were supposed to be looking for stills down the road," he told Conners. After the phone call, they were apologetic. Conners offered them a drink, then another. Eventually Conners sent them on their way with a thousand dollars each and a quart of rye. "They were so drunk I was afraid they wouldn't be able to drive back to town, and offered to have one of my men act as driver," he said.

The Cincinnati police were just as venal. "Several city detectives were working for us on the side," Conners told Anderson. "Each one would dig up a few customers — saloons or private parties. The detective would give us an order, tell us how much to deliver, and what to collect. Sometimes the detective would go along on the truck when the delivery was made. This would protect the truck, and assure the buyer he was getting protection and wouldn't be raided."

Altogether, Conners said, there were over a thousand salesmen on the force, working for Remus. In other cities, in other circumstances with other bootleggers, the situation was much the same.

The Cincinnati detectives did not cost Remus much, but in spite of his exceptionally well-organized legal front, his expenses were enormous. (Al Capone, a much smaller operator than Remus as far as liquor was concerned, later told investigators that bootlegging was a losing game: "Too many overheads.") At every level, in every state where his whiskey ended up, Remus parted with enormous sums to keep the government, the Prohibition Bureau, and the police off his back. He later estimated that half his gross earnings were spent in bribes. Since, at the peak of his activities, Remus was grossing about $40 million a year, this meant that $20 million went into the hands of corrupt officials. The pattern was the same all over America, whether law enforcement officials were dealing with whiskey certificate bootleggers such as Remus or with the more adventurous rumrunners. Remus told Anderson that in his entire career he only came across two people who turned down his bribes — and they were, in time, to contribute to his downfall. One was Burt Morgan, the Prohibition director of Indiana, who "could have had $250,000" to look the other way. The other was Sam Collins, the Kentucky Prohibition director, whom Remus offered $100,000 simply to quit his job and take up a far more remunerative appointment as the manager of a soft-drink plant. As state Prohibition directors, Morgan and Collins earned $4,600 a year each. With his mixture of showmanship and genuine panache, Remus would later pay tribute to the "untouchables." "You didn't sell out; I want to shake hands with you, sir," he told Collins when he met him.

Remus was not the only victim of Collins's integrity. John Langley, the Indiana State congressman who had appointed Collins Prohibition director in the first place, and expected him to be an obedient pawn, found this out to his cost. Collins had him indicted for protecting bootleggers and taking their bribes. But Morgan and Collins were remarkable exceptions to the rule.

Remus's money "sweetened" not only poorly paid officials but senior members of the Harding administration, including the very man charged at the highest level with upholding the law — the attorney general himself. Prohibition and all that went with it — corruption, bribery, the complicity of the very people supposed to fight it — can only be understood within the wider political context of 1920s America and the iniquitous Harding administration as a whole.

8

HARDING AND
THE RACKETEERS

Prohibition was part of a far larger scandal — the scandal of the Harding presidency. Warren Gamaliel Harding was, if not the worst, certainly the weakest, most indecisive president in American history. This need not have been disastrous — America faced no major external threats between 1920 and 1923 — had not the start of Prohibition coincided with the beginning of his presidency. As it was, "the Harding Administration was responsible in its short two years and five months for more concentrated robbery and rascality than any other in the whole history of Federal Government."[1]

Harding was not an evil man, nor was he, personally, exceptionally corrupt by the standards of the time. The abysmal record of his administration was partly due to a "character flaw" inherent in the man — his excessively good-natured, amicable disposition. A former colleague in his early days noted that "he wanted to be everybody's friend . . . a small town play boy." His entourage was well aware of his craving to be liked and exploited this weakness to the hilt, knowing that he was too dependent on his friends to deal with them harshly even when their corrupt practices led to public scandals. Many judges and law enforcement officers, including those dealing with Prohibition, took their cue from what they saw happening at the top.

The cronyism of the Harding administration was such that for as long as he was in office the white-collar criminals known as "the Ohio gang" who had grown up with him and become his intimate friends knew they were immune from prosecution, that Harding would protect them from the rigors of the law. Harding's own belated realization of the extent of their corruption in all likelihood contributed to a physical and mental collapse leading to his sudden, early death. His ineptitude could not possibly be ignored, even by political allies out to praise him posthumously. At a Harding Memorial Association meeting in June of 1931, President Herbert Hoover, in a singularly ambiguous eulogy, noted that

> Harding had a dim realization that he had been betrayed by a few of the men whom he had believed were his devoted friends. It was later proved in the courts of the land that these men had betrayed not only the friendship of their staunch and loyal friend but that they had betrayed their country.

Harding grew up in the small town of Marion, Ohio, where his father, an unsuccessful homeopathic doctor, earned a supplementary income as a small-time junk dealer. Even as a boy, Warren was hail-fellow-well-met, easy-going — a gregarious youngster who preferred billiards, poker, and small-town gossip to books, but was smart enough to make a good living. His first job — as editor of a small, local paper, the Marion *Star* — suited him perfectly.

He was nineteen when he first bought shares in the paper, later winning the remaining shares in a poker game. His innate deviousness made him an excellent poker player. Tall, handsome, dignified looking, he stood out in any gathering, and knew it. But he was not what he seemed: the ultimate hollow man, he looked more impressive than he was. "No man could be as much of a Roman senator as Harding looked," Mark Sullivan wrote in *Our Times*. According to the *Saturday Evening Post*, Harding "needed only a toga to complete the illusion he had come out of the ancient world."

Florence Kling was the daughter of the richest man in Marion. She was 31 and already had a daughter by a first marriage when she married Harding, then 26. His marriage was no love match but a calculated move on his part, a social as well as a financial stepping-stone. She was tall, plain, and square-jawed, "lacking any kind of charm." Although she dressed expensively, flaunting a wilting kind of femininity, she had huge hands and moved awkwardly. She had also inherited her father's dictatorial manner and "his determination to get what he wanted out of life."[2] Her household servants, and Harding himself, lived in constant terror of her incessant nagging. Because of her imperious manner, she was known in Marion as The Duchess, and the nickname stuck, right through to her White House years. Not surprisingly, the Hardings' sex life did not last long, and they had no children — for Harding, a bitter disappointment. His personal charm was considerable: in early middle age he turned into a consistent, if somewhat lazy, sentimental philanderer.

As editor and owner-publisher of a small-town paper, Harding was well placed to enter state politics. "His conception of political progress was to make no enemies," a friend noted. Partly for this reason, he became a valued member of the Republican party, then, in Ohio, dominated by forceful, unscrupulous "Tammany Hall" type personalities such as George "Boss" Cox and "Fire Engine" Joe Foraker, who ran the state like a private preserve. Harding showed little interest in the world at large: "Books did not enter into his scheme of life in any important sense. . . . He cannot fairly be called illiterate, although some of his verbiage, when he strives to attain the impressive, furnishes a sad example of the grandiloquently inept," a local newspaperman wrote. The beginning of his speech for Taft as presidential nominee in 1912 (Taft would lose to Woodrow Wilson) — "Progression is everlastingly lifting the standards that marked the end of the world's march yesterday and planting them on new and advanced heights today" — is a fair example of his rhetoric, which reminded H. L. Mencken, the great satirist and social critic of the time, of a "string of wet sponges" and "dogs barking idiotically through endless nights. . . . It is rumble and bumble. It is flap and doodle. It is balder and dash." "It is so bad," he wrote, "that a sort of grandeur creeps into it."

His amiable, conciliatory record in state politics, combined with his impressive good looks and statesmanlike (if spurious) "presence" singled him out as an above-average player, so much so that the Ohio Republican party machine encouraged him to stand as a senator. "It costs such a lot of money to live in Washington," Florence Harding told a *Marion Star* employee. "If he was only a corporation lawyer and could pick up a lot of business on the side, I'd say yes. But he couldn't do anything there. No: I don't know as we can afford it yet."[3] Harding did finally make up his mind and went to Washington in 1915, as senator for Ohio — and immediately regretted that he had not done so earlier. The Senate, as he discovered, was the most congenial club in the world for pleasure-loving, sports-loving extroverts such as himself. He enjoyed himself immensely, especially when The Duchess was not around, and failing health kept her in Marion most of the time. George B. Christian, his confidential secretary and devoted friend, writing later about these "six years of happiness," shrewdly noted that "He didn't like being a Senator, he liked being in the Senate." Voting records show his attendance was sporadic, to say the least. He was far more often on the golf course, in the Senate bar, in a poker game, or out chasing women than in the chamber itself, and "his contribution to legislation was practically nil." Like other Ohio Republicans, Harding was a consistent supporter of Prohibition only because it was a sure-fire vote-getter. But though "politically dry," he was a steady drinker.

It was during his early political apprenticeship in Ohio that two men far more flawed than he spotted his political potential, and became his faithful aides, fixers, and boon companions. The chief usefulness of Harry Micajah Daugherty, a lawyer and failed politician, was as a veteran insider, fully conversant with the devious workings of Ohio's notoriously corrupt Republican party machine. Infinitely more cynical and manipulative than Harding, and aware, after his own abortive career in state politics, that his real talent was that of a wheeling-and-dealing, back-room boy *éminence grise,* he soon became indispensable to Harding as both mentor and strategist. Jess Smith, twelve years younger than Daugherty (they came from the same home town, Washington State House), began handling Harding's financial affairs in the late 1890s. The pair would play a major role in the Prohibition saga, and the unraveling of the Harding presidency must be laid at their door.

Although both were unprincipled, utterly ruthless operators, temperamentally they were very different. Daugherty had married a beautiful local heiress, but their life together was joyless; her serious health problems soon turned him into a devoted but harassed nurse. Their son, an alcoholic, was in and out of clinics all of his adult life. A secretive political operator, quick to take advantage of the weaknesses of others, he was also on the extreme far right of his party, obsessed with the "Bolshevik peril," seeing communist conspiracies everywhere. Ideologically, he was a striking forerunner of Senator McCarthy — his smear techniques just as outrageous.

Jess Smith, a dandy, mother's boy, dilettante store-owner, man about town, and inveterate gossip, was Daugherty's devoted admirer, aide, and hireling. Almost certainly homosexual, Smith left his mother's company only once in his life, to marry Roxy Stinson, a spectacularly good looking redhead with a showgirl's figure. It didn't last, and Smith went back to his mother, but he and Roxy remained firm friends. Smith frankly admitted his lack of manly, physical courage to her, and she, in turn, became, in time, and after his mother's death, a mother-surrogate and confidante. Smith's timorous nature made him an ideal Daugherty foil — the cringing, subservient slave-buffoon to a dominant master. The Daugherty-Smith relationship, in its brutal intimacy, is reminiscent of the protagonists in Samuel Beckett's *Waiting for Godot*. In later years, Daugherty and Smith would live together in Washington, sharing first a house, then a hotel suite, sleeping in adjoining bedrooms with the door always open, for Smith was afraid of the dark. In many respects their relations mirrored that of J. Edgar Hoover and his lifelong friend Clyde Tolson.

Daugherty and Smith were so close to Harding that he could have no secrets from them. They knew all about his philandering, including his five-year liaison with an attractive married neighbor, Carrie Phillips. They also knew about his relationship with a twenty-year-old shopgirl, Nan Britton, which began in July of 1917 (Harding was fifty-one at the time) and continued long after their child, Elizabeth Ann, was born in 1920. Harding was well aware that were this liaison to become public knowledge it would wreck his political career, and there is no doubt Daugherty and Smith took advantage of the situation, turning an already inherently weak Harding into an unwilling accomplice of their crimes.

Nan Britton wrote at length about their liaison in a book published in 1927, including a description of "the night I became his bride" that had all of the elements of a Feydeau farce.[4] They had checked into a hotel on Broadway "where his Washington friends had intimated to him that they had stopped under similar unconventional circumstances with no unpleasant consequences." But no sooner had they made love than two men — detectives on the lookout for prostitutes — burst into the room. "They've got us!" was Harding's reaction. "Let this poor little girl go," he begged them. They told him "he should have thought of that before," Britton wrote.

> I remember he told them that I was twenty-two years old and I, not realizing that he wanted to make me as old as he safely could, interrupted him and stated truthfully that I was only twenty. To almost every argument he advanced on my behalf they answered "You'll have to tell that to the judge." About that time one of the men picked up Mr. Harding's hat. Inside was his name, in gold lettering, and upon seeing the name they became calm immediately. Not only calm but strangely respectful. . . . We packed our things immediately and the men conducted us to a side entrance. On the way out Mr. Harding handed them a $20 bill. When we were in the taxi, he remarked explosively, "Gee, Nan, I thought I wouldn't get out of that under $1,000!"

In his relationship with Nan Britton, he was both infinitely devious and extraordinarily naive. He made elaborate travel arrangements for her before her pregnancy, smuggling her into his hotel room during dozens of out-of-town senatorial speaking engagements or official business trips to New York; making reservations under assumed names, but dining with her in well-known New York restaurants; going to popular New York plays with her in crowded theaters, running considerable risk of discovery — his chief concern neither the press nor public opinion but The Duchess. At the same time he wrote her forty-page love letters promising eventual marriage and an idyllic future together. He often smuggled her into his Senate office. "He told me he liked to have me be with him in his office, for then the place held precious memories and he could visualize me there during the hours he worked alone." In January of 1919, she would later write: " . . . we stayed [in his office] quite a while that evening, longer, he said, than it was wise for us to do so, because the rules governing guests in the Senate offices were rather strict. It was here, we both decided afterwards, that our baby girl was conceived. . . ."

Harding, she wrote, seemed genuinely excited by the news, and looked forward to being a father. He loved children, he said, and had always wanted a daughter. This may have been another example of Harding's deviousness, for he never allowed Nan Britton to show him their child, though once he became president she was frequently smuggled into the White House, where they made love in a broom closet adjoining his anteroom. She too obtained her share of perks: halfway through his presidency, $75,000 was appropriated to enable her, at length, to "investigate the raw silk market in the Orient."

Following Woodrow Wilson's stroke in office, both Harding's nomination as Republican presidential candidate and his subsequent election campaign also had farcical undertones. At the start of the 1919 Chicago Convention, he was no more than a favorite son, a rank outsider. There were four main contenders, all of them far more worthy presidential material. Daugherty, Harding's campaign manager, found it difficult to raise money and openly admitted, at its start, that "poor old Warren hasn't a Chinaman's chance." But during the subsequent, increasingly deadlocked convention, Daugherty worked hard in smoke-filled rooms to convince the Republican party bosses that Harding was the ideal compromise candidate. Halfway through the proceedings, George Harvey, a prominent Republican and editor of the *North American Review,* asked Harding to "tell us, in your conscience and before God, whether there is anything that might be brought up against you that would embarrass the party, any impediment that might disqualify you or make you inexpedient, as candidate or President." Harding said he needed time to consider his reply, but a short while later, almost certainly after consulting Daugherty, told him he was clean. As Harvey then told reporters covering the convention, "There ain't no first-raters this year. . . . Harding is the best of the second-raters."

By the sixth ballot, it became known on the floor that, thanks to Daugherty's efforts and patronage pledges, Harding had become the choice of the party bosses. After the eighth ballot, which showed a steep rise in the number of votes for him, the cry went up: "Climb on the bandwagon."

He finally made it on the tenth ballot, and his singularly down-to-earth reaction, on winning the nomination, was that of a born gambler, remarkable for its lack of cant or ethical content. "I feel," he said, "like a man who goes in with a pair of eights and comes out with aces full."

The party bosses were unaware of Nan Britton and her daughter, but they did know about his former mistress, Carrie Phillips. They offered her a deal: an immediate lump sum ($20,000) and a monthly allowance for as long as Harding remained president, as well as a world tour for herself and her husband. She accepted immediately.

It was Jess Smith's turn to step into the limelight. As Harding's campaign manager, he came up with two deliberately low-key, singularly uninspiring campaign slogans: "Think of America first," and "With Harding and back to normal." They proved singularly effective. After the heady interventionist days of Woodrow Wilson, the trauma of the Great War, and the unprecedentedly violent coal miners' and steel workers' strikes of the previous year (as brutally repressed as the strike of Boston's policemen, which had deeply shocked the public), America longed for a return to the good old days. The temptation to withdraw into a secure cocoon, as Charles Mee noted in *The Ohio Gang*,[5] was irresistible, and the vote for Harding, implying as it did a refusal to get involved with cynical Europeans, legitimized the American withdrawal from the League of Nations. It also explained the subliminal attraction of Prohibition, with its promise of a return not only to sobriety but to social harmony in a refreshingly simple, family-oriented, church-dominated America.

Although Jess Smith operated a campaign headquarters in Washington out of the shabby New Ebbett Hotel (Harding's penny-pinching was legendary), he believed that Harding's homespun, folksy image could best be projected by having him campaign mostly from his front porch in his home town. It was Howard Mannington, another Daugherty crony — later a notorious deal-maker, bootlegger, and shady go-between — who handled the endless stream of visitors to Marion, with Harding putting on a convincing act as a loving family man and the incarnation of small-town America's virtues and down-to-earth qualities. After visiting Harding in Marion, and watching Mrs. Harding sweep the front porch herself, Chicago Mayor "Big Bill" Thompson came away elated. "Where but in America could that happen?" he asked, prophesying that Harding would be "one of our greatest Presidents." Nan Britton was told in no uncertain terms to stay away until well after the election.

Harding may have fooled the public, but he didn't fool himself. He discovered, very soon after his election, that the United States presidency, even in the less complicated world of the 1920s, required qualities he simply did not possess. He admitted the fact, semipublicly, time and time again. "I don't think I'm big enough for the Presidency," he told a judge after a round of golf. "Oftentimes, as I sit here, I don't seem to grasp that I am President," he admitted to a newspaper columnist. "I can't make a damn thing out of this tax problem," he said to an aide. "I listen to one side and they seem right, and then, God! I talk to the other side and they seem just as right and here I am where I started. I know somewhere there is a book that will give me the truth, but Hell! I couldn't read the book!" When Arthur Draper, of the New York *Tribune,* returned from a trip abroad and sought to brief the President, Harding told him: "I don't know anything about this European stuff. You and Jud [his political secretary, Jud Welliver] get together and he can tell me later. He handles these matters for me." Harding was also famous for his malapropisms, as when, questioned about the (then alarming) 1.5-million unemployment figure, he replied that "the figures are astounding only because we are a 100 million, and this parasite percentage is always with us."

There were some able men in his administration, though on the financially archconservative side (Herbert Hoover; Andrew Mellon, a millionaire with extensive distilling interests; and an able secretary of State, Charles Evans Hughes, later to be Supreme Court chief justice, who made up for Harding's ignorance of the world at large), but they were outnumbered by mediocre Republican party hacks, dubious Ohio gang cronies, and downright crooks. Several (Secretary of War John Weeks and Labor Secretary John Davis among them) were there simply because they were poker-playing sycophants, but his most unsuitable appointment, by far, was that of Harry Daugherty as attorney general. Daugherty wanted the Justice Department and Harding owed too much to his kingmaker to refuse him anything — though he did balk at giving Jess Smith a cabinet appointment.

It didn't make any difference: Jess Smith moved into the Justice Department anyway, with an office (and a stock-market ticker-tape machine) across the anteroom from Daugherty. He had no clearly defined job, but he did have a secretary, unlimited access to Justice Department files, and a Bureau of Investigation badge, and was soon regarded as Daugherty's second in command, an unofficial deputy attorney general. There was a constant stream of shady visitors in and out of Smith's office. Thomas Felder — lobbyist, veteran member of the Ohio gang, bootlegger, and con man with underworld connections — practically used it as his own. So did Howard Mannington, now a prominent Washington bootlegger. Mannington was the Harding crony who had masterminded Harding's "front porch" election campaign in Marion with his sidekick Bill Orr, a former journalist. In a later book, *The Inside Story of the Harding Tragedy,* remarkable for its lack of substance and self-serving, mealy-mouthed ingenuity, Daugherty made almost no mention of Smith and claimed that he had known nothing of his activities until too late. But he never did explain in the book why Smith had an office in the Justice Department across from his own anteroom and what he was doing there.

Myron Herrick, the Republican party's Ohioan elder statesman, did his best to prevent Daugherty's appointment. "Harry Daugherty will wreck your administration," he told Harding — and was packed off to Paris as ambassador. Later, but only after he had been forced out of his job, the *New York Times* would belatedly write that "from the first day, Daugherty had been a gross misfit as Attorney General."

Alice Roosevelt Longworth, ex-President Teddy Roosevelt's daughter, observed the new White House social scene with patrician distaste. Under Harding, visitors came in two categories. The run-of-the-mill guests were kept downstairs, where they were served fruit juice. But Harding's cronies, and other privileged guests, were invited upstairs, where liquor flowed like water. On her first visit to Harding's study, she wrote that

> . . . no rumor could have exceeded the reality: the study was filled with cronies (Daugherty, Jess Smith), the air heavy with tobacco smoke, trays with bottles containing every imaginable brand of whiskey stood about, cards and poker chips ready at hand, an atmosphere of waistcoat unbuttoned, feet on desk, and spittoon alongside.[6]

Harding, she added, "was not a bad man. He was just a slob." Had she been allowed to visit those parts of the Senate reserved for the select few, she would have found a similar ambiance. Part of the

Senate Library had been curtained off, and had become "the best bar in town," well stocked thanks to regular visits from ingratiatingly subservient customs officials bringing with them confiscated liquor.

Harding was similarly showered with gifts of liquor. Because excessive overt flaunting of Prohibition rules was bound to attract attention, Ned McLean, the wealthy playboy son of John R. McLean, owner of the *Cincinnati Enquirer* and the *Washington Post,* provided Harding with a safe house. This was the "little green house on K Street," a short walk from the White House, where Harding's cronies met, drank, played billiards and poker, and, behind Harding's back, plotted their nefarious schemes. There was another, even safer house for Harding and his cronies outside town: a hunting lodge at Deer Park Creek, unknown even to The Duchess. All the while, the ritual of Prohibition was being ostentatiously observed. When the dreadnought *Washington* was launched in 1924, a congressman's daughter broke a bottle of river water over its bow, and Dr. Charles Foster Kent of Yale was hired to rewrite the Bible, removing all references to wine.[7]

The scandals of the Harding years came in quick succession. Under Woodrow Wilson, 13,000 post office jobs had been removed from patronage and placed under nonpolitical Civil Service regulations. Harding, under Republican pressure, annulled the ruling. The officials were fired, and the jobs parceled out to political appointees. But this was negligible compared to the scams Harding's cronies indulged in with total impunity.

Colonel "Charlie" Forbes was a close friend of Harding's — perhaps the most constant member of his poker-playing circle of intimates. Harding appointed him Health secretary and head of the Veterans Bureau, a sizeable department with a $550 million annual budget. Forbes proceeded to asset-strip his own department with all the skill of a Mafia boss. Harding's sister, Carolyn Votaw, who had married a Seventh-Day Adventist clergyman (Harding had appointed *him* federal superintendent of prisons), knew Forbes well, and introduced him to a friend of hers, a wealthy construction company executive called Elias Mortimer and his very pretty, ambitious wife Kate. There was a pressing need for veterans' hospitals, and Mortimer promised Forbes huge kickbacks for every building contract awarded to his firm. Forbes let him see the supposedly secret rival bids. For every new hospital, Forbes got a cash payment of $50,000 and up. On the pretext of looking at possible sites, the threesome took expensive trips all over America, where Forbes was lavishly entertained (and also slept with Mortimer's wife), with Mortimer footing the bill.

Forbes milked the Veterans Administration in other ways. He paid hugely inflated prices for hospital land (up to $95,000 for sites whose market value was $17,000), splitting the difference with the sellers. He disposed of brand-new hospital equipment at token prices, in return for kickbacks, then replaced what he had sold for practically nothing with brand-new items for which the Veterans Administration paid hugely inflated prices, again getting a cut. In subsequent investigations he was shown to have paid ten times the market price for 35,000 gallons of floor cleaner and 32,000 gallons of floor wax — a hundred-year supply. In all he was shown to have squandered $33 million — or several hundred million dollars in current values.

The trashing of the Veterans Administration became common knowledge. Harding duly learned of his poker buddy's practices, and flew into a rage, but protected him from the law by sending him abroad on a spurious mission. Although Forbes was eventually sentenced (in 1925) to two years in jail and fined $10,000, his real problems only began after Harding's death.

Albert Fall, secretary of the Interior, another close Harding crony, was resourceful in other, more imaginative ways. He was an intimate friend of two oil tycoons, Edward Doheny and Harry Sinclair, both, hardly coincidentally, heavy contributors to Harding's campaign fund. Before World War I, President William Howard Taft had ordered large tracts of oil-bearing land to be handed over to the U.S. Navy to ensure adequate supplies at the lowest possible cost. Thanks to a three-way scam involving Navy Secretary Edwin Dealey, Interior Secretary Albert Fall, and — in the wings — Justice Department Secretary Daugherty, the two oil tycoons ended up with most of the Navy's priceless oil-rich land.

As a first step, Navy Secretary Dealey (who later had to resign) had the site ownerships secretly transferred from the Navy to the Department of the Interior. Then Fall worked out a deal to hand them over to Doheny and Sinclair. There was a semblance of legality: in exchange for the land, Doheny and Sinclair were to build storage tanks for the Navy and provide the Department of the Interior with oil certificates (at favorable rates) to be used by U.S. Navy ships.

These arrangements were not publicized, and there were no bids from competing oilmen — Fall invoking the overriding need for secrecy in "matters affecting national defense." He himself received kickbacks amounting to several hundred thousand dollars, resigning shortly afterward to take up a well-paid sinecure in Sinclair Oil. The payoff was a tiny fraction of the hundreds of millions of dollars that Doheny and Sinclair made out of the scam, known since as the Teapot Dome scandal.

Daugherty, a later investigation showed, must have been aware of Fall's scheme (the Justice Department was required to give its stamp of approval to deals of this importance), but nothing was ever proved. Only later did it become known that he had invested in Sinclair stock before it started booming as a result of the Navy deal. Daugherty was a difficult man to catch in flagrante, operating as he did behind his front man Jess Smith. He was also utterly ruthless with the small handful of liberal Republican politicians who tried to bring him down.

Later, as investigation after investigation revealed the scandalous depths of the Harding administration, Daugherty would claim — a tactic later emulated by Senator McCarthy — that there was "abundant proof" that it was all part of "the hellish designs of the Communist International." When Senators Burton K. Wheeler and Smith W. Brookhart did succeed in launching an investigation into his Justice Department activities, he told the *New York Times* (the interview was published on April 24, 1924) that

> ... the two senators, who spent last summer in Russia with their friends, were part of an effort to capture, by deceit and design, as many members of the Senate as possible and to spread through Washington and the cloakrooms of Congress a poison gas as deadly as that which sapped and destroyed brave soldiers in the late war. The enemy is at the gate, he [Wheeler] aims at nothing short of the overthrow of the institutions which are your protection and mine against tyranny.

Even by the lax standards of the 1920s, Daugherty's conduct while attorney general was remarkable, not just for the extent of his corruption but for its eclecticism. No transaction was too trivial for him. In the Washington brownstone on H Street Daugherty shared with Smith, the Armour meat processing company regularly delivered sides of bacon and ham, while uniformed police officers paid for past and future favors with confiscated liquor. No one, at the time, seems to have been preoccupied by the discrepancy between Daugherty's salary ($12,000 a year) and his household expenses ($50,000 at least, for he entertained heavily) — and Smith did not draw an official salary at all.

Roxy Stinson, Jess Smith's ex-wife, testifying before the Senate investigation on Daugherty, was later to be an unwilling but inexhaustible source of information. She told how Smith had boasted to her of the windfall Daugherty expected to collect from the proceeds of a pirated film of the Dempsey-Carpentier match. Smith had acquired the film on Daugherty's behalf and expected to sell it all over America. She remembered Smith telling her that Daugherty's friends had made $33 million in five days over the Sinclair Oil land deal. "Were you [i.e., Daugherty and Smith] in on it?" she asked him. "No," said Smith, "that's what we're sore about." But she also remembered how, shortly after the Sinclair Oil deal, Smith had shown up in Ohio where she lived, and proudly boasted that he had seventy-five $1,000 bills on him. She told of Daugherty and Smith's innumerable expensive junkets to New York, paid for by Joe Weber, of Weber and Fields, a big theatrical entrepreneur, who provided them with lavish accommodation, theater tickets, "and all sorts of other favors." It turned out that Weber wanted parole for his wife's brother, currently in jail. But Daugherty wanted hard cash as well as a good time in New York, and she remembered Smith telling her: "I don't know whether we'll bother with him or not. He is awful cheap and wants something for nothing."

In this immediate postwar period, there was a great deal of litigation arising out of irregular wartime contracts and seizures made under the Enemy Appropriations Act. As attorney general, Daugherty was at the center of things: he could expedite, delay, and settle cases virtually at will. In some cases, documents simply disappeared. Captain H. L. Scaife, a former Justice Department investigator, told Senator Wheeler how he had resigned in disgust after discovering that his patient investigation into the Standard Aircraft Company affair had been mysteriously "lost." The company had been paid millions of dollars during the war to provide fighter aircraft, but not a single plane had been made or delivered. It was later discovered that a representative for the Japanese Mitsui company, which had acquired the Standard Aircraft Company, had met with Jess Smith. Money had changed hands, and the proceedings just stopped.

Daugherty was equally diligent in speeding cases up, for a suitable fee. The $6 million assets of the American Metal Company, owned by the Metallgesellschaft und Metall Bank in Frankfurt, had been seized during the war. Daugherty and Fall, the secretary of the Interior, used John King, a middleman who often worked for Jess Smith, to bargain with German lawyers. $441,000 changed hands. King took a fee, with the bulk of the money going to Jess Smith. As Daugherty's bagman, he is thought to have handed over some of it to the attorney general himself.

As Senator Wheeler found out to his cost, proving Daugherty's financial involvement in these scams was not easy. There was a simple reason why Jess Smith was so invaluable to Daugherty: Smith's brother, Mal, owned the Midland National Bank of Ohio, and it was through this small bank that a lot of the money was laundered. The bank was capitalized at only $100,000, but received huge deposits regularly. When investigators finally succeeded in getting permission to look at the records, Mal Smith destroyed them, but not before Wheeler discovered that there were large fluctuating deposits there in Daugherty's name.

But Daugherty and Smith's biggest money-earner came from Prohibition. Millions of dollars passed through Jess Smith's hands provided by those shrewd enough, and wealthy enough, to buy immunity from prosecution. George Remus may not have been Smith's biggest single contributor, but he was the most notorious — for the simple reason that when, finally, his huge cash payments failed to buy him the promised exemption, he decided to spill the beans.

9

REMUS UNRAVELS

Every bootlegger, Prohibition agent, nightclub owner, and affluent private customer in the Midwest knew about Remus, his parties,
his ostentatious generosity, and his inexhaustible supply of high-quality
liquor. He was convinced he was untouchable. All of the politicians
and law enforcement agencies of the city of Cincinnati were in his
pocket, and he had what he knew was a unique relationship with the
"deputy Attorney General," Jess Smith. But his luck was not to last,
and when it went, like Job, he was assailed with every conceivable
woe.

There were a number of reasons for his downfall — his overcon-
fidence and excessive greed, to begin with. In 1922, he was well on
the way to establishing a whiskey monopoly. This was not to the liking
of other bootleggers with underworld connections, and he may well
have been the victim of a conspiracy to bring him down at all costs. His
German origins, too, were almost certainly held against him in these
hysterically anti-German years, though his immediate fall stemmed also
from the ingenuity of the two people in the world he found he could
not bribe — the Prohibition directors of Indiana and Kentucky. But

most of all his nemesis came when Jess Smith, Daugherty's front man and operative, fearful that he was about to be indicted at long last and unwilling to betray his mentor, committed suicide in December of 1923.

When, a year later, Senator Wheeler finally persuaded the Senate to look into Daugherty's record, Remus became one of the star witnesses of the investigative committee. His cross-examination explained why he had been so sure he would never come to grief, even if indicted. Remus told the committee how his lawyer, Elijah Zoline, introduced him to Smith and then "gracefully withdrew."

> WHEELER: Did you know he was close to Daugherty?
>
> REMUS: Well, having practiced criminal law, we knew these matters. It was a matter of public record that he was pretty close to the Attorney General.
>
> WHEELER: What did he say?
>
> REMUS: He said that for a consideration he would obtain permits, if I would pay him so much for the permits per case.
>
> WHEELER: What did he say with reference to your being indicted in these matters, or prosecuted?
>
> REMUS: That there would never be any conviction — maybe a prosecution, but no ultimate conviction, that no one would ever have to go to the penitentiary.
>
> WHEELER: How much did you pay him on this first occasion?
>
> REMUS: Fifty thousand dollars.
>
> WHEELER: And the money paid to Jess Smith was for protection, was it not?
>
> REMUS: Yes, he was to do what he could, to make connections as far as the withdrawal of these permits was concerned.
>
> WHEELER: Did the payment involve him getting the permits for you?
>
> REMUS: No, that was a different arrangement. The person withdrawing the liquor would pay $15 to $21 a case. A case contains three gallons. That you would consider overage expenses. That would be in addition to the $21 to $25 a case you would pay to the warehouseman.

WHEELER: Did Smith get any of that?

REMUS: Yes, he got about — we figured at the time he and I talked — about $1.50 to $2.50 a case.

WHEELER: Are payments of that kind included in this $250,000 to $300,000 that you paid him (for protection)?

REMUS: Oh, no, Senator.

WHEELER: That was in addition?

REMUS: Yes.

Remus told the committee of meetings with Smith in hotels in New York, Washington, Cincinnati, Indianapolis, and Columbus, Ohio (the dates, times, and places had been carefully logged), each meeting invariably concluding with cash payments, or checks made out to "pay cash." On one occasion, in Indianapolis, he saw Smith and Daugherty together but Daugherty was never directly involved in the transactions. Wheeler asked Remus whether there was any friendship between the two men, or was it "a pure-cold-blooded proposition." "Not a bit of sentiment attached to it," Remus replied. Again and again, the Senate investigators returned to the subject of Remus's promised immunity.

WHEELER: Did you discuss with him anything with reference to your indictment? [Remus was currently in jail.]

REMUS: Yes. The Department of Justice would put up a vigorous battle, but ultimately I would never see the penitentiary.

WHEELER: And that vigorous prosecution was going to be done just as a blind? Was that it?

REMUS: I am sorry to say that is not true, Senator.

WHEELER: But that is what he told you?

REMUS: Yes. He said that while there might be a conviction before the jury, the matter would go to the Court of Appeals and the case would be reversed.

WHEELER: Did Jess Smith not say to you that it did not make any difference if the Court of Appeals did confirm it, he could get you out of it?

REMUS: Yes.

WHEELER: When did he say this?

REMUS: A short time after my conviction — May 1922.

WHEELER: Even after the conviction?

REMUS: Absolutely.

WHEELER: He told you you would never serve a day, that he would see to it that you got out of it?

REMUS: Absolutely.

WHEELER: Where was this?

REMUS: At the Washington Hotel.

WHEELER: Did you pay him any money at this time?

REMUS: About twenty or thirty thousand dollars.

WHEELER: The way he would get this suspension of sentence or anything would be through the Attorney General?

REMUS: Yes. He said he was assured there would be no ultimate sending away of Remus or his men to a penitentiary.

WHEELER: And who did he say assured him of that?

REMUS: The general.

WHEELER: He called him the general, did he?

REMUS: Yes, sir.

WHEELER: How many times did he tell you that?

REMUS: I should say twice or three times.

WHEELER: Did he tell you that if the Supreme Court affirmed that decision you would still be granted a pardon, or that you would never have to serve a day in jail?

REMUS: Yes, he said that. On account of his friendship with the general, he said he would do everything he could to see that the matter would be reversed.

The indictment that Jess Smith promised would be quashed was the work of the two "untouchables": Burt Morgan, the Prohibition director of Indiana, and Sam Collins, Prohibition director of Kentucky. Luck was on their side. In 1921, a regular Death Valley Farm customer, Nathan J. Goldman, was flagged down in Indiana with cases of whiskey in his car. In court, he pleaded guilty, and received a $500 fine and a ninety-day jail sentence. In the time-honored bootlegging tradition, he had refused to say where he had obtained his liquor, but Morgan was certain it had come from Death Valley Farm, which he had heard about, though he knew nothing of its whereabouts. Since it was in another state, the chances of involving Remus seemed slim.

But Morgan went to see Goldman in jail and proposed his immediate release in return for his cooperation. Goldman accepted. He even agreed to take Morgan by car to Death Valley Farm to show him where it was. They drove there, turned around, and went back to Indiana. Unlike Cincinnati, Indiana really was a dry state, and its agents, under the "untouchable" Morgan, were less ready to be paid off, but Morgan knew he would have a hard time getting the cooperation of his Cincinnati colleagues.

Another "untouchable," Sam Collins, the Kentucky Prohibition director, was also on Remus's track. His agents had, by chance, arrested two runners from a Chicago saloon after their cargo of whiskey spilled into the street after a car crash. They too agreed to cooperate, and admitted it had come from Death Valley Farm.

Morgan and Collins got together. Since they had no jurisdiction outside their own states, they knew they would have to get the Cincinnati Bureau to issue a search warrant, and to do that they would have to trick their corrupt Cincinnati colleagues into cooperating with them. Once more, luck was on their side. Although Remus invariably insisted on cash payments so that his involvement could not be traced, he had made an exception for Goldman, who had paid for his consignment in part with a $250 check to Conners. By oversight, after Goldman's arrest, it had not been canceled, so here was invaluable proof.

Morgan and Collins, and their teams, came quietly and unannounced to Cincinnati and set up headquarters in the Sinton Hotel. They called their Cincinnati colleague, Robert E. Flora, and asked him to join them without telling him the reason for their presence. Only when Flora showed up was he told that the purpose of their visit was a raid on Death Valley Farm. After studying the evidence, he had no alternative but to issue a search warrant. Virtually under house arrest himself and unable to make a telephone call (Morgan and Collins were well aware that the Cincinnati Prohibition Bureau would tip Remus off if given the chance), Flora was compelled to go along with them on the raid.

The raiders used unmarked cars that Sunday noon, and did not have to use force, as the men at the gate assumed they were customers. Once inside, they showed their search warrant, and quickly discovered the cellars, the bottling plant, and hundreds of gallons of whiskey.

Conners and Gehrum had been to the races the day before, and did not show up at Death Valley Farm until late that Sunday afternoon. The search was still in progress. Conners pretended he was simply "looking for a friend," and he and Gehrum left in a hurry. They immediately drove to the Remus mansion to tell him of the raid.

With his extensive network of contacts, Remus had in fact heard rumors that a strange Prohibition agent was in town, but was not too concerned. Gehrum had told him there were hardly any stocks of liquor inside the farm. He had lied, it was later revealed, because he had some of his own customers lined up and wanted to make a profit on the side. Nevertheless, Remus sent a messenger down to the farm early on Sunday morning, to collect some money. The messenger was told to be sure and tell the men on duty to clear out all of the liquor, because there were strange men in town. The messenger forgot to relay the message.

Remus's first reaction, on hearing of the raid in progress, was to mount an armed expedition and rout the raiders with guns. A weeping Imogene begged him not to ("I know you'll be killed! Then what will I do?"). Remus arranged bail for those on the farm who had been arrested. Three weeks later, Conners and Remus were themselves arraigned. In May of 1922, Remus, Conners, and eleven of his staff went on trial, and were found guilty. Remus received a two-year jail sentence, and the maximum $10,000 fine. Conners and the others got sentences ranging from one year to eighteen months and fines ranging from $5,000 to $10,000. All appealed to a higher court and were allowed further bail until the next hearing.

Remus was still not overly worried, convinced that the protection money he had spent would prevent any of them from ever going to jail. "When you have Washington fixed," he told Anderson, "you don't need to go below." Even with Death Valley Farm closed, his five other halfway houses — in Reading and Hamilton, Pennsylvania; Glendale, California; Buffalo, New York; and New York City — were doing well. He carried on business almost as usual, if on a slightly smaller scale. But his extraordinary luck had deserted him, and with Smith's suicide, he had lost his expensive link to Daugherty. The Supreme Court refused to consider his case, and in January of 1924, all appeals exhausted, Remus, Conners, and his eleven subordinates began their jail sentences in Atlanta.

Remus was engaged in another major operation during the time he remained free on appeal: he had become part of a St. Louis and Indianapolis syndicate that had bought the Jack Daniel's distillery. His partners, prominent local politicians and state officials, including a congressman and the St. Louis director of Internal Revenue, assured him that their stature and influence guaranteed them all full immunity.

It was while he was in jail that this syndicate not only tricked him out of any return on his investment but behaved so ineptly that they would later be arrested, charged, and convicted. Against Remus's advice, instead of paying expensive intermediaries for withdrawal permits, and proceeding by stealth, a few cases at a time, they simply emptied the Jack Daniel's distillery of its 31,000 gallons of whiskey, replacing the barrels with water and wood alcohol. Then they committed what Remus regarded as the most unpardonable crime of all: before selling the Jack Daniel's whiskey to private customers, they watered it down — to such an extent that the purchasers demanded their money back. The case went against them, and the sensational trial that followed (Remus was originally slated to be a prosecution witness) was probably triggered by furious customers in high places.

Remus's departure from Cincinnati to an Atlanta jail was one of the highlights of the social season. Remus, in pearl-gray suit, spats, and diamond tiepin, and Imogene by his side, turned the trip into yet another party. Accompanied by federal marshals (whom he treated like honored guests), Imogene, George, Conners, and the eleven other sentenced men boarded a specially hired luxury railroad car, hitched to the regular Atlanta train. On board was a specially hired chef. Waiters served gourmet meals. On his arrival, knowing he would have to wear prison garb, Remus presented the porter with his silk shirts and reporters and photographers were on hand to interview the "Bootleg King." Remus told them he hoped to lose weight in prison.

By this time he had put his affairs in order. Imogene got a huge check to cover all expenses for the next two years. Remus also gave her power of attorney, so that she could run his business for him while he was in jail. That was to prove his biggest mistake — and the cause of even greater problems.

10

THE ADVENTURERS

Coast Guard to Long Island fisherman: "See you tonight, Charlie."
Fisherman to Coast Guard: "Not if I can help it!"[1]

While George Remus was taking advantage of loopholes in the Volstead Act to build his bootlegging empire, others, more adventurously, became smugglers — and folk heroes. The very history of the United States gave them considerable legitimacy: as lawyers constantly reminded the courts, John Hancock, a founder of the Republic and one of the signatories of the Declaration of Independence, had himself been a smuggler, openly defying the British and their hated Stamp Act at the start of the Revolutionary War. He soon became the rumrunners' patron saint. Lawyers also used to compare their clients to those heroes who had patriotically challenged the pre–Civil War Fugitive Slave Act, smuggling runaway slaves out of the South and into Canada.

In actual fact, importing liquor into America during Prohibition involved more than rum-running. It required considerable complex advance planning, usually in more than one continent, in a pre-satellite era when transatlantic communications were far more easy to monitor. Just as present-day drug traffickers constitute only part of a sophisticated organization with international ramifications — involving networks of farmers, middlemen, and money launderers from as far away as Afghanistan, Lebanon, Myanmar (ex-Burma), and Pakistan — so the rumrunners, from 1920 onward, were only bit players in a series of complicated, often European-based, operations.

But the forerunners of today's drug barons and money launderers were not underworld figures but respectable merchant banks and brokerage houses in Paris, London, Bremen, Hamburg, and Kiel, with equally respectable commission agents in Africa, Canada, Latin America, the West Indies, and the French islands of St. Pierre and Miquelon, off the Canadian coast, where liquor was exceptionally cheap (a quart of gin cost 25 cents, rum 50 cents a gallon, and a bottle of champagne $1). Prohibition would give St. Pierre and Miquelon a level of prosperity that is still remembered there with nostalgia. They are the one place in the world where their benefactor, Al Capone, even at this remove in time, remains a hero. Many of the houses still standing there are made out of the wooden cases the champagne bottles originally came in.

Increasingly, U.S. diplomats abroad were enlisted in the war against bootleggers — so much so that they began complaining that they were spending more time on anti-bootlegging activities than on their regular duties. Washington received a constant stream of information from U.S. consulates around the world relaying details of suspect ships' departures, cargoes, and probable destinations. A report from the U.S. Consulate in Copenhagen is typical of many. "The German steamer *Apis* has sailed from Copenhagen with 437,000 liters of liquor," it informed the State Department in 1923. The cargo was "falsely billed as destined for Africa but the intent is to smuggle the cargo into the United States." The reluctance of America's allies to help stamp out the liquor traffic caused diplomatic rifts similar to those that would later plague America's relations with her Latin American partners over drugs.

America's neighbors all profited from Prohibition — to the extent that European shippers of gin, whiskey and champagne began shipping stocks previously sent directly to the United States to convenient relay stations such as Mexico, Canada, and St. Pierre and Miquelon. Export records from the famous French champagne firm Moet et Chandon show that its champagne consignments to Canada increased more than tenfold from 1922 to 1929. After the end of Prohibition, exports to Canada dropped dramatically.[2]

The Bahamas became a privileged halfway house — the Medellín of the Prohibition era. Sir Harry Cordeaux, governor of the Bahamas, in a speech in Montreal in 1921, openly acknowledged that "the healthy condition of the island's finances is largely due to its liquor traffic" — so much so that 250,000 pounds were spent on harbor improvements. In the House of Commons, some teetotaling Scottish MPs criticized the British government's passivity. W. G. A. Ormsby-Gore, Colonial Office under-secretary, told the House that "practically the whole of the large increase in imports of wine and spirits into the Bahamas last year [1922] was due to Prohibition in America." Asked whether, "for the sake of friendship with America," these colonies could be rationed, Ormsby-Gore was brutally frank. "No," he said, for the traffic "would only go to Haiti or some other convenient island belonging to another nation."

To the law enforcers' fury, many prominent Americans openly aided, abetted, and praised the lawbreakers. Prohibition had only been in force eighteen months when Democratic Senator Owen Stanley broke into song on the floor of the Senate, reading into the Congressional Record the popular "Song of the Moonshiners" (to the tune of "My Country, 'Tis of Thee"):

> My country, 'tis of thee,
> Land of grape juice and tea,
> Of thee I sing.
> Land where we all have tried
> To break the laws and lied!
> From every mountain-side
> The bootlegs spring. . . .

Roy A. Haynes, the first Prohibition commissioner, wrote, in his book *Prohibition Inside Out*,[3] that "rum and narcotics smuggling, evasion of the immigration laws, and diamond smuggling run hand in hand," but that liquor was by far the most lucrative cargo. Over fifty ships of 5,000 tons and over operated out of the Bahamas in 1922, "the shippers of their lawless fleets drawn chiefly from the scum of the American waterfronts." As would be the case later with narcotics, some investments were virtually risk-free, on a "forward buying" credit plan. "If the runner is known, the local liquor importer will trust you for as many cases as you care to gamble on at $5 a case. You pay him the cost price per case until the vessel returns with the money — one of them cleared $200,000 in a few months."

Investors found as many ways of circumventing the law at sea as Remus did on land, and the methods used were strikingly similar to those used by embargo-evading arms dealers today. A Bahamian shipping owner got clearance to ship liquor to a fictitious British, Canadian, or French port. If apprehended within territorial waters, reduced in 1923 from twelve miles to three, the ship's captain simply claimed this was merely an innocent voyage between two foreign ports. After disposing of the cargo, he entered a U.S. port for clearance "on ballast," to refuel, pick up a legitimate cargo, and go on his way.

Because the U.S. Coast Guard had the right to board and search suspect vessels flying the American flag, even on the high seas, there was a rush to switch to flags of convenience — a standard procedure to get around the law. "A British merchant institutes libel proceedings against a certain (American) yacht owner who has defaulted on stores or debt, and claims he can't pay. His boat is sold. The British merchant buys it. It is now a British ship, rum-running with the same crew." Once at sea, it also became common practice to alter ships' names after a few round trips, to confuse the Coast Guard.

After the 1929 Wall Street crash, bootleggers had a huge choice of luxury yachts — the former toys of once-wealthy speculators. As Sally Rand, later the famous "fan dancer" star, recalled,

> These beautiful yachts that cost half a million dollars were sitting around (on the West Coast) with barnacles on them. These are the people who jumped out of windows. Who's gonna buy a yacht? A man came up to me and said, "Hey, any of these yachts for sale?" I said: "Are you kiddin'? They're all for sale." The guy was a bootlegger. So I sold half-million-dollar yachts to bootleggers. For five or ten thousand dollars. And took my six percent commission on them. Beautiful.[4]

The bootleggers, she said, "decorated them with pretty girls in bathing suits, like going out for a little sail. Load up and come back. . . . The interiors were done in rosewood, gold handles on the toilets and all that jazz, great oil paintings in the salons. They're now jammed up with loads and loads of wet alcohol . . . the interiors of them were gutted and ruined."

There were still easier ways of circumventing Prohibition. Just as Remus legitimately obtained B Certificates (permits) to withdraw liquor from distilleries for medicinal purposes, American distillers could, just as legitimately, export their own liquor in bulk for so-called "medicinal use" abroad. Hundreds of thousands of gallons of whiskey thus purchased, on paper at least, by businessmen in Scotland, British Columbia, New Brunswick, Germany, Cuba, and even Tijuana never reached their fictitious destinations.

> If we believed the tales of all who apply for liquor permits [wrote Haynes], we would naturally come to the absurd conclusion that the whole world is sick and desperately in need of distilled spirits. . . . Does anyone believe that Scotland, home of whiskey, is really in need of 66,000 gallons of American whiskey for non-beverage purposes? . . . It is the irony of ironies, a wet world, come to dry America to beg for liquor.

As with the later war on drugs, the goal of the law enforcers was to catch the truly major operator. "The conviction of one such," Haynes wrote, "is worth the conviction of twelve small operators. Their identities are mostly well known — but they have to be caught in the act, to establish evidence which will prove guilt in the courts." As the recent BCCI scandal showed, current drug operations have also involved at least one established bank, but during the Prohibition years the list of prestigious British and American banks providing services to rum-runners, knowingly or unknowingly, was huge. In operations involving major players, by no means confined to the underworld, money was deposited in banks in advance, held in trust, and only remitted after shipments were completed, the transactions invariably referred to as "unspecified goods or commodities."

Haynes wrote that "one finds names that once epitomized honor and power and community esteem steeped in the same befouling brew with names of thieves, thugs and murderers." Joe Kennedy, father of President John F. Kennedy, was one of those "epitomizing honor and power" who could not resist an occasional risk-free flutter, though he was careful to hide behind a screen of dummy companies.

While bankers and entrepreneurs on both sides of the Atlantic got rich on the proceeds, a new mythical hero emerged as part of Prohibition folklore: the risk-taking, devil-may-care rumrunner, even though reality seldom measured up to the legend. At least one of them was a woman. "Spanish Marie" assumed command of the boat she renamed *Kid Boots* when her husband and ship's captain fell overboard after a surfeit of cargo sampling (rumor had it that she may have given him a final push).

> She strutted about with a revolver strapped to her waist, a big knife stuck in her belt and a red bandanna tied round her head. Legend had it that she was about as tough as she looked. She was captured in March 1928 while unloading liquor at Coconut Grove, and was released on five hundred dollars bail on the plea that she must take care of her babies. The bail was increased to $3,500 when investigators found the children at home with a nurse and Spanish Marie at a speakeasy.[5]

Although millions of gallons of liquor ended up on American shores, rum-running expeditions all too often came to grief as a result of incompetence, communication failures, greed, and mutual mistrust, with expeditors and ships' captains sharing the blame.

In America's National Archives are records of several instances of undercover penetration wrecking otherwise perfect plans. Everett S. Allen, in *The Black Ships*, tells the story of a somewhat boastful London entrepreneur, Thomas Godman of the Schooners Association of London, who bragged of his unique relations with corrupt American officials. He claimed to have access to detailed Coast Guard surveillance schedules. But his letters were intercepted and his operations went terribly wrong. In 1927, he reported "a rush of orders from my friends for whiskey to meet the Christmas trade" and made plans for a $488,700 cargo to unload off Montauk Point, at the extreme tip of Long Island — a favorite landing place. But crew members deserted, fought one another, got drunk on pilfered cargo, and almost ran their boat, the *Tom August*, aground. Others went on strike or jumped ship when they learned that their wives had not been paid as promised. Godman's cargo failed to meet up with its expected customers either at sea or on shore until the crew members who remained on board began taking cases ashore themselves — and not returning. Profits on a successful run were huge, but only if it did not take too long, and the *Tom August*, cruising up and down the Long Island coast for weeks, cost Godman far more than he could afford to lose. He retired from the game a near bankrupt.[6]

Although rum-running ships such as the *Tom August* feared pirate hijackers far more than the Coast Guard, ships' officers seldom trusted even their own crews. There was always the possibility they would be tempted to themselves hijack the ship and sell the liquor. Rival syndicates also represented a constant threat. The potential rewards made for a climate aboard of distrust and permanent, brooding violence. The rumrunner *Mulhouse* was owned by a powerful French company that maintained a permanent sales representative in New York during the first few Prohibition years. It was boarded at gunpoint in Sheepshead Bay. Of its cargo of 23,000 cases of liquor, 7,000 were transferred aboard the hijacking schooner, the remaining 16,000 cases sold off to unidentified buyers in powerful speedboats as the French crew was held hostage below decks. The French syndicate's sales representative had been set up by rivals posing as respectable wholesale buyers. A mysterious bootlegger known only as "Big Eddie" was suspected of masterminding the scam.

Norwegian crews had an exceptionally bad reputation. The Coast Guard cutter *Seneca* boarded the Norwegian merchant ship *Sagatind* off the East Coast. The ship was found to be carrying 13,000 cases of liquor and $26,000 in cash. "All of *Sagatind*'s crew were stupefied with drink except for three whose jaws were broken. One man had a broken leg and many had black eyes."[7]

Although the East Coast — especially the Hamptons, Nantucket, and Martha's Vineyard — were favored off-loading areas, Puget Sound was also a favorite bootleggers' haunt, being convenient for smuggling operations initiated either in Mexico or elsewhere in the Pacific. Liquor cargoes ended up in Oregon, Washington State, and California. In some cases, Coast Guard crews responsible for policing the area actually did some rum-running themselves.

Increasingly, as the rumrunners stepped up their activities, their predators did likewise. A new breed of pirates, preying on officially commissioned smuggling ships, began intercepting cargoes, killing crews, and either sinking the vessels or leaving them disabled and motionless in the water — twentieth-century equivalents of the mysteriously abandoned *Marie Celeste*. Pirate ships operating out of Nova Scotia were particularly feared.

As with later drug operations, law enforcement agencies managed, with some success, to infiltrate the bootlegging world. One undercover agent (code name: London) surfaced in Bremen, posing as a member of a European consortium eager to invest in a rum-running operation, and managed to convince one Wilhelm Huebers, of the respectable German Products and Trade Corporation, that he was a bona fide speculator. The German firm lost its entire shipment.

The Prohibition Bureau also made considerable use of informers. Agents were authorized to pay snitches two dollars a day for information. The newly formed FBI was more generous, but the smugglers, like drug dealers later, were often one step ahead of them — they too adept at disinformation. Haynes cites the example of "Hippy" Werner, a well-known bootlegger, who told the FBI that the British trawler *Minerva,* out of Barbados, was about to land 4,000 cases of Scotch whiskey at Warwick Beach in the middle of the night, and that the landing operation would be protected by three Coast Guard boats in the smugglers' pay. A major operation was mounted, and the cargo was seized. But the *Minerva* turned out to be a decoy boat with a cargo of cheap methyl alcohol flavored with fusel oil. While the FBI and reliable Coast Guard units were busy with the *Minerva,* other boats unloaded huge amounts of valuable Scotch whiskey further down the Rhode Island coast.

The best-known, most revered rumrunner of all time was Bill McCoy, who gave rise to the well-known expression "the real McCoy," which originally referred to the high quality of his liquor. A former merchant navy first mate — who, with his brother, opened his own boatyard in Jacksonville, Florida, after the First World War, custom-building luxurious speedboats for millionaires — McCoy became a bootlegger for the money, but also out of a passion for sailing. He was fonder of the *Arethusa,* the spectacularly beautiful sloop he was able to buy with the profits of his first few runs, than he was of money, even though his returns were considerable.

McCoy made the Bahamas, where whiskey cost a mere $8 a case, his base. Total expenses for a run from the Bahamas to Martha's Vineyard and back amounted to $100,000 ($40,000 for the whiskey, $60,000 for the crew and the ship's running expenses), the average net profit per trip amounting to $300,000. The *Arethusa* (like most rum-running vessels in the West Indies area, it flew the Red Ensign) was not only a beautiful ship to look at, but was better equipped, and better run, than any other bootlegging boat. McCoy ran a tight ship. Although a reporter who went aboard later wrote that "the crew resembled as wicked a gang of cutthroats as ever bade a victim to walk the plank," they were intensely loyal to him. Pay was good, discipline stern, drinking aboard forbidden, and sales techniques highly sophisticated. McCoy's motto was "We do business day and night." Because storage space was at a premium, he packaged the liquor in pyramid-shaped, six-bottle burlap-wrapped packs rather than in wooden cases, and these were then wrapped in container-size gunnysack bales.

Others imitated him, and such was his reputation that all over America, unscrupulous domestic moonshiners, pretending that their whiskey was "straight off the boat," wrapped *their* inferior, adulterated liquor in similar burlap bags, often soaking them in salt water to give them an authentic "McCoy" appearance.

The *Arethusa* was a floating liquor store, with shelves of samples for visitors. Tasting was encouraged, but only two prospective buyers were allowed aboard at the same time — not so much to prevent law enforcement raids as to deter the hijackers, almost as numerous on the high seas as they were outside Remus's Death Valley Farm. On deck, a swiveling machine-gun emplacement was prominently in view, and every time an unidentified speedboat hove to alongside the *Arethusa*, it remained trained on the visitors throughout their shopping expedition.

Despite his precautions, McCoy's luck did not hold. He had to abandon the *Arethusa* to subordinates for a while, living as a fugitive from justice with friendly, discreet Indians on remote reservations because "they don't ask questions, they haven't any particular regard for the law."[8] Eventually his luck ran out altogether. In November of 1924, the Coast Guard cutter *Seneca* fired on the *Arethusa* off Seabright, New Jersey, and rather than risk losing his boat, McCoy surrendered, was charged, and went to jail.

Another bootlegger who achieved mythical status was Seattle-based Roy Olmstead. When Prohibition was introduced in Washington State (ahead of the Volstead Act), he was the youngest lieutenant on the Seattle police force. His superiors were unaware that their most promising detective was moonlighting as a bootlegger, using his police connections across the Canadian border to buy his supplies from trusted middlemen, some of whom were also serving or retired police officers.

He first came to prominence in March of 1920 when Prohibition agents staged an ambush on Brown's Bay, near Meadowdale, and seized a huge cargo of Olmstead's liquor. Fined and dismissed from the force, he immediately became a full-time operator, the head of an eleven-man syndicate running an operation that included not only navigators, delivery crews, and salesmen, but bookkeepers, many of them serving police officials.

The Canadian government cynically exploited the Volstead Act, officially imposing an export duty ($20 a case) on all liquor destined for the United States. Olmstead arranged for his consignments to be shipped (on paper) to Mexico, avoiding the levy. This made it possible for him to undersell his competitors, and he boasted that his brand-name Scotch and Canadian whiskey was barely more expensive in dry Seattle than in Canada. The *New York Times* described Olmstead as "the king of one of the most gigantic rum-running conspiracies in the country." The scale of his operations was huge. In 1922, the Prohibition Bureau estimated that 1.5 million gallons of bootleg whiskey came from Canada.

By 1924, Olmstead was a millionaire, dealing exclusively with wholesalers. With net profits of at least $200,000 a month, he acquired a palatial home in Mount Baker, Seattle's choicest suburb, as well as the American Radio Telephone Company, Seattle's first radio station (KFOX), which his wife Elsie ran from their home. Like Remus, Olmstead entertained on a lavish scale, and, like Remus, acquired a new glamorous companion. The elite of Seattle, including the mayor, were proud to be his friends. As a Seattle newspaper commented in 1924, "It made a man feel important to casually remark: 'as Roy Olmstead was telling me today . . . ' "

His police connections were invaluable, as the following wiretap extract proves:

> Roy phoned the police station. M — came to the phone and said: "Hello, Roy, what's on your mind?" Roy said: "One of your fellows picked up one of my boys." M — replied: "Who is it?" Roy replied that it was B — "I don't give a damn what they do but I want to know before he is booked." M — replied, "I'll take care of it for you, Roy."

In another wiretapping extract, a policeman was heard telling Olmstead that he had arrested one of his men. "He was loaded clear to the axle. I could not do anything else." Olmstead quickly got to know that his phones were tapped, and exploited this to his advantage. He started giving fake orders on the phone, using an untapped telephone booth to give his staff genuine instructions.

But eventually the law caught up with him. Mabel Willebrandt, the deputy attorney general who pursued Olmstead as diligently as she did Remus, was convinced that his radio station was used to transmit coded instructions to his reception committees and wholesalers, and that key words were broadcast in specially written children's bedtime stories read on the air by Olmstead's wife. It was during one such transmission, made from Olmstead's mansion (which had its own transmitting studio) that Prohibition agents finally made their raid, and arrested him. In 1926, he stood trial for "conspiracy to possess, transport and import intoxicating liquors," and was sentenced to four years in jail.

His trial made legal history because the judge authorized hitherto illegal use of wiretaps. Olmstead's career did not end there. After his release from McNeil Island federal prison, he became a born-again Christian Scientist and devoted the rest of his life, and the remains of his considerable fortune, to charitable work with convicted prisoners. Mc-Coy, released at the same time, retired to Florida, also with substantial funds. After the territorial waters limit was reduced to three miles, it became essential for valuable ships such as McCoy's *Arethusa* to remain at a safe distance from the coast, and a new category of player emerged — the fishermen who ferried customers to the floating liquor supermarket ships and back (also hiring themselves out to bring the liquor ashore, braving Coast Guard interception). Their exploits were celebrated in sea shanties, including these famous lines:

> Oh we don't give a damn
> For our old Uncle Sam
> Way, oh, whiskey and gin!
> Lend us a hand
> When we stand in to land,
> Just give us time
> To run the rum in!

Everett Allen, author of *The Black Ships*, grew up during Prohibition in New Bedford and remembered not only the friendly bantering between fishermen and Coast Guards but that "on most days there would be twelve to fifteen rum boats testing their engines and roaring around New Bedford harbor while a patrol boat kept an eye on them. Then, as it got later, one by one they would disappear."

Local New Bedford fishermen found rum-running far more lucrative than catching and selling fish, and many became minor dealers themselves. "You knew right away when a man stopped fishing and started running rum," a local New Bedford resident told Allen. "In the first place, his family began to eat proper and you could tell by what they bought at the grocery store, when they had had to run up a grub bill all winter." A fisherman called Manuel stored liquor in his cottage water tank, selling it to private customers by the bottle straight out of a water spigot. In wintertime, peddlers sold rubber hot water bottles containing whiskey from pushcarts in the New Bedford streets.

Freelance fishermen's "shuttle services" often operated without prior knowledge of any "floating supermarket" arrivals, for there was a constant flow back and forth. A former Coast Guard officer turned rumrunner told Everett Allen: "At night on 'rum row' [the stretch of the Atlantic nearest New Bedford] you'd think there was a city out there." Isabelle Mairs, an East Hampton teenage flapper in the 1920s, remembers watching Coast Guard vessels pursue fishing boats in spectacular chases clearly visible from East Hampton's exclusive Maidstone Club — which, though serving every conceivable type of liquor, was not raided once during the Prohibition years. Its members were far too influential, and East Hampton's police chief, a frequent guest at the club, would get so drunk that his car ended up in the lake several times.

At first, the fishermen-bootleggers used their own boats to take the liquor ashore, but as Coast Guard patrols became more experienced, and their engines faster, fishermen's boats became increasingly vulnerable. Jimmy McGhee, a motor mechanic in Manorville, near Southampton, helped save the situation for the bootleggers. His brilliant, never-patented creation was a speedboat of his own devising. It was a pared-down floating platform powered by twin water-cooled airplane engines (bought cheaply from stocks of First World War surplus) and capable of speeds of up to 65 miles an hour — far faster than the fastest Coast Guard boats. McGhee's powerboats ran on aviation fuel and required skilled, cold-blooded crews, for there was a constant risk of engines overheating and blowing up at high speeds.

McGhee became a well-known figure in the Hamptons, and was in great demand not only as a mechanic but as a boat designer. Like McCoy, he was more interested in boats than in money. Although he was, in a sense, the Coast Guard's worst scourge, he never did anything illegal, consistently refused to take a cut on the liquor cargo his boats transported, and was never arrested. Long after Prohibition, this entirely self-taught mechanical genius became a well-known figure in racing car circles, and during the Second World War was hired as an adviser by Grumman, the maker of fighter aircraft.

Boats such as McGhee's, built in discreet workshops in New York and all along the East Coast, were also acquired by notorious underworld bosses whose men ran the Coast Guard gauntlet themselves. Their one-man torpedo boats were armor-plated, with bullet-proof windshields, and carried up to 400 cases and moved at 35 knots. Some of these craft have survived, including one once owned by Dutch Schultz, the notorious gangster, and are now valuable collectors' items.

The war at sea was continuous. Fishermen used their nets to foul the engines of pursuing Coast Guard boats. Regardless of the weather, veteran residents recall, there were noisy water ballets off the Hamptons coast involving fishermen's boats and their Coast Guard pursuers. In 1925, Coast Guard boats were ordered to mark suspected rum-running vessels at all times. Many of the speedboats were equipped with radios, and used codes to communicate with their land bases, even though the penalty for using an unauthorized radio on a rum-running speedboat was a $7,000 fine. The FBI knew that rumrunners ferrying liquor from parent ships to shore used accomplices, sometimes fronting as local radio station employees, to broadcast cryptic messages in Morse that only the initiated could understand.

The bootleggers' codes got increasingly sophisticated as time went on, and were not confined to radio, for they knew their mail was routinely opened, and were careful to conceal details of their shipments as best they could. As the Coast Guard's cryptanalysis improved, so did the exporters' methods. One of the biggest bootlegging conglomerates, the Consolidated Exporters' Company, hired a retired Royal Navy expert to devise and modify their codes every few weeks, paying him a $10,000 retainer.

David Kahn, in *The Code Breakers*,[9] quotes Elizabeth Smith Friedman, a senior cryptanalyst for the Coast Guard, as saying that "at no time during the [First] World War, when secret methods of communication reached their highest development, were there used such involved ramifications as are to be found in some of the correspondence of the West Coast rum-running vessels." Testifying in a New Orleans court against the Consolidated Exporters' Company, she gave this example of encoded instructions: "Anchored in harbor. Where and when are you sending fuel?" became

"MJFAK ZYWKH QATYT JSL QATS QSYGX OGTB."

Largely at her insistence, the Coast Guard eventually launched the CG-210, a patrol boat packed with high-frequency receivers and direction finders, and staffed with trained cryptanalysts that could listen in on a large number of coded messages simultaneously. It was, in a way, a high-tech breakthrough comparable to today's AWACS plane, and Kahn makes the point that without prior work on bootleggers' code-breaking, progress in World War II cryptanalysis against Germany and Japan would have been far less successful.

The Coast Guard would doubtless have gained the upper hand had it had superior craft, but when President Calvin Coolidge, Harding's successor, asked for appropriations to buy faster powerboats, legislation was often held up by wet Congressmen, including a hard-core minority known to be in the pay of rum-running financiers.

The Coast Guard was a tough adversary, but its rate of interception never rose above 5 percent of the total traffic — roughly the equivalent of law enforcement scores today involving drugs — and even this elite force of 11,000 men was by no means above suspicion. As a boy, Everett Allen recalled two uniformed Coast Guard personnel "coming into Vineyard Haven drunk enough so they tried to sell liquor in bottles right off the street."[10] On Block Island, a notoriously corrupt Coast Guard captain systematically looked the other way, and Allen remembers seeing sixty cases of whiskey awaiting collection in broad daylight within a few hundred yards of a Coast Guard station.

"It became as necessary to exercise vigilance over the Coast Guard as over the smugglers," A. Bruce Bielaski, a former federal Prohibition enforcement chief for the whole of the Atlantic seaboard, told the *Sat-*

urday Evening Post.[11] For letting fishing boats land liquor at Fort Point Bay, near Montauk, Coast Guard captain Frank J. Stuart got $2,000, the equivalent of a year's pay. Bielaski told the *Post* that some Coast Guard crews actually helped in the transfer of liquor from rum runners to speedboats. "When the schooner *Dawn*, with 2,000 cases of whiskey on board, was captured and towed into New Bedford, she suddenly sank. A report was sent through that she had gone down with 200 cases on board. We knew better. Later she had to be raised, and not a bottle of whiskey was found on her." There were also large numbers of situations in which Coast Guard crews protected the rumrunners by sending U.S. Navy destroyers trying to apprehend them off on false trails.

Because Coast Guard authorities were reluctant to admit to failings in the ranks, courts-martial were invariably held in secret, and the press was informed much later, if at all. In 1932, the Coast Guard commandant reluctantly admitted that the Coast Guard officer in charge of Georgica station, Long Island, had been sentenced to one year in the Portsmouth naval jail for "certain offenses." That same year, three boatswain's mates were convicted of "scandalous conduct" for conniving with bootleggers around Fire Island.

So incensed was one anonymous citizen that he wrote a letter to a senior Washington official asking for a loan to buy and equip "a good submarine chaser with gun, a load of torpedoes and a few machine guns. I will supply a crew. We will go to sea and sink without trace every rum boat we can find. . . . I am sick of seeing foreigners thumbing their noses at the U.S. Am I for Prohibition? Hell, no. Just tired of fiddling, fooling and graft." The writer's political agenda was clear. "I'll clean the seas of the graft as Forrest cleaned the woods of niggers." The reference was to the infamous Major General Nathan Bedford Forrest, who massacred black Union troops at Fort Pillow in 1864 — the letter itself a reminder that Prohibition supporters included not only devout Christians and moralistic Anti-Saloon Leaguers but the equivalent of today's extremist militias; that is, the then extremely powerful — and teetotal — Ku Klux Klan, which at its peak had over four million members.

Coast Guard morale was not high, even among impeccably honest crews, for several reasons. One was the grotesquely ham-handed public relations policy of the times. In January of 1923, Edward Clifford, assistant secretary of the Treasury Department, which supervised all law enforcement relating to Prohibition, recommended that "Prohibition officials be requested not to talk to newspapermen, in fact to give no publicity whatever as to what they are doing. This is also to apply to the Coast Guard. This matter cannot be handled successfully by giving out information to the press." This meant that Coast Guard exploits were seldom mentioned in the press. The consequence was that the corrupt reputation of the Prohibition Bureau spread to the far less corrupt Coast Guard.

The Coast Guard's original mission had been to ensure the safety of ships at sea, and rescue vessels in distress. But after some rum-running vessels began using fake distress signals to draw Coast Guard ships into ambushes, few humanitarian missions were attempted. As one of its supervisors, Rear Admiral Frederick C. Billard, wrote in 1927, "marked enthusiasm for this kind of operation could not be expected on the part of the average, old-time Coast Guard sailor," who felt that he was "fighting a war with one hand tied behind his back."

There were some spectacular successes. A huge rum-running vessel called the *Taboga* (which had changed its name to *Homestead* and sailed under a Costa Rican flag) surrendered at sea to two Coast Guard vessels after a running battle. It had 2,000 cases aboard — a major disappointment for the boarders, for it had enough storage space for 50,000 cases. In another case, a young Coast Guard lieutenant called Duke single-handedly boarded the *Economy* and forced its crew to surrender at revolver point. But at other times Coast Guard ships simply looked the other way as "black ships" steamed straight into New York, unloading liquor within spitting distance of Brooklyn Bridge. A black ship crew member recalled that "the wharf was full of carts and they had a gang there to unload us. All of the front street was blocked off. Cops were keeping everybody off the wharf."[12] Former Coast Guard lieutenant Joseph Slovick (who retired in 1952, having signed up as a teenager in 1928) gave a vivid description of the hazards involved. "There was no radar then, and we never knew where the ships were going to be,"[13] he said.

> Their ships were always faster than ours, and they had protection from the local community. There were spotters out there alerting

them. I remember once we were chasing a rum-running fishing vessel off Fire Island and I saw a man drop off and make for the shore. He was warning the people waiting for the consignment that they were being chased. It was a cat and mouse game, and the smugglers made great use of sandbars. We knew that within our Coast Guard station there were informers working for the bootleggers.

As seaman second class, Slovick earned $36 a month. To his knowledge, there were no black sheep among his crew mates, but there were plenty among customs officers.

A lot of the time, when we had seized some liquor, we didn't bring it into the Customs house during the daytime because we didn't want any contact with the customs men. They wore great big brown overalls and they would stash bottles of liquor in them as they carried the stuff into their trucks, as many as they could — they would keep it for their own purposes, or to sell.

11

"PROHIBITION WORKS!"

> The Prohibition Department has made, and is making,
> substantial progress.
>
> — *President Warren Harding, in a preface to*
> *Roy A. Haynes's book* Prohibition Inside Out, *1926*

Twenty months after Prohibition became effective, the Internal
Revenue Bureau, as it was then called, reckoned that bootlegging had
become a one billion dollar business, and a senior official urged the
government to take steps to recover $32 million from bootleggers in
excess profits taxes. Americans consumed 25 million gallons of illegal
liquor in 1920, the Bureau claimed, noting that another 30 million
gallons had been released to consumers for medicinal purposes by the
new Prohibition Unit.[1]

For all this disastrous beginning, Prohibition apologists felt they
had good grounds for believing that the long-awaited millennium was
at hand. Statistics could be made to prove that, at any rate in the first
few years of its existence, Prohibition worked, was indeed spectacularly
successful.

"Deaths from alcoholism took a terrific tumble in 1920," wrote
the *Literary Digest,* the best-informed, most influential American
magazine of its day. Many years later, in occupied France, when

supplies of wine and hard liquor disappeared from the shops (all stocks had been requisitioned by the Germans), there was a marked drop in cases of delirium tremens, cirrhosis of the liver, and other alcohol-related illnesses — and this was also true of America, at least until the bootleggers got organized. State budgets all over the United States, in 1921 and 1922, reflected Prohibition's impact. During those years, hospitals had fewer patients with alcohol-related illnesses; there were fewer cases of alcohol-related crimes, including street drunkenness; and there was a corresponding drop in the prison population. In Chicago, the DTs ward of Cook County Hospital was closed, as well as one wing of the Chicago City Jail.

Although Wheeler and the ASL naturally attributed the improvements exclusively to Prohibition, the Volstead Act alone was not responsible. In actual fact, as 1900–1910 statistics showed, per capita liquor consumption had steadily declined since the turn of the century, America had turned partially dry long before 1920, and in the 1917–1918 war years, many drinking American males were serving abroad.

Some health figures *were* impressive. In the years immediately before America's entry into the First World War, the death rate from alcoholism had oscillated between 4.4 and 5.8 per 100,000 people. In 1917–1918 the drop was spectacular — from 5.2 to 2.7. To Prohibitionists, this was sufficient proof that America was indeed on the threshold of the much-vaunted millennium. In 1920, the death rate from alcoholism went down still further, from over 2 per 100,000 to 1. In 1921, there was a modest rise (1.8). In 1922, the level had climbed to 2.6 — still an improvement over the 1917 figure. In 1923, it climbed still further (to 3.2), and from then on the rise became vertiginous, even if deaths caused by adulterated liquor poisoning are excluded from the count.

As late as 1925, Wayne Wheeler could, with some legitimacy, argue that the benefits of Prohibition were huge — though some of his reasoning was specious. "Prohibition is decreasing crime," the *Literary Digest* reported in January of 1925. Violent domestic crime *was* down, as were arrests for drunkenness and brawling. "Prohibition has saved a million lives," Wheeler announced that year. "The welfare of little children is too eloquent a voice to be howled down," the *Grand Rapids Herald* acknowledged.

Prohibition enthusiasts also used statistics to argue, again before bootlegging operations got into their stride, that cash once spent on liquor was now being used to buy more and better food, and that consequently people were healthier. Statistics showed that grocery stores were doing better business, and that American families were putting more money into savings accounts.

"It makes me sorry we did not have Prohibition long ago," wrote the editor-owner of the Seattle *Times*, who had originally opposed Prohibition. "Yes, sir, we have found in Seattle that it is better to buy shoes than booze."[2] The Prohibitionists naturally claimed that the Volstead Act was uniquely responsible. This was by no means certain, for the revitalized postwar economy was almost certainly a likelier reason for the new spending patterns. In any case, benefits were only temporary, and long before 1929, such claims were no longer being made.

Wheeler declared that Prohibition had "doubled the number of investors" and was fueling America's growing manufacturing boom — a "post hoc ergo propter hoc" argument, but one enthusiastically supported by most American industrialists, at least until the Great Crash of 1929.

One major but anonymous industrialist told Prohibition Commissioner Haynes that "before the Volstead Act, we had 10% absenteeism after pay day. Now it is not over 3%. The open saloon and the liquor traffic were the greatest curse to American morals, American citizenship, thrift, comfort and happiness that ever existed in the land."[3] Men such as Rockefeller (at least at first) and Edison were also Prohibition supporters. And much was made of the fact that certain skilled labor unions, such as the Brotherhood of Locomotive Engineers, had come out in favor of Prohibition.

Wheeler's most vocal and influential Prohibition ally was undoubtedly Henry Ford — a major Anti-Saloon League contributor from the start. Ford's rationale was simple: neither a principled nor a religious man (insofar as he had any moral convictions, these were based on the superiority of the white, Aryan race), his sole concern, as an innovative car manufacturer, was efficiency: hangovers slowed down the pace of the assembly line and provoked accidents. The Volstead Act did not make Henry Ford disband his private police, but their task became simpler, for they no longer had to keep watch over a multitude of saloons and liquor shops.

Halfway through Prohibition, Ford himself issued a stern warning in the *Pictorial Review*.

For myself, if booze ever comes back to the U.S. I am through with manufacturing. I would not be bothered with the problem of handling over 200,000 men and trying to pay them wages which the saloons would take away from them. I wouldn't be interested in putting autos into the hands of a generation soggy with drink.

With booze in control we can count on only two or three effective days work a week in the factory — and that would destroy the short day and the five-day week which sober industry has introduced. When men were drunk two or three days a week, industry had to have a ten- or twelve-hour day and a seven-day week. With sobriety the working man can have an eight-hour day and a five-day week with the same or greater pay. . . . I would not be able to build a car that will run 200,000 miles if booze were around, because I wouldn't have accurate workmen. To make these machines requires that the men increase their skill.

Other automobile industry tycoons shared these views, and the Carnegie Institute's tests on the effects of alcohol on human efficiency added credibility to Ford's remarks. But the arguments in favor of Prohibition were not confined to industrialists. Some of the social arguments advanced no longer used the hysterical rhetoric favored by the ASL and the WCTU, which equated Prohibition with salvation. One of the few totally honest members of the Harding administration, Mabel Willebrandt, the deputy attorney general (and the infamous Daugherty's "real" number two), argued that even if they drank in speakeasies, women were Prohibition's greatest beneficiaries.

Herself one of America's early feminists, who had defended prostitutes and victims of domestic abuse at the start of an impressive law career and had gone on to campaign for better conditions in women's prisons — scandalizing some of her more straitlaced legal colleagues by becoming an early "Murphy Brown," adopting a baby girl after her divorce — Willebrandt defended Prohibition in dispassionate, modern terms. She recognized that there was little interest in Prohibition "among those who congregate in country clubs and who have plenty of leisure and very little work." Nevertheless, speaking as a woman in a male-dominated society, she wrote that

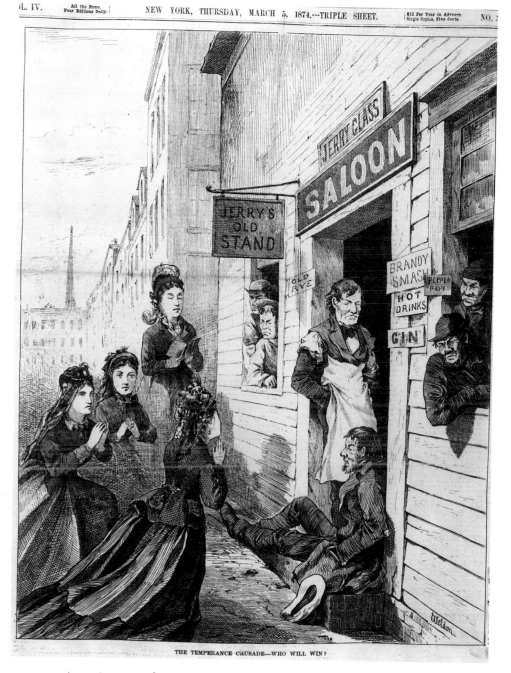

THE TEMPERANCE CRUSADE—WHO WILL WIN?

An early cartoon (1874) showing Woman's Christian Temperance Union volunteers picketing a saloon full of drunks. *(Library of Congress)*

Carry Nation praying in her jail cell in Wichita, Kansas. *(Library of Congress)*

Wayne Wheeler, power broker
and Anti-Saloon League boss.
(Library of Congress)

President and
Mrs. Warren Harding.
(Library of Congress)

Andrew Volstead (1869–1947),
Minnesota congressman, author of
the Volstead Act, which brought
Prohibition into being in 1920.
(National Archives)

Warren Harding and members of his cabinet. Seated, left to right: John Weeks, Andrew Mellon, Charles Evans Hughes, Warren Harding, Calvin Coolidge, and Edwin Denby. Standing, left to right: Albert Fall, Will Hays, Harry Daugherty, Henry Wallace, Herbert Hoover, and John Davis. Daugherty was bootlegger George Remus's man in the Harding administration. *(Stock Montage, Inc.)*

Jess Smith, Harding intimate and a close friend of Attorney General Harry Daugherty, was Daugherty's bagman and effective number two in the Justice Department. *(Jack Doll/Delhi Historical Society)*

A St. Louis wine cellar chockablock with vintage French wines being inspected by a Prohibition official before it was sealed off (1920). *(National Archives)*

A Prohibition Bureau agent smashes seized liquor (1923). *(Library of Congress)*

A bootlegger's car, which crashed during a police chase
in Washington, D.C. (1926). *(Library of Congress)*

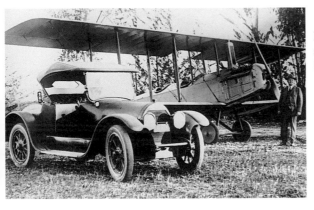

FBI agent with captured plane
and getaway car near the Mexican
border (1928). *(Library of Congress)*

Prohibition Bureau
agents raid a speakeasy in
Washington, D.C., at 922
Pennsylvania Avenue (1923).
(Library of Congress)

Special garter and miniature
flask for ladies. *(Library of Congress)*

New York's largest illegal beer
brewery being dismantled (1930).
(National Archives)

An Anglo-American crew
of rumrunners under
arrest, posing with
Prohibition agents.
The top section of this
composite photo shows
their two-masted
British schooner.
(National Archives)

Coast guardsmen survey
their latest capture in
New York harbor,
gunnysack-stitched
whiskey bottles, like
"the real McCoy," while
thirsty citizens look on.
(National Archives)

In Grosse Pointe, Michigan, a customs agent displays a long submarine cable used to pipe whiskey from Canada to the United States. *(National Archives)*

Prohibition agents breaking up New York's largest whiskey still (1927). *(National Archives)*

Inside the Remus mansion, Remus and guests pose for a photograph before a dinner given to celebrate completion of the $100,000 swimming pool. Remus is seated at the head of the table. Imogene is standing at his right. Stepdaughter Ruth is standing to his left with her arms around George's shoulders. His sister is seated at his left. *(Jack Doll/Delhi Historical Society)*

George Remus behind bars in 1924. Remus sold $75 million worth of liquor in a two-year period. At the same time he was said to have spent $20 million to pay off various federal, state, and local officials for their silence. Eventually arrested and prosecuted, he served five sentences for liquor law violations. *(Jack Doll/Delhi Historical Society)*

George Remus.
(Jack Doll/Delhi Historical Society)

The former Imogene Holmes,
Remus's second wife.
(Jack Doll/Delhi Historical Society)

Remus's adopted daughter, Ruth. She was
nineteen at the time of the murder trial.
(Jack Doll/Delhi Historical Society)

Al Capone.
(National Archives)

Free soup kitchen
in Chicago, paid for
by Al Capone (1930).
(National Archives)

Prohibition agents smashing up a bar just prior to the end of Prohibition.
(*National Archives*)

"Big Bill" Thompson, mayor of Chicago during Prohibition years, and friend of gangsters.
(*National Archives*)

The beginning of the end: anti-Prohibition slogans on cars (1930–31). *(Library of Congress)*

Anti-Prohibition demonstration in New York in 1932. *(National Archives)*

In 1933, but *before* the end of Prohibition, applicants for licenses to sell draft beer line up in New York. *(National Archives)*

At Prohibition's end, there were no liquor stores, and such was the thirst for legitimate liquor that some banks turned over their premises temporarily (1933). *(National Archives)*

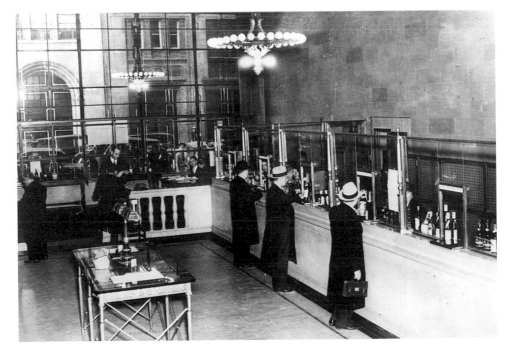

Happy workers celebrate
the reopening of their
brewery (1933).
(National Archives)

In Philadelphia,
a bar scene immediately
after Prohibition's
end (1933).
(National Archives)

Anyone who mingles freely with all classes of women is bound to discover very soon that the majority are opposed utterly and unalterably to reestablishment of open saloons. . . . Most women still lean economically upon men, their fathers or their husbands. Even if they have property they let men in the family handle it. The saloons deprived women not only of the companionship to which they thought they were entitled but absorbed money which the women felt they were entitled to share. For selfish reasons, quite as much as moral reasons, the women of the country will continue to cast their influence for prohibition. There is better furniture in the homes throughout the country than ever before, simply because a woman is able to divert a larger part of her husband's income to household uses. There are more luxuries in which the family can share: automobiles, music lessons for the children and the like.

The modern girl, who makes no protest when her escort to dinner produces a pocket flask and shares its contents with her, has no present stake in prohibition enforcement. But the moment that girl marries, she probably will, whether consciously or not, become a supporter of prohibition, because she always will be unwilling to share any part of her husband's income with either a bootlegger or a saloon-keeper operating legally. I am convinced that as far as the women of the country are concerned, prohibition has come to stay.[4]

The arguments of Roy A. Haynes, the luckless Prohibition commissioner appointed by Harding on Wheeler's recommendation (he too was part of the Ohio gang but one of the few honest ones), were far less convincing. Faced with an untenable situation, he was compelled to take an uncompromising moral stand: "It is no longer a question as to whether we are for or against that legislation, but whether we are for or against the United States Constitution."

Haynes recognized that Prohibition was hideously difficult to police. The frontier between Canada and the United States was over a thousand miles long, and Detroit was a privileged entry point. No pursuit was possible on the river separating Canada from the United States in Detroit, for spy ships "financed by Canadian brewing interests" were on a permanent lookout for Coast Guard and Prohibition Bureau craft, and the "smugglers have to be caught in the act." But his contention was that Prohibition was under control "and that control becomes more complete and more thorough every day. . . . The clamor of a dwindling clique cannot drown the voice of truth."

"The bootlegger's life is increasingly one of fear, dread and apprehension," Haynes claimed, with some truth. He failed to add that the financial rewards were such that the risks were worth taking, even if, as he noted, the bootleggers were constantly preyed on by politicians, public officials, police, and lawyers.

He was correct to say that "few men in any line or calling are subject to the temptation which besets the Prohibition enforcement agent." Bribes *were* on a phenomenal scale. A group of brewers offered some agents a monthly $300,000 retainer to look the other way. The bootleggers, Haynes wrote, regarded the agent's badge as "nothing but a license to make money. . . . Bootleggers brag of top political connections, with representatives in the Department of Justice, the Bureau of Internal Revenue and the Prohibition Unit itself." In most cases, though Haynes did not say so, such accusations were well founded.

There were indeed a few untouchables in the Prohibition Bureau, as George Remus found out to his cost. Haynes devoted a chapter to thirty "fallen heroes," agents shot and killed between 1920 and 1925, either in running gun battles, in ambushes, while searching for stills, or as a result of being lured to lonely and deserted places where they were gunned down in cold blood. These included some authentic heroes, but some "executions" involved the paying off of old scores — the price some Prohibition agents paid for failing to make good their promises to "look the other way."

Haynes could not avoid the issue of corruption within his own Prohibition Bureau. There were, he admitted, "weak men, few in number," who could not "withstand the strain of temptation placed in their way [by the bootleggers]." Invariably, Haynes wrote, Prohibition agents were advised that if they accepted bribes, they would simply be adhering to an almost official code of conduct, for "claims are made by rich and apparently influential cliques that they have connections by which they can control the action of the 'higher-ups' in the various government departments. These claims are groundless."

They were not, as he well knew. According to Haynes, only forty-three Prohibition agents were convicted in the courts between 1920 and 1925, which proved that "The force was 99% honest. . . . Let our enemies make the most of the fall of these forty-three unfortunates. I am thinking of the other 3,957 who kept the faith."

According to Haynes, of the forty-two convicted, twenty-three were found guilty of offenses involving corruption, and eight of drunkenness; one committed murder; one had a false expense account and tried to influence a grand jury; one committed theft; and the remaining eight suffered small police-court cases. "Of real corruption, therefore, the ratio stands at about one half of one per cent," Haynes claimed.

This was nonsense, even if Haynes was compelled to add that those caught "are, doubtless, but a fraction of those who are guilty," for the Prohibition Bureau's record was, on the whole, appalling. As records would later show, between 1920 and 1930, some 11,926 agents (out of a force of 17,816) were "separated without prejudice" because their criminal involvement could not be proved, and another 1,587 were "dismissed for cause," that is, for offenses that could be proved but might not warrant sentencing, or that would involve costly, publicized trials.

The discrepancy between Prohibition agents' low salaries and their life-styles was staggering — some of them even showing up for work in chauffeur-driven cars. Not just subordinate agents but senior Prohibition Bureau officials were involved in bootlegging activities. In Philadelphia in 1921, the local Prohibition director was shown to have been part of a plot to remove 700,000 gallons of whiskey (with a street value of $4 million) from government-bonded warehouses. Daugherty promptly ordered the upright local prosecuting attorney, T. Henry Walnut, who uncovered the conspiracy, to resign, and the case was dropped. And though it was reopened, thanks to Walnut's behind-the-scenes doggedness, all accused were discharged: the evidence against them in possession of the Justice Department mysteriously disappeared.

There were sufficient cases of this type to trigger a response from Harding himself. In his State of the Union message in December of 1922, he referred to "conditions relating to enforcement which savor of a nationwide scandal."

Even after 1925, when a major reorganization of the Prohibition Bureau took place under the auspices of retired general Lincoln C. Andrews, the situation hardly changed. Andrews eliminated state barriers, and did his best to make the Prohibition Bureau a part of the Civil Service, but this failed to eliminate corruption, for the simple reason that three-quarters of the Prohibition Bureau's staff failed to pass the necessary Civil Service test. By 1928, only two-thirds of the vacancies had been filled. In Pittsburgh, a congressman stood for reelection after serving a jail sentence for using his influence to allow 4,000 cases of whiskey to be released from bond into the hands of bootleggers. Not only was he reelected, but the ASL helped him win back his seat: he had always voted dry.

Haynes — who was not entirely the paragon of virtue he made himself out to be, for it was later learned that he had been paid a monthly retainer by the ASL while commissioner — preferred to lay the blame elsewhere, *outside* the Prohibition Bureau and related law enforcement agencies: "There are large communities where the entire machinery of government, municipal, county and state, is such that federal enforcement officials can get little if any cooperation whatever." In a large number of cases, judges systematically sided with the accused and against the law enforcers. "In some cases it is difficult for an observer in the courtroom to tell whether the bootlegger or the Prohibition agent is on trial." This would not be the case, he said, "if some of our better citizens would attend the courts. Friends of bootleggers throng the courtroom but friends of the law stay away."

The complicated predicament of some judges, caught between their need to be seen upholding the law and their loyalties to those who had voted for them, can be gauged from this Haynes anecdote: Some Prohibition agents were stopped for speeding while chasing a bootlegger along a highway, hauled into court, and heavily fined. The judge then called them into his chambers, returned the fine, and told them: "I'm in politics and I can't afford to let you fellows off."

Not all Prohibition agents were corrupt or intimidated by proof of collusion at the highest levels. Izzy Einstein and his partner, Moe Smith, rapidly became the two most famous Prohibition agents in America. Einstein, "the man of a thousand disguises," accounted for 20 percent of all arrests for violations of the Volstead Act in Manhattan from 1920 to 1925.

Einstein was a postal clerk on Manhattan's Lower East Side when he volunteered his services. His superior, Chief Agent James Shevlin, said he "didn't look the type." Einstein was five feet tall and weighed

225 pounds. "There might be some advantage in not looking like a detective. I could fool people better," Einstein told him. He was hired, given a gun (which he never used) and a badge, and immediately became a star.

As he later wrote,[5] he made his first arrest dressed as a working man. He went into a bar serving soft drinks and legal near beer. "The barman asked: would I like a little lollypop on the side. There was quite a laugh. I told the bartender I was a stranger who didn't know the ropes but I'd buy a pint of whiskey if it wasn't too expensive. He sold me a pint and I arrested him."

In order to keep evidence intact, Izzy invented a device, a small glass funnel easily concealed in a pencil pocket, connected by tube to a bottle hidden in the lining of his coat. Despite his unforgettable appearance and build, he fooled thousands — dedicating his book "To the 4,932 persons I arrested." His gimmicks included a straightforward proposition: "Would you like to sell a pint of whiskey to a deserving prohibition agent?" But there were also elaborate disguises involving crutches, fishing gear (in Long Island), and German, Polish, Hungarian, and Italian impersonations. Fluent in Yiddish, with unmistakably Jewish features, Einstein had great fun conning fake rabbis out of their stocks of sacramental wine.

He soon became notorious. One suspicious bartender said: "Eat this ham sandwich with the compliments of the house, and then I'll give you a drink." Izzy got rid of the ham, ate the sandwich, ordered the drink, and made the arrest. In a speakeasy with a sports clientele, he arrived in football clothes, smeared with fresh mud. In a musicians' club, he was asked to play an instrument. "I'll play you the revenue agents' march," he said. He wrote that one Pole offered him his wife in exchange for ten barrels of whiskey he had seized. He often made twenty to thirty arrests in a single day. The Brooklyn *Eagle* wrote: "Izzy does not sleep. He's on the job day and night and accomplishes more for the drys than half a dozen anti-saloon leagues." Wayne Wheeler wrote him: "The bootlegger who gets away from you has to get up early in the morning."

"By becoming a character I popularized prohibition," Einstein wrote. In fact, Izzy the showman had no strong objections to liquor. An irrepressible extrovert and a born character actor, who realized early on in life the futility of his father's ambition — that he should become a rabbi — he was never happier than when impersonating a socialite (he posed as the judge in a beauty contest before making an arrest), a southern colonel (at a Democratic convention) or a foreign dealer. So successful was he that a whole school of impersonators sprang up, pretending to be Izzy Einstein and demanding $25 shakedowns from saloon keepers.

Although Izzy later fell out with his partner, Moe, he owed much of his success to him. A favorite gimmick was for Moe Smith to pose as a rich out-of-town businessman, and Einstein as his fawning New York subordinate. The two men would sit through a meal in a fashionable New York restaurant, Einstein talking loudly about the Broadway shows Moe should see, and Moe telling him, making sure the waiter was in earshot, that what he really wanted was to find something decent to drink. Einstein would take the waiter into his confidence, the liquor would be produced, and the arrest made. Since both men were easily recognizable — Moe Smith was even fatter than Einstein, weighing in at close to 300 pounds — the naiveté of their victims seems, in retrospect, unbelievable. Their record number of arrests was due, first and foremost, to the laziness, passivity, and corruption of almost all of their Prohibition Bureau colleagues.

Izzy and Moe's out-of-town exploits were less successful. In New Orleans, a local paper carried Izzy's picture on the front page on the day of his arrival, warning that the dreaded agent provocateur was in town. Disguise apart, he and Moe Smith were capable of solid detective work. In true gumshoe fashion, they hired a room overlooking the premises of the Pure Olive Oil Company in Lower Manhattan, observing the comings and goings of its trucks for days at a time, eventually seizing a cargo of rye whiskey worth $50,000. Einstein also arrested a dealer who had imported hundreds of cases of liquor into the city who turned out to be the commercial attaché at the Peruvian consulate in New York. Because he enjoyed diplomatic immunity, Izzy recalled, "we had to give him back his liquor."

Although the Peruvian consul's dealings may have been an exception, diplomatic immunity meant that liquor could be imported for diplomats' private use, and was even served at official parties. Few ambassadors were as respectful of the law as Sir Esmé Howard, British ambassador in Washington in 1929, who not only banned the serving of wine or champagne at cocktail parties but told his staff that, out of respect for the Constitution, anyone caught ordering liquor through the "diplomatic bag" would be sent back to London in disgrace. His staff staged a huge party when his successor was named.

The trade in fake sacramental wine for religious purposes gave Izzy and Moe unlimited opportunities to perfect their provocation techniques. Practicing Jewish families were allowed one gallon per adult member per year, and sacramental wine was rationed — amounts determined by the number of registered worshippers in New York's synagogues. Needless to say, the system led to monumental abuse. As Izzy and Moe discovered, a 600-member synagogue turned out to be a laundry; a delicatessen was another. A thousand gallons of wine had been drawn for a synagogue that was no more than a postal address in a Lower East Side tenement building. They also exposed an entirely fictitious "Assembly of Hebrew Orthodox Rabbis of America," whose members consisted of one person, who, it turned out, was neither orthodox nor a rabbi, nor even Jewish, but an Irishman called Sullivan.

There were innumerable other scams. American cigar makers — among those officially entitled to alcohol for the manufacture of their products — also took advantage of the Volstead Act and the ignorance of the civil servants who administered the Bureau of Industrial Alcohol responsible for delivering it. A Philadelphia cigar maker who had spent $480 on alcohol in the previous eighteen years obtained an official permit for 420,000 gallons of alcohol a year — more than enough to soak all the cigar tobacco leaf in the world, the Prohibition Bureau later claimed. Prohibition agents also fought a losing battle with thousands of fly-by-night manufacturers of hair restorers, skin conditioners, and other toilet preparations smelling of whiskey, gin, or rum.

Hardly surprisingly, there is no mention of Izzy and Moe in Haynes's book. The reason is that their career came to an abrupt end. They had been too successful, offending too many people in the upper echelons of the police, state, and federal agencies — and in Congress. In November of 1925, pretexting an "administrative reorganization," Haynes, himself under considerable political pressure, abruptly fired them both.

For all his official optimism, Haynes's discouragement emerges in his long catalogue of prominent citizens battening onto bootleggers' bribes. In one "mid-Western industrial city" (unnamed, but probably

Cincinnati) "the mayor, the sheriff, the judge of the city court, a former prosecuting attorney, a detective sergeant, a justice of the peace, lawyers, deputy sheriffs and cabaret staffs and singers were all involved," and proprietors of places where liquor was sold illegally were "systematically protected by the police in cognizance of higher officials." A mayor of Atlanta was sentenced to eighteen months for participating in a bootlegging ring. New Jersey was "a stamping ground for bootleggers doing volume business." In a case involving 100,000 gallons of impounded wine and property worth $2 million, "the wine growers, a prominent citizen and the ex-Governor of the state of California all testified in favor of the accused." On the West Coast, one bank president, fourteen wholesalers, a lawyer, and a deputy collector of internal revenue aggregated 31 years in jail and $167,000 in fines in a case involving liquor worth $4 million.

In the face of evidence of this type, "The Federal Government," Haynes insisted, "*is* reaching big operators, the 'higher-ups,' with ever-increasing success." At the time of his writing, as later statistics would show, liquor was America's biggest industry. Americans were consuming 200 million gallons of hard liquor, 684 million gallons of malt liquor, and 118 million gallons of wine a year, and the bootleggers' overall income amounted to four billion dollars a year.

Rather than expose in detail instances of corruption among politicians, the Justice Department, the police, and the state judiciary all over America, Haynes preferred to lay the blame for his bureau's failures on a powerful international wet conspiracy. He quoted Lord Astor, who claimed in a speech in 1923 that "people are working in England to misrepresent the attitude and actions of America." He attached great importance to a (1922) "anti-Prohibition Congress" in Brussels attended by politicians from Belgium, Canada, Spain, Finland, France, Britain, Denmark, Italy, Norway, Sweden, and Switzerland, which, he said, was plotting to undermine American institutions under the pretext of "defending individual and commercial liberty." He claimed there was a powerful movement in France, headed by Count Albert de Mun, to "provide wets" with ample funds "and the active support of a hundred million European advocates." Hardly coincidentally, Haynes noted, Count de Mun was "president of one of the largest champagne companies in France and was formerly an extensive exporter to the U.S." Tourist and advertising agencies boosted France as a tourist haven and a drinker's paradise, "appealing to the comradeship that existed between Yank and poilu[6] in war days" and asserting that "in all our cities throughout our entire wine-growing region, you will not meet a drunken man."

In America itself, Haynes wrote, no fewer than forty-two organizations had been set up to fight Prohibition. The most powerful, the Association Against the Prohibition Amendment, got massive financial support from former liquor manufacturers and dealers associations. It "practically paralleled in organization method the Anti-Saloon League"; that is, it systematically backed wet congressional candidates (with considerable success, in that Volstead himself would lose his seat as a result of their efforts).

In the last resort, for all the occasional fascinating glimpses he gave of his real problems, Haynes's book never dared explore in depth the crucial problem at hand: that for all the infrequent incorruptibles, law enforcement officials' hands were tied and the Prohibition Bureau doomed because of a web of collusion — a tacit conspiracy to batten onto Prohibition involving politicians, the judiciary, the banks, and the police extending from Washington to every state of the Union and even involving the attorney general himself from 1921 to 1924.

Instead, Haynes preferred to repeat, Coué-like, the conviction that "Prohibition has come to stay" and highlight the perils of drink in any form. "Who drinks bootleg drinks with death," he wrote, citing the example of a promising actress who killed herself "because the effects of the liquor drunk at a party had caused her to seek death as a relief," and the case of the "young woman on a Hoboken ferryboat who took a drink from a flask, almost immediately staggered to the stern, plunged into the Hudson and died." That such deaths were directly attributable to Prohibition, and the nonavailability of quality liquor, seems never to have occurred to him.

But perhaps Haynes, who knew all about the drinking habits and corrupt practices of the Harding administration, deliberately wrote his book tongue in cheek. He was, after all, a Daugherty appointee, and was well aware of the latter's appalling reputation, though he did pay a somewhat ambiguous tribute to him in his book. "There can be no doubt as to the attitude of the nation's chief law enforcement officer, Attorney General Daugherty," he wrote, "to whose department is entrusted the task of prosecuting violators of the prohibition laws."

It was symptomatic of the hypocrisy of the Prohibition era that, in 1921, the American Bar Association decided to hold its annual meeting in Cincinnati — the very town where almost the entire police force was on George Remus's payroll, either as convoy guards or as salesmen on commission. In Daugherty's presence, it solemnly declared that

> The people of the United States have undertaken to suppress the age-long evil of the liquor traffic. When for the gratification of their appetites, lawyers, bankers, merchants, manufacturers and social leaders, both men and women, scoff at this law, or any other law, they are aiding the cause of anarchy, and promoting mob violence, robbery and homicide.

After hours, many of those attending the meeting were haunting the speakeasies they denounced. Every lawyer present must have been aware that "the General" was on the take, using Jess Smith as his bagman not only to dispose of controversial cases but to protect big bootleggers and even peddle B permits to them. But even the most cynical among them must have listened to Daugherty's keynote address with wry amusement.

"I do not mean to impute moral turpitude to him who is opposed to the Eighteenth Amendment," Daugherty conceded magnanimously,

> But when public sentiment has crystallized into law there can be no question as to the duty of good citizens. They may still debate as to the wisdom of the law, but there is only one course of conduct, and that is obedience to the law while it exists. . . . To refuse or to neglect to enforce a valid enactment of the legislative department of government, or to enforce it mechanically or half-heartedly, or to wink at its violation, is without justification on any sound theory of government. Those who ask or expect this not only contribute to lawlessness, but destroy the basis upon which their own security rests. Our safety and happiness lie in obedience to law by every man, woman and child.

There was loud, prolonged applause.

12

"PROHIBITION DOESN'T WORK!"

No one who is intellectually honest will deny that
there has not yet been effective nationwide enforcement.
— *Mabel Willebrandt, deputy attorney general
in charge of Prohibition enforcement, 1929*

Shortly after resigning her post in 1928, Mabel Willebrandt published *The Inside of Prohibition*,[1] from notes accumulated during her eight years in office as deputy attorney general in charge of Prohibition enforcement. Her book was in sharp contrast to Haynes's. Unlike him, she had no reason to pull any punches: she owed her appointment not to the Ohio gang but to former president Taft, who had strongly recommended her to Harding. And though she did pull *some* punches, (here, too, references to Daugherty are tongue-in-cheek, though criticism is clearly implied), she did not balk at allocating responsibility for failure where she felt it was due. The bootleggers and rumrunners, she made it clear, were less responsible for the Prohibition mess than the corrupt, hypocritical *system* that battened onto them.

From today's standpoint, one is tempted to ask what all the fuss was about. Who cared whether a network of speakeasies and middlemen kept Americans supplied with liquor, good or bad, while police and Prohibition agents systematically looked the other way? But the perspective was different in the twenties. The fact is that, as Willebrandt wrote, ever since the United States became a republic, *"No political, economic or moral issue has so engrossed and divided all the people of America as the Prohibition problem, except the issue of slavery. . . .* Nor will it be denied that Prohibition enforcement remains the chief, *and in fact the only real political issue of the whole nation."*2

Willebrandt was one of the few in authority to point to the folly of passing a law and simply expecting it to be obeyed. Of course, such a controversial issue required teeth ("the problem of enforcement will not solve itself"), but neither the transgressors nor the corrupt Prohibition agents were really to blame. "The Federal Government's record in all these things is not such as to produce exaggerated pride in one who has been a part of it," she conceded.

Willebrandt acknowledged the quandary facing any administration, defining it as follows:

1. It was clearly impossible to prevent immense quantities of liquor from entering the country.

2. The media had perhaps exacerbated the problem, but "certainly it would be ridiculous for me to deny that liquor is sold in large and small quantities throughout the country, and that practically anyone who possesses simultaneously a thirst and as much as a quarter dollar can partly assuage that thirst."

3. At the same time, repeal of Prohibition's stricter measures, making wine and beer legal again, was "practically impossible," for she was convinced that a majority of drys would vote against any modification in the law, however much it was disobeyed. Her assessment, as a well-informed Republican, was that "Congress remains overwhelmingly dry in its votes, *whatever the personal habits of the members may be,"* and *"a Congressman who comes up for re-election every two years cannot afford to be wrong about the wet or dry sentiment of his district. He knows!"*3

The real culprit was the American political system itself. Traditionally, liquor interests had "financed city and state campaigns, controlled city councils, boards of commissioners, state legislatures. Through political allies they prevented enactment of early closing-hour ordinances and Sunday closing laws, the breweries and whiskey wholesalers were always willing to chip in to help elect a county or state's attorney, a member of the legislature or the city council."

Despite the swing in public opinion in favor of Prohibition — provoked by church militancy, the ASL, and, above all, America's entry
into the First World War — Willebrandt was convinced that such influence had simply passed into the hands of the bootleggers, moonshiners,
still owners, and all those with vested interests in the status quo. "The
influence of liquor in politics begins down in the City wards and often
in county districts, *but it extends if it can up to the Cabinet and the
White House in Washington.*"4

> After George Remus, king of the bootleggers, had been convicted
> and lost his appeals, the rumor reached me that he would never serve
> a day in Atlanta prison. I set it down as only the bragging of the
> defendant. But a few days later, a phone call came from the White
> House, stating that a respite of 60 days would be granted Remus if
> the Attorney General would send over the necessary papers. Promi-
> nent politicians . . . had intervened with the President.

She did not, of course, infer that they had, in all probability,
included the attorney general himself.

In a case involving another prominent bootlegger, "every conceivable political and personal appeal, including an appeal by a Cabinet official, was made to quash the case. Attorney General Daugherty called
me to his office and told me of the pressure that had been brought
on him to call off any further investigation into this matter." Again,
she must have known that Daugherty was playing games with her, but
chose not to mention this. Most readers, she knew, would draw their
own conclusions.

Even more damaging to those who genuinely wanted to uphold
Prohibition laws was the government's neglect of the end use of industrial alcohol. In 1926, she revealed, every month some 660,000
gallons of "denatured" alcohol were sold to a variety of customers, including pharmaceutical industries, beauticians, and drugstores — and
a tidy amount, duly flavored and sometimes lethal, had ended up in
bootleggers' whiskey bottles.

Even those relatively innocent congressmen without any bootlegging connections brought the political system into disrepute by chal-
lenging the validity of one of the laws embodied in the Constitution.
In the first place, "many originally in favor are now opposed to it," or

had become convinced that Prohibition could not be enforced, and were lobbying for its repeal.

> Many others have been antagonized by the discovery that the very men who made the Prohibition law are violating it and that many officers of the law sworn to enforce Prohibition statutes are constantly conspiring to defeat them. How can you justify prison and fines when you know for a fact that the men who make the laws and appropriate the money for Prohibition are themselves patronizing bootleggers?

It was common knowledge that "Senators and Congressmen appeared on the floor in a drunken condition," that "bootleggers infested the halls and corridors of Congress and ply their trade there," and that no attempts had ever been made to expel them. What she failed to say, but must have known, was that bootleggers kept huge stocks of liquor in the House of Representatives and Senate cellars so that orders could be met without delay. It was common knowledge that well-connected retailers had unlimited access to Senate and House of Representatives offices, with home deliveries of every conceivable type of liquor.

Congressmen and high government officials, Willebrandt noted, believed they were above the law, and customs officers were told to extend the usual courtesies and free entry privileges to them — as they would to foreign diplomats. When one congressman was caught smuggling a barrel of rum into the country after a West Indies cruise (a customs officer's attention had been drawn to a broken bottle of rum, part of thirty quarts of smuggled liquor), he was indicted but acquitted. In her book, Willebrandt failed to add that the politician concerned was Republican Congressman Everett Denison of Ohio, one of the most intransigent Prohibition propagandists in the House. Elected by rural church-going voters, like so many other publicly dry, privately wet politicians, he was compelled to toe the Prohibition line, at least in his speeches and voting record or risk losing his seat to an even more hypocritical rival. For years, men such as Denison would be the pliant tools of Wayne Wheeler's Anti-Saloon League, refusing him nothing — one of the reasons why the Prohibition albatross poisoned the political life of America for so long.

For those lacking political clout or money for lawyers there was

no such leniency. In her book, Willebrandt made no mention of police persecution of small-time violators or of measures in both Michigan and New York that provided drastic mandatory sentences to those
convicted for a fourth time for violations of the Volstead Act.[5]

There were some appalling travesties of justice. Both Fred Palm
of Lansing and a mother of ten elsewhere in Michigan got life sentences for possession of a pint of gin. Michigan was "the wettest state in
America," the *New York Herald Tribune* pointed out with heavy irony,
"with tens of thousands violating the Volstead Act daily if not hourly
. . . so we suggest a further simplification: instead of sentencing to life
imprisonment those of its citizens who insist on harboring pints of gin
in their homes, let Michigan sentence them to the chair. . . ."

"The truth is," Willebrandt wrote, "that in New York as in other
cities, it is immensely profitable to the politicians to let the speakeasies
flourish: politicians never lack for poll workers on election day." Prior
to Prohibition, she noted,

> . . . the saloons were the assembling places and allies of crooked
> politicians who manipulated elections in the interests of the grab-
> bers of franchises for street railways, electric light and gas plants and
> other seekers of special privilege. It is those political machines that
> are still functioning . . . the so-called decent citizens have done little
> anywhere permanently to curb the reign of the corrupt manipulators
> of city affairs.

Few were really prepared to fight for "decent city government."
Until they did so, "there would not be honest enforcement of either
Prohibition or any other laws. If the searchlight of Prohibition has
revealed the city as our national shame, then it will have served more
widely than the framers of the 18th Amendment ever dreamed."

But the change could not be imposed from above. Anticipating
the Republican tidal wave victory in the November 8, 1924, elections, Willebrandt, in a prescient chapter titled "The Seceding States,"
noted that "the people of America do not want and will not permit an army of offices of the Federal Government to enforce law and
order in local counties and cities. Nothing in the country is more
contrary or repugnant to basic principles of our form of government."

The trouble was, as Mabel Willebrandt well knew, in some states the federal government was all that was left to enforce Prohibition — for starting with New York State (in 1923, with the assent of Democratic Governor Al Smith, an acknowledged wet), a handful of states (New Jersey, Montana, Nevada, Wisconsin) *had* repealed Prohibition, at least insofar as state law enforcement was concerned, putting the entire burden on the FBI, the Justice Department, the Treasury, the Prohibition Bureau, and the federal courts.

In New York State alone, Willebrandt pointed out, there were some 3,000 state police, a 17,000-strong city police force, 113 state supreme court judges, and 62 county prosecutors. From the end of 1923 onward, they were all ostentatiously refusing to enforce Prohibition laws. This did not mean that in these states Prohibition no longer existed; on the contrary, the introduction of the Jones Act (passed in 1925) sharply increased sentences for violations of the Volstead Act (up to five years in jail instead of two, and $10,000 fines instead of $1,000 fines, double that for recidivists), and a new "padlock" rule, admittedly only partially enforced, resulted in the permanent closure of speakeasies whose owners had come before the courts. But it did mean that federal agencies, and the highly corrupt Prohibition Bureau, could no longer enlist the aid of state authorities in their fight against bootlegging.

Furthermore, the federal judiciary, as Willebrandt well knew, was often even more reluctant to convict Prohibition offenders than the state judiciary was. Haynes had hinted that this was so, but Willebrandt gave instance after instance of federal judges and prosecutors openly mocking Prohibition law enforcement efforts, siding with the accused they were supposed to prosecute, either because they disagreed with the law, had been bought, or were actually in business partnership with the bootleggers and speakeasy operators. "With the right kind of prosecutors the bootleggers will go out of business," she wrote, but "during my eight years as Deputy Attorney General a large part of my time and energy was devoted to prosecuting prosecutors."

She cited examples of assistant attorneys responsible for enforcing the Prohibition laws being convicted of association with bootleggers, sometimes as co-owners of illicit breweries or stills, and of how judges had in court openly attacked the integrity of Prohibition Bureau officials, quoting one of them as saying: "I want to instruct the witness that a prohibition agent is not the law and most of them whom I have seen are about as far away from it as could be imagined."

There was an additional impediment to justice. U.S. commissioners were the "middlemen" who decided whether the accused should go before a grand jury. Whether they handled one case a day or ten, they were only paid a fee for the one case, which scarcely made for speedy procedures. But worse than that, many of them were unbelievably corrupt, tipping off speakeasy operators in advance so that when federal officers went on raids, all they discovered were innocuous soft drink bars with church music playing in the background. Some commissioners were known to receive monthly fees of between $50 and $75 from each speakeasy operator in town. Jury selection being their other prerogative, some deliberately selected for jury duty men and women whose anti-Prohibition bias was well known to them, or else intimidated juries to acquit accused bootleggers.

And even when speakeasy owners *were* fined, these sentences were usually excessively low (except for notoriously dry states such as Kansas), and what was even a $10,000 fine to millionaires such as George Remus and Willie Haar? In some cities and counties, bootleggers and speakeasy owners came up before local courts every month, their fines going straight into municipal accounts — barely disguised, pre-Prohibition era saloon license fees.

It was partly because state law enforcement agencies no longer handled Prohibition offenses in urban centers such as New York and actively wet states such as New Jersey that the federal authorities devised new, sophisticated techniques to convict offenders, many of them anticipating those later used by the Drug Enforcement Agency (DEA).

In 1925, for example, a speakeasy called the Bridge Whist Club opened at 14 East Forty-fourth Street in New York. It was an undercover operation, entirely financed by secret federal funds, the purpose being to obtain incriminating evidence about bootleggers and their supplies.

Surveillance techniques were primitive but effective: there were no automatic recording devices in the 1920s, but wire-linked microphones, built into the club's lampshades, were connected to the earphones of a battery of stenographers working around the clock on a shift basis. Thanks to these taps, agents did apprehend a major bootlegger, but owing to informers within its ranks, clients soon knew all

about the operation. Also, much of the information gathered was deliberately planted disinformation, including references to the drinking
habits of well-known politicians, clergymen, and even senior Prohibition officials.

The Justice Department also tapped Remus's phones. Many years
later, in a *Collier's* article, Bill Mellin, a former agent, described how
he did this. He was sent to Columbus, Ohio, where Remus had
booked into a hotel suite. For nine days, Mellin waited in vain to be
contacted by special agents. In the *Collier's* piece, he noted that he
was probably followed during this period to make sure he was not secretly in league with Remus or his associates: "They were suspicious of
some of their own agents in that city." He was given a duplicate key
to Remus's suite (room 707), and a room next to it was booked for
Mellin.

Mellin proceeded by stages. First, he connected the 707 exten-
sion to his own room telephone so that he could listen in on all of
Remus's telephone conversations. Learning that he would be away for
twenty-four hours, Mellin entered the Remus suite, picked a suitable
spot on the wall and, boring a hole, inserted a mike, using soap to fill
in the drill holes and painting the surface to match the wall. "It was
a smooth, perfect job." In his own room, Mellin connected the wires
from the mike to a handset, and installed a device that switched on
a red light every time a conversation started in Remus's room. "That
way, you don't have to keep the headphones on your ears all the
time."

Two government stenographers were then sent in. They worked
in shifts in Mellin's room, recording all of Remus's conversations with
his visitors. They learned a good deal about Remus's bootlegging operations, including the fact that eighteen freight cars would soon be discharging liquor for Remus at a railroad siding in Covington, Kentucky
(near Death Valley Farm).

But the operation also revealed the degree of corruption prevalent
in Columbus. "One day alone, Remus had forty-four people in, and
some of them were Federal prohibition agents or deputy marshals,"
Mellin wrote. "He paid them an average of $1,000 apiece. When I had
summarized all the information, I went to a United States official in
Cincinnati, and said: here's the dope. He looked at me for a full minute
without talking. Then he said: 'My boy, come back tomorrow.' "

I went back the next day. He said: "Son, where is your home office?" I told him it was in New York. He said: "Son, there are times when a man has to be practical in this business. It's only a few weeks to election, and the information you've dug up is political dynamite. The men you spied on — the agents and marshals — are political appointees. Go back to New York and forget it." I didn't go back to New York. I went to Washington and squealed. But it didn't do me any good. Nothing ever happened on the Remus information.[6]

There were equally flawed government-funded speakeasy operations in Washington (where a banquet for major bootleggers was sponsored by the Prohibition Bureau in the Mayfair Hotel) and Norfolk, Virginia, and one curious aspect of the New York "Bridge Club" operation was that long after surveillance had ceased, it continued to function without ever being raided.

In light of all this, was Willebrandt's contention that "Congress remained overwhelmingly dry" a tenable proposition? The answer is that, in 1924 at any rate — for all the grotesque law enforcement failures, the open secession of New York State (the other five were still to come), the disgust shown by honest people at blatant corruption, and the consequent growing damage to the American body politic itself — the mood of the country was such that repeal was not just unlikely, but impossible.

A crucial test came that year with the Democratic presidential nomination. Al Smith, the popular governor of New York State, was the Democratic front-runner. Despite the fact that he was a Catholic, and therefore deeply suspect to Southerners and the Ku Klux Klan, he was the only candidate who stood a chance of beating Calvin Coolidge. The latter, though Harding's vice president, had been one of the few totally honest members of the Harding administration, and, because Harding had died while still in office, was already a temporary White House incumbent — almost always a considerable advantage for a presidential contender.

Al Smith had the backing of Tammany Hall, that network of largely corrupt politicians and entrepreneurs who ran the city, but there was no hint of major scandal in his own political past — and the fact that the 1924 Democratic Convention was being held in Madison Square Garden was a huge plus. But convention proceedings not only revealed an element of schizophrenia among grass-roots representa-tives as far as Prohibition was concerned, but dramatically underlined the veto powers of the Anti-Saloon League — its ability to ensure that any American president continued to do its bidding.

Both Wayne Wheeler and Izzy Einstein made notable appearances at the convention. It was yet another pretext for Izzy to disguise himself as a goateed Southern colonel, though by now he was so well known that his presence was not so much a disguise as a warning that those attending the convention had better moderate their drinking, at least in public. (They did not: according to witnesses, some of the delega-tions openly drank out of paper bags during the proceedings, and the galleries stank of whiskey.)

Wheeler had a far more serious purpose: to prevent Al Smith's nomination. As a committed Republican, he wanted Coolidge, a "sound" Prohibitionist, to become president, and knew this was a foregone conclusion unless Al Smith became a contender. Wheeler had done his homework: he controlled one-third of all the delegates (mostly from southern and midwestern states) who would never vote for a wet. But Franklin D. Roosevelt, a rising star in the Democratic party, made a keynote speech nominating Al Smith that had a galvaniz-ing effect. "Ask your Republican friends whom they would least like to see nominated," he told the delegates, and got a huge ovation.

Al Smith himself was well aware that his real opponent was not his likeliest rival candidate William Gibbs McAdoo — a nonentity dry whose strongest credential was that he happened to be the late presi-dent Woodrow Wilson's son-in-law — but Wheeler himself. While the convention proceeded without them, the two men met secretly in a New York club.

Their long discussion was surprisingly cordial. Smith asked Wheeler why the ASL had been so adamant in banning real beer, and told Wheeler that if elected, he would probably increase its alcoholic content. But he said nothing about repealing Prohibition, hinting that he was perfectly aware of the extent of dry sentiment outside New York State, especially in the South and Midwest. He told Wheeler that "be-ing President of the United States would be quite different from being Governor of New York." But Wheeler had the last word. When Smith made an allusion to his own possible future presidency, Wheeler told him: "Governor, you will never enter the White House."[7]

In the contest that followed, Al Smith's supporters wrecked McAdoo's chances, but Wheeler's dry delegates effectively blocked Al Smith (there were over a hundred ballots). In the end, as Wheeler had both anticipated and planned, the Democratic delegates selected a lackluster compromise candidate for the nomination — an obscure West Virginian political hack named John W. Davis. Coolidge won easily, and Prohibition was given a new lease on life.

Al Smith was not the only impeccably honest wet politician whose anti-Prohibitionist views stemmed solely from moral convictions. New York Congressman Fiorello La Guardia, who would become New York's mayor in 1929, replacing the arch-corrupt Tammany Hall figure Jimmy Walker, was another.

A brilliant media manipulator, La Guardia was almost as much of a showman as Izzy Einstein. In 1926, after tipping off the press, he marched into Room 150 of the House Office Building in bartender's uniform and proceeded to demonstrate how easy it was to make real beer, mixing near beer with malt extract, which could be bought legally. Inside Congress, he knew he was immune from prosecution, but when the news came from Albany, where the headquarters of the state's Prohibition Bureau was located, that anyone caught making "La Guardia" formula beer would be arrested, the *New York Times* announced that "Representative La Guardia will walk into a drugstore at 95 Lenox Avenue, purchase the necessary ingredients and mix his brew with a kick. Then he will stand by to be arrested." Little Flower, as he was known, was exceedingly disappointed when no Prohibition agent showed up, and a city policeman refused to arrest him. Newspapers all over America carried stories of his exploit, and one city editor wired him: "Your beer a sensation. Whole staff trying experiment. Remarkable results."[8]

Although such antics seemed at the time to make him out to be a political lightweight, his opposition to Prohibition was no mere electioneering gimmick but stemmed from his conviction that it was destroying the nation. As early as 1919, he had told Volstead that "this law will be almost impossible of enforcement. And if this law fails to be enforced — as it certainly will be as it is drawn — it will create contempt and disregard for the law all over the country." Excessive drinking, he insisted, could be curbed only by education, not legislation.

A born iconoclast, he openly proclaimed what other politicians believed but dared not even whisper. Consequently, he attracted a large number of enemies in Congress from the dry Midwest and the South. Southern congressmen, he told the House, knew full well that the moonshiners down south favored Prohibition because it increased their business ". . . if the people from the dry states would keep out of New York City, we would have no drunks there." And if they were all for Prohibition, he told a constituent, it was because Prohibition "was only enforced among the coloured population," whereas "the white gentleman openly and freely can obtain and consume all the liquor he desires." He could in fact have expanded on this theme. A detailed survey of "police blotter" cases involving Prohibition offenses in the *Easthampton Star* from 1920 to 1933 reveals that no socialites, or even "respectable" wealthy householders, were ever arraigned in the Hamptons: the victims of local Prohibition agents' zeal were invariably working-class artisans or small potato farmers, often recent immigrants with exotic Polish names.

La Guardia returned to the theme of two-tier justice (not only concerning Prohibition enforcement) again and again. "May I remind the gentleman from Georgia," he replied to a congressman who had urged him to respect the constitutional sanctity of the law, including its Prohibition provisions, "that there is also a 14th amendment to the Constitution? The 14th Amendment deals with human rights and liberties and it is as dead as a doornail in certain sections of the country."

After a decade of Prohibition, he commented with some bitterness, ". . . politicians are ducking, candidates are hedging, the Anti-Saloon League prospering. People are being poisoned, bootleggers are being enriched, and government officials are being corrupted."

Will Rogers, the famous American humorist, may have joked that "Prohibition is better than no liquor at all," but to La Guardia, it was no laughing matter, for all its tragicomic undertones: as an Italian-American, he had a special reason to seek the end of Prohibition. He knew that the longer it lasted, the more the Italian-American image would be tarnished in the eyes of public opinion.

In fact, in New York at least, the underworld was by no means exclusively Italian-American. Frank Costello — one of its masterminds, and a brilliant businessman in his own right — took an Irish name, but he was born Francesco Castiglia, although he did his best to conceal the fact. However, his front man, "Big Bill" Dwyer; Tammany Hall operative Alfred J. Hines; and Larry Fay, owner of a taxi company that operated a mobile bootlegging operation, *were* Irish-Americans. Arnold Rothstein, one of the biggest owners of speakeasies, clip joints, and New York nightclubs (and the man who fixed the 1919 World Series), was Jewish. So were "Dutch" Schultz (Arthur Flegenheimer); Meyer Lansky, probably the most astute entrepreneur of all; and Benjamin ("Bugsy") Siegel. Nor did the Italian-American gangsters operate in a vacuum. Albert Anastasia had an official, police-approved bodyguard who was not an Italian-American. "Lucky" Luciano trusted his Jewish underworld partners more than his fellow Sicilians. A leading Mafia hit man suspected of killing the anti-fascist refugee Carlo Tresca had a direct line to the (largely Irish-American) New York police department.

Chicago was where Italian-Americans came to dominate gangland during the Prohibition years — but the problem was not simply that Al Capone, Johnny Torrio, and the infamous Genna brothers were Italian-Americans and active in the *Unione Siciliana*. In Chicago, Prohibition resulted in so blatant a collusion between underworld figures and those supposed to be fighting them that during the three terms of Chicago Mayor "Big Bill" Thompson, Capone and Torrio between them "ran and directed the political, police and federal enforcement agencies of Chicago and Cook County."[9]

13

CHICAGO

The *Untouchables*, that hugely popular TV series starring Robert Stack as Eliot Ness, with Walter Winchell's gravelly voice-over narration, gave viewers all over the world a pretty good idea of American gangland activities during Prohibition — or so they thought. In fact, the series bore as much relation to reality as a Stalinist film of the 1950s glorifying the Soviet regime. Made with the close cooperation of the FBI, under J. Edgar Hoover's supervision (he monitored the series and the FBI had censorship rights), *The Untouchables* was a complete travesty — a blatant propaganda exercise eulogizing Hoover and the FBI, bending the facts to suit him.

First shown in the early 1960s, *The Untouchables* celebrated the triumph of the forces of righteousness over absolute evil. The FBI's war on gangsters took place in a vacuum, with not the slightest hint that the underworld bosses were so aggressive because they knew they were aided and abetted by so many respectable individuals, including members of the judiciary and the police. Nor were there any references to politicians and elected officials on the take, to district attorneys and judges in collusion and even in business partnership with bootleggers, or to bribed, bent, or terrorized juries.

In fact, it can be argued that some of America's biggest villains during the Prohibition era were not the Al Capones, Johnny Torrios, Gus Morans, Dutch Schultzes, or Frank Costellos but the political bosses in New York, Chicago, and elsewhere who used the underworld to their considerable advantage, and the many venal, conniving police and law enforcement officials who supplemented their incomes with mobster money.

New York's mayor and Tammany boss James Walker — until defeated by Fiorello La Guardia in 1929 — enjoyed a cozy relationship with New York's gangland. But nowhere was the collusion between politics and organized crime more spectacularly evident than in Chicago, where Mayor "Big Bill" Thompson's three-term reign led to a virtual breakdown in law and order, and a situation in which — on a par with "Papa Doc" Duvalier's Port au Prince, Medellín (Colombia) in the 1980s, and Moscow today — gangs virtually ran the city. "Thompson," wrote Fletcher Dobyns, "made Chicago the most corrupt and lawless city in the world."[1]

It had been a wide-open town long before Prohibition became an issue. The old-time First Ward (district) Democratic bosses, "Bathhouse John" Coughlin and Michael "Hinky Dink" Kenna,[2] both sons of Irish immigrants, owed their clout, and their considerable wealth, to handouts from the brothel owners they routinely protected. "I always entertained state legislators free in the Everlight Club," Minna Everleigh, owner of Chicago's most famous and expensive brothel, told a Chicago judge after her retirement. That was the least of her favors.

"Hinky Dink" Kenna was a dour saloon owner whose generous "schooner" measures made it the most popular drinking place in town. He was also, for several decades, a hugely influential inner city Democratic party figure, who had devised a foolproof way of ensuring his partner Coughlin's reelection.

It was called chain voting: genuine ballots were spirited away and marked for "Bathhouse John." They were then distributed to floating voters, who were driven to the polling booths, where they voted, using the already marked ballots and picking up fresh ones, which they surrendered to "Hinky Dink's" henchmen, collecting a small fee in return. These were then recycled, and used with another batch of voters, ensuring that "every vote paid for was really cast for Coughlin."[3]

Long before 1920, the Chicago gangs had established a tacit but effective *modus vivendi*, sharing out their most lucrative activities — gambling, prostitution, "protection," and strike breaking — throughout the various inner city wards. Paradoxically, the fact that local politicians (including Coughlin and Kenna) were so intimately involved in the management and protection of Chicago's many brothels meant that violent crime was relatively rare. The politicians' vested interests gave Chicago's red light districts an aura of respectability — all those involved knew that bloodshed and gangland violence drove the customers away.

Prohibition brought this era to a close. The reason Chicago became synonymous with gang warfare — from 1920 to 1933, nearly eight hundred gangsters were killed in shoot-outs with other gangsters — was the irresistible profit motive. With no legitimate source of liquor left, clubs, speakeasies, and private dealers were compelled to turn to the bootleggers, and these, increasingly under the thumb of underworld bosses, became a ready prey.

From 1920 onward, a new breed of gangsters emerged to take advantage of the new situation. Underworld leaders — the term is inappropriate because they made little attempt to conceal their activities — used their links with politicians and politically appointed city officials, including the police and even the judiciary, to eliminate their rivals with virtual impunity. Given the cozy, mutually rewarding relationship that existed in Chicago between politicians and mobsters even before Prohibition, the gangland saga that followed was eminently predictable, even though the gangsters' political allegiances had always been notoriously fickle.

From 1910 onward, "Big Jim" Colosimo, the slot machine and brothel king (and owner of Chicago's celebrated saloon Diamond Jim's), had worked closely with "Hinky Dink" Kenna and "Bathhouse John" Coughlin — though he would campaign for Republican "Big Bill" Thompson for mayor in 1919. His demise, in 1920, shortly after Prohibition came into being [4] (Johnny Torrio, his bodyguard, almost certainly had him killed after "business differences" arose between them), marked the passing of an era. His was the first of the hugely expensive, ostentatious funerals that would later become a ritual. Congressmen; aldermen; members of the Chicago Opera Company; countless public officials, including district attorneys; and over a thousand First Ward Democratic party stalwarts solemnly paraded through the city behind his coffin.

In pre-Prohibition days, many brewers and distillers had behaved like loan sharks, buying up saloons and then squeezing the saloon keepers for ever-increasing profits. From 1920 on, the new, younger, greedier gangs behaved far more ruthlessly, using terror as a weapon. It was, as Remus's aide, George Conners, noted, a seller's market: with good liquor constantly in short supply, saloon keepers and nightclub and brothel owners were now compelled to buy set quantities of liquor at set prices in return for "protection." The purchasers knew that if they protested too much, the penalties could be fatal.

The police rarely intervened in such disputes, and underworld members, including those of non-Italian origin, respected a form of *omerta:* even on their deathbeds after fatal shootouts, they seldom cooperated with the police. Nor did the police intervene when rival gangs began hijacking each other's liquor. As long as no law enforcement officers got hurt, it was a private war that did not concern them. As in Cincinnati in George Remus's heyday, suitably remunerated uniformed police in Chicago even routinely escorted delivery vans belonging to specially favored bootlegging gangs.

In all fairness to Chicago, New York was not far behind. "Lucky" Luciano claimed he controlled every New York police precinct, and had a bagman deliver up to $20,000 a month to New York Police Commissioner Grover Whalen in used notes. He also maintained that after the 1929 stock market crash, he loaned Whalen $35,000 to cover his margin.[5]

Hijackings occurred with increasing frequency. The rationale was not only to acquire liquor stocks for free but to eliminate business rivals for good. "Crime," John Huston has a character say in *The Asphalt Jungle*, "is just a left-handed form of human endeavor," and in many ways there was a parallel between gangland history during the Prohibition era and that of the new industrial empires, also coming of age from 1920 onward. Gangs, like respectable conglomerates, competed for an ever larger share of the market because it was soon clear to both that they had to keep on growing or go under, gobbled up by more powerful rivals.

Chicago was unique because it became, in the early 1920s, not just a microcosm of corrupt, *affairiste* Washington under the Harding Administration but at times a virtually lawless city. "Big Bill" Thompson, its mayor, was no Daugherty. The latter was careful to maintain a respectable front while in office, using bagmen such as Jess Smith to do his dirty work.

"Big Bill" Thompson's front men tended to control *him*, for this testy, foul-mouthed tub-thumper with a child's attention span and only moderate intelligence lacked Daugherty's shrewdness, discretion, and political experience. Thompson's weapons were blustering invective, crude intimidation, and an entirely spurious, hail-fellow-well-met charm. "Big Bill" and Prohibition were certainly made for each other, and Prohibition's impact on Chicago cannot be fully explained without a closer look at one of the oddest political phenomena in American history.

In terms of damage done to Chicago's image, there was not much to choose between "Big Bill" Thompson and Al Capone. Capone was certainly by far the more sophisticated operator. He had an innate public relations sense — whether paying the hospital expenses of a middle-aged woman bystander who had been severely wounded in the eye in a shoot-out aimed at killing him in Cicero or opening soup kitchens for the destitute after the 1929 crash, even as he was about to go to jail for tax evasion. A superb media manipulator, he even convinced some respectable newsmen that he was merely a somewhat unscrupulous businessman who deplored violence and was invariably singled out as a convenient suspect even when he was totally innocent — and could prove it.

"Big Bill" 's cowboy image, popular at first, rapidly degenerated into caricatural, swaggering megalomania. Unaware of his failings, and surrounded by venal flatterers, Chicago's mayor saw himself as a pioneer, "the big builder." Although he was indeed responsible for some of Chicago's new city infrastructure, he had no real vision — he was no Robert Moses — and his anti-British, anti-Washington, anti-intellectual obsessions eventually degenerated into near-lunacy. Like Daugherty, he was an authoritarian who believed in conspiracies and favored strong-arm methods almost rivaling Capone's. Only in the Prohibition era could such a figure have dominated America's second city for so long. Without him, it's unlikely that Chicago, or Capone, would have acquired their mythic status.

William Hale Thompson's father, the scion of a wealthy Bostonian family, settled in Chicago to take advantage of the real estate boom, becoming a millionaire. "Big Bill" 's own aversion to school was such that he never graduated from high school, let alone Yale, where his overindulgent father had hoped he would follow him. From childhood, young William became obsessed with the Wild West: his single-minded passion was such that he even dressed as a cowboy, riding horses through Chicago streets. His father, in 1881, reluctantly allowed his fourteen-year-old son to "go West" and live out his fantasies at first hand instead of merely reading about them — at first as a brakeman on the Union Pacific at the height of the Gold Rush, then as a greenhorn cowboy in Cheyenne, Wyoming. At least he would no longer have to bail out his son for rowdy behavior in Chicago.

Young Thompson never became a full-fledged cowboy (he was assigned work as a camp cook), and, to please his father, continued to follow winter courses at Chicago's Metropolitan Business College, but he did acquire the brash, macho ways of the cowboys he so admired. He also learned how to run a ranch, and, in 1888, his father bought him one in Nebraska. It did well, and Thompson was all set to remain there when his father died and his mother begged him, as the oldest son, to take over the family business. Back home, his father's office more or less ran itself. Bill joined the Chicago Athletics Club, becoming one of its outstanding water polo and football stars, and making his mark as a yachtsman.

In 1900, he entered politics, as a Republican alderman in Chicago's Second Ward. He did so for a bet, but the hard-drinking, all-male world of Chicago politics, revolving around saloons and brothels, soon became a substitute for the "Wild West" of his youth, and he never looked back. A playboy who continued to devote more time to sports than to his alderman's job, he quickly acquired the tricks of the politician's trade, and his tub-thumping speeches, though at first barely literate, proved effective.

His local standing as a member of a prominent, wealthy family and his popularity as an athlete, along with his shallow, lazy approach to politics, convinced a small caucus of unscrupulous businessmen that he was an ideal front man behind whom tidy fortunes could be made. They got together to sell "Big Bill" Thompson to Chicagoans as candidate for mayor. Among them was William Lorimer, a prominent Chicago

Republican. As he put it, Thompson "may not be too much on brains, but he gets through to the people."

The career of "Blond Boss" Lorimer, his earliest patron, had already unraveled. Although the former streetcar conductor had had a meteoric rise, becoming, briefly, senator for Illinois, he had not remained one for long. In return for large campaign funds from a local lumber company, Lorimer, whose bristly mustache made him look like a Mack Sennett cop, had voted in favor of high lumber tariffs, and this came to the attention of the Chicago press, forcing his resignation. Thompson, who remained loyal to Lorimer, never lost his hatred of the *Chicago Tribune* and other Chicago papers responsible for destroying Lorimer's political career.

Another even more valuable mentor was Congressman "Poor Swede" Fred Lundin, an ex-shoeshine turned street hustler who had peddled homemade "juniper ade" on the streets of Chicago, and still invariably wore his hustler's outfit — a long black frock coat, Windsor tie, plains hat, and huge gold watch — as a trademark.

Lundin applied the same brash organizational talent to "selling" Thompson he had shown parlaying his juniper ade tonic into a profitable company. He worked the streets, recruiting local "street captains" as election agents, leaving cards behind to be filled in with names and numbers of likely Thompson voters. "On each card was a space for a notation of what kind of job the precinct captain wanted in case of victory."[6]

Although "Big Bill" campaigned only intermittently — at one crucial stage he left for Cowes to race his motor launch *Disturber III*, making a gracious speech after losing (his anti-British sentiments not yet to the fore) — his oratory was that of an earnest reformer. "I am going to clean up the dirt of the rotten administration in power," Thompson promised. "No policeman will be sent to the cabbage patch if he offends some politician; not while Bill Thompson is your mayor." For all his expressed good intentions, some of his most assiduous campaigners were gangsters; men such as Jake "Greasy Thumb" Guzik and Jimmy Mondi, owner of the Sportsman's Club, an underworld hangout.

Thompson also undertook to "protect the fair womanhood of Chicago." On a more practical note, he promised to introduce cheaper streetcar fares, improve public transportation, and build more and better schools. To Chicago blacks, arriving in large numbers from the South, he said: "I'll give you people the best opportunities you've ever had." He seems to have been genuinely anti-racist at a time when this was relatively rare in mainstream Chicago politics, but was also aware that the black vote would be crucial in several wards.

With the start of the First World War, Thompson also realized the importance of gaining the support of another minority group: Chicago's 600,000 Germans and Austrians. His anti-British, anti-Royalist bias, later to become an obsession, first became apparent as his campaign for mayor got under way in 1914. An honorary member of Chicago's German-American Alliance, he delighted in quoting excerpts from the articles of another even more pro-German Thompson — who happened to have been, until recently, U.S. consul in Berlin, and who had written extensively about the "hysterical" anti-German campaign in the British and American press. Most listeners assumed the quotes were his own. So rabid did Thompson's anti-British rhetoric become that many Chicagoans started calling him "Kaiser Bill."

The Prohibition issue was crucial, and Thompson's rival, Democrat Robert M. Sweitzer, had the support of the drys. "Ice cream, soda water, ginger ale and pop! Sweitzer, Sweitzer always on top!" was his opponent's ringing, singularly apolitical slogan. A dry Chicago parade saw a turnout of 12,000 marchers carrying appropriate banners, such as "Booze brutalizes" and "Boozers are losers." But they were vastly outnumbered, shortly afterward, by 40,000 wets, organized by the saloon and liquor lobby, the United Societies for Local Self-Government whose secretary was Anton J. Cermak, later a Thompson rival who would become mayor himself. With the help of the wets, and the support of the German, Austrian, and Afro-American minorities, Thompson won handsomely.

His reformer image did not last long. Although he did bow to dry opinion by promising to implement the Sunday closure laws, favored saloons (including "Big Jim" Colosimo's establishments) were never raided, and city workers hired on a patronage basis found they had to kick back part of their salaries to a William Hale Thompson Republican Fund (each new garbage team contributed $5 per horse and cart).

Lorimer had rightly surmised that Thompson was no intellectual giant, and that his clique of helpers would be free to plunder the city. With "Big Bill"'s tacit consent, "Poor Swede" Lundin virtually ran

Chicago, and the misrule began. Violent crime increased by 50 percent in a single year, and Colosimo's vice empire — and that of other underworld barons — flourished, in part as a result of the men Thompson chose to fill the unenviable post of police chief. The new chief of detectives, Nicholas Hunt, was a dandy with an expensive life-style and abysmal reputation, who had already been compelled to resign from the force in 1912 for protecting brothels in the Hyde Park district. So had another prominent Chicago detective, Mike Ryan, once on Colosimo's payroll.

One of Thompson's many police chiefs, Charles Healey, came to trial in 1917, and his "little green book," produced in court, showed weekly cash payments from brothels and saloons and lists of places not on the take that "can be raided." Despite overriding evidence of corruption, Clarence Darrow, the famous Chicago lawyer, won him an acquittal, thanks to a singularly understanding, appropriately selected jury.

Even before gangsters became Chicago's real masters, thanks to Prohibition, citizens were complaining that the police consistently looked the other way. John A. Carroll, head of the Hyde Park State Bank, told reporters that in order to get results, he had been compelled to hire private detectives to investigate a $272,000 bank robbery. The police were "simply not interested."

The escalating breakdown in law and order, even before Prohibition, was largely Thompson's doing. He ordered the scaling-down, then the demise, of Chicago's Morals Division, and introduced a zoning system, devised by "Poor Swede" Lundin, that made independent police work virtually impossible. In each of the city's wards, a suitably pliant police captain was selected to act as a liaison man, routinely receiving orders from a ward committeeman relaying "guidance" from Thompson and Lundin. A number of honorary precinct captaincies were created. One of them went to "Big Jim" Colosimo shortly before he was gunned down.

There were rumors, later substantiated, of payoffs and illegal profits in almost every field of city activity — school and hospital construction, public works, tramway and bus concessions. Able, honest administrators were systematically removed, and — in at least one case — driven to suicide as a result of campaigns against them. City departments were run by political hacks, whose personal loyalty to

Thompson was the sole prerequisite. The Lundin fund-raising techniques anticipated those of Colonel Charlie Forbes, soon to become the Harding administration Health secretary and prime asset-stripper. But the "Big Bill" electoral magic still worked, and he was elected for a second term in 1919.

Shortly afterward, the choice of Chicago as the site of the Republican Convention was a further boost to his career. Thompson enthusiastically endorsed Harding as candidate — like Thompson an isolationist "America firster" — but Harding's victory mattered less to him than that of his candidate for governor of Illinois, Len Small, a benign-looking farmer and unprincipled political hack. During his own campaign meetings, Small, aware of his mediocre oratorical talent, invariably cut short his own speech with groveling humility. "I'm sorry to be taking up your time," he told the crowds, "for I know you want to hear the greatest mayor Chicago ever had — the greatest man in the United States."

Until they fell out, several years later, Governor Small would protect Thompson and his clique from trouble of all types, granting pardons not only to Thompson appointees but to gangland members. Thompson's first political eclipse, in 1923, was largely the consequence of Governor Small's appearance before a grand jury for corruption. Although Thompson was acquitted (later there was ample evidence that the jury had been tampered with), their friendship did not survive. The law also caught up with Fred Lundin, who promptly left town. He too was subsequently acquitted on corruption charges, in one of the murkiest trials Chicago had yet seen. Lundin too, in later years, would turn against the man whose career he had fashioned.

In his early days, Johnny Torrio, who inherited the Colosimo empire of speakeasies, breweries, and brothels — and who was soon in partnership with *his* bodyguard, the youthful, up-and-coming New York Lower East Side expatriate Al Capone — had relied more on Democrats than on Republicans to expand his business empire — men such as Morris Eller, a trustee of the Chicago sanitary department and a prominent figure in local Democratic politics, as well as respectable attorneys and at least one former U.S. deputy marshal. But with Thompson's election as mayor, the Torrio-Capone gangs established close ties with Republican ward-heelers, aldermen, and the new Thompson political appointees.

Thompson's second spell as mayor was plagued with scandal from the start. The removal of honest city officials had taken its toll: the city was sliding into bankruptcy. Thompson knew that if he wanted a third term, his election campaign would be an expensive one. In 1921, he raised the money in ways that would later become standard practice among politicians hard pressed for cash from Grenoble to Valparaiso. He hired experts, at a cost of $3 million, to carry out a number of urban planning studies. After receiving their commissions, they discreetly turned the money over to his secret campaign fund. These funds remained unused for a long time. As Chicago's problems worsened, Thompson tried to shore up his waning popularity in increasingly demagogic ways, but was sufficiently astute to see the writing on the wall, and in 1923 announced he would not seek a third term. Chicagoans elected William E. Dever, an upright, Democratic judge — and committed dry.

Without entirely loosening their hold on Chicago — Dever's attempts to enforce Prohibition would in any case be a resounding failure — Torrio and Capone promptly shifted their activities to Cicero, a small, hitherto peaceful Chicago suburb in Cook County.

That they were able to do so was directly attributable to the local Republican party machine. Ed Konvalinka, a soda fountain owner and rising star of the local Republican party, struck a deal with Torrio and Capone: if they would work for the election of the Republican candidates in Cicero, the Republican political bosses, if elected, promised not to interfere with their activities. Torrio-Capone speakeasies, brothels, and greyhound racing tracks there were soon bringing in hundreds of thousands of dollars a month. Lauterback's, one of Capone's many Cook County investments, was both a saloon openly serving whiskey (at 75 cents a shot), beer (35 cents a stein), and wine (30 cents a glass), and a casino whose roulette stakes were almost certainly the highest in the world, often amounting to over $100,000 worth of chips on the table per spin of the wheel. "Overnight," wrote Fred D. Pasley in his *Life of Al Capone,* "Cicero seceded from the Volstead United States and went wilder West, and wilder wet, than Chicago [itself]."

The 1924 Cicero election was a textbook example of gangsterdom in action. It did not have to be rigged. Voters known to be opposition Democrats were hijacked and driven out of town, and voters were forced to cast Republican votes at gunpoint. When, alerted by outraged citizens, police arrived on the scene, there were gunfights. Among the dead was Frank Capone, one of Al's brothers.

The results were never challenged, and consequently, under nominal Republican leadership, Torrio and Capone virtually ran Cicero — its puppet mayor, Joseph Z. Klenha, soon living in mortal fear of the gang he had ushered into power.

In Chicago itself, even during Thompson's temporary eclipse, collusion between politicians and gangsters was almost as blatant. Dan O'Banion, its most powerful, colorful gangland boss, had long had a working relationship with the Democratic party. A former choirboy and lifelong devout Catholic, he had started out in life as a professional killer and strong-arm enforcer, and by the time of his violent death was accredited with twenty-five murders, though he was never brought to trial for any of them. But there was another side to this teetotaling, devoted family man, with an impeccable, Irish lace-curtain private lifestyle: he loved flowers and was the proud owner of a fashionable flower shop, which was both his official place of business and his "front." The elaborate bouquets he put together for selected clients were highly prized.

Shortly before the 1924 elections, both to reward O'Banion for past services and to remind him where his future interests lay, the Democratic party staged a testimonial dinner for him, attended by scores of gangland figures. Also present were prominent Chicago policemen such as Chief of Detectives Michael Hughes, a former prominent DA; County Clerk Robert M. Sweitzer (the same Sweitzer who had been Chicago's leading dry protagonist in 1915); and Colonel Albert A. Sprague, commissioner of public works in the Dever Administration and Democratic nominee for the Senate. After keynote speeches by Sprague and Sweitzer, O'Banion was presented with a platinum watch set in rubies and diamonds. All of this did not prevent him, weeks later, from throwing his weight behind the Republicans, in exchange for a more lucrative deal.

Law enforcement agencies and the judiciary were almost equally corrupt, and ineffective. Out of 136 gangland murders that took place in Chicago during the first five years of Prohibition, only six led to trials, and of these, all but one ended in acquittals (the sixth involved a gangster who had blown off the head of a rival inside a police precinct during an official inquest on the latter's brother's death). In a three-year period, the Board of Pardons and Paroles freed 950 felons. Illinois Governor Len Small personally intervened to pardon professional killer Walter Stevens (in return for some strong-arm work on a grand jury looking into his own questionable activities). O'Banion himself, caught red-handed robbing a labor office safe in 1921, was acquitted by a bribed and otherwise terrified jury. Al Capone proudly displayed a gun permit delivered by a Chicago magistrate in 1923.

But perhaps the most flagrant example of police collusion had to do with the infamous Sicilian Genna brothers. In the first five years of Prohibition they were Chicago's biggest bootleggers. Although their criminal record was a long one, they had obtained a license to make large quantities of industrial alcohol, farming the job out to slum-based Sicilian families using primitive home stills, who delivered the liquor to a Genna-owned warehouse factory within four blocks of the Maxwell Street police station, one of the largest in town.

Here the raw alcohol was turned into whiskey and gin — 40,000 quarts of alcohol at about 50 cents a quart producing 120,000 quarts of bootleg "ersatz" whiskey and gin costing anything from $15 to $60 a bottle.

No attempt was made at concealment. In any case, the factory ingredients — creosote, iodine, burnt sugar, fusel oil, cane sugar, oil of juniper — gave off considerable telltale odors, which only the Maxwell Street policemen seemed unable to detect.

A former manager later told investigators the factory operated on shifts, twenty-four hours a day, with heavy trucks constantly parked outside.

> The warehouse was run openly and in full view of everybody, unmolested by the State authorities other than an occasional raid. But notification of 24 hours was always given to the Gennas. Sometimes the very letters sent out by the police ordering the raid were shown to them. There would be a clean-up, then a raid, then a re-opening. . . . During all the period that I worked there the entire Genna enterprise was done with the full knowledge, consent and approval of the Chicago police.[7]

Needless to say, the Genna brothers spent a great deal on such protection. They maintained payroll records, not just of police but of

Cook County DA representatives, checking their identities when they showed up for their money, making sure they were paying the right people. The Maxwell Street station also routinely provided uniformed police to protect truck convoys of liquor. When proof of the pay-offs reached public prosecutors, all that happened was that some 187 uniformed policemen were transferred elsewhere.

The Genna brothers were prominent members of the Italian Republican Club, and in 1924 staged a banquet at the Morrison Hotel for their friends. Those attending included a prominent DA, a clerk of the Circuit Court, a county recorder, the head of the Cook County Republican party, and friends and cronies of an Illinois senator.

The Gennas' influence did not last. One by one, they were killed off, eliminated by Capone's gunmen as he moved in on his rivals. Although such killings invariably made front-page news, only one of the many violent deaths of 1926 became a cause célèbre. William McSwiggin, twenty-six, a police sergeant's son and prominent Cook County DA, was shot dead from a moving car outside the Pony Inn, a well-known Cicero saloon. Two other people, Jim Doherty and Tom Duffy, both well-known underworld figures and Capone rivals, died with him. A third, Myles O'Donnell, escaped.

Although McSwiggin's office claimed he had only been "trying to obtain information" at the time of his death, it was soon clear that the ambitious, up-and-coming DA had been far closer to the three men than he should have been. He was probably killed accidentally, simply because he happened to be in their company, but the testimony of Al Capone illustrated his contempt for all those connected with law enforcement. A leading suspect, Capone told the press: "Of course I didn't kill him. Why should I? I liked the kid. Only the day before he got killed he was up at my place and when he went home I gave him a bottle of Scotch for his old man. I paid McSwiggin and I paid him plenty, and I got what I was paying for." There was no trial, and the murder was never solved.

Even out of office, Thompson was seldom far from the public eye. His isolationist, anti-British, anti-Prohibition rhetoric invariably gained him media attention, as did his campaign against city school officials responsible for "tainted," insufficiently patriotic school books. He also showed an imaginative flair for publicity, as when he embarked on a highly publicized expedition to the South Seas aboard his yacht

Big Bill to bring back a mythic tree-climbing fish to a Chicago zoo — a voyage that petered out in New Orleans.

In 1927, he decided the time was ripe for a comeback. Dever tried to put Thompson on the defensive, focusing his campaign on "Big Bills"'s appallingly corrupt, gangster-ridden record.

Thompson presented himself as "Billy the Builder." His campaign was based on a vague anti-Prohibitionist, "America First," "Make Chicago Hum" program, and he answered none of Dever's specific charges of mismanagement or corruption. He made it perfectly clear he intended to defy the Eighteenth Amendment rules. "If I catch a policeman crossing the threshold of a man's home or place of business, I will fire that policeman right off the force" he told his supporters. "When I'm elected, we will not only reopen places these people have closed, but we'll open up ten thousand new ones."

Not only Capone but the fast-diminishing band of anti-Capone rivals were quick to respond, openly supporting Thompson for a third term. As Frank J. Loesch, president of the Chicago Crime Commission, noted at the time: "It did not take me long to discover that Al Capone ran the city. His hand reached into every department of city and county government." Over Capone's desk, Loesch noted, were three large oil portraits, of George Washington, Abraham Lincoln, and "Big Bill" Thompson.

A Capone campaign contribution (later estimated at $260,000) reached Thompson's headquarters through a local Republican ward-heeler, Daniel A. Serritella, known to be on Capone's payroll. Another gangster, Jack Zuta, who ostentatiously flaunted his William Hale Thompson Republican Club membership card, contributed $50,000. "Big Tim" Murphy; Abie Arends, the former manager of "Big Jim" Colosimo's nightclub; and Vincent "The Schemer" Drucci (he had been one of O'Banion's men, but had rallied Capone since his master's death) also became Thompson campaigners. Drucci distinguished himself by raiding (and wrecking) the offices of Alderman Dorsey R. Crowe, a leading Dever supporter, a week before the election, and on polling day, Capone's men patrolled polling booths as they had in Cicero in 1924. Thompson won, but with a diminished majority.

His third term unraveled more quickly than his second. There was an ominous presage on election night itself: the overcrowded yacht belonging to his "Fish Fans Club," aboard which he and some 1,500 supporters were celebrating his victory, slowly sank, settling on a sand-bank. There was no loss of life, but the proceedings were considerably dampened.

Thompson was no longer, as he had been for so long, the maverick, slick populist athlete-turned-politician whose turn of phrase galvanized unsophisticated crowds. Except for his own Chicago *Journal,* he was now anathema to the press, not only in Chicago but all over America. He himself had changed, physically and mentally. The once tall, trim athlete had become jowly and overweight, his public appearances now often downright embarrassing, revealing a growing confusion of mind.

His gangland supporters duly reaped their rewards: one of Thompson's first moves, after his election, was to appoint Daniel A. Serritella city sealer, or official verifier of shopkeepers' weights and measures. Not that Serritella did much checking: he simply haunted City Hall, unofficial ambassador to the "Mayor of Crook County," as Capone was called, conveying his master's requests.

Thompson's reelection marked the apogee of Capone's power. He began spending less time in Cicero and more in Chicago itself, renting fifty rooms, including a large conference hall, on two floors of the Hotel Metropole. Jake Guzik and Harry Mondi, Thompson's underworld campaigners during his first campaign for mayor, also became key figures in the Capone gang, running his gambling empire.

Capone had good reason to congratulate himself on his judicious funding. Shortly after his reelection, Thompson told a crowd: "We'll throw every damn dry (Prohibition) agent in jail." "I will do all in my power," he pledged, "to save Chicago citizens from any more suffering at the hands of thugs and gunmen sent here by the Federal Government."

Against all evidence, he claimed that Chicago was no more gangster-prone than any other large American city. "Sure we have crime here," he told reporters. "We will always have crime. Chicago is just like any other big city. You can get a man's arm broken for so much, a leg for so much, or beaten up for so much. Just like New York, except we print our crime and they don't."

Despite Thompson's now abysmal reputation as far as many Chicagoans were concerned, he was deluded enough to believe he might win the next Republican presidential nomination (Coolidge had let it be known he would not run for a second term) and embarked on a 10,000-mile trip through the United States to gauge his chances, on the pretext of raising funds for flood control. In a series of banquets and meetings, Thompson was suitably coy. "There are a lot of reports I want to be president," he told a San Francisco audience. "That's not true. My one ambition is to protect the people of the Mississippi valley from the floods of the future." But this denial was belied by the pamphlets handed out by his aides. The cover was a red-white-and-blue target whose bull's-eye was "America First." Inside, Thompson asked Americans to "shoot at the bull's-eye for American prosperity" through "united action," urging delegates to the next Republican Convention to work for the four "Thompsonian principles": America First, farm relief, inland waterways, and national flood control.

Like an earlier attempt to sound out his chances of gaining a seat in the Senate, his presidential ambitions did not last. On his return to Chicago, he faced deep trouble. An election for state's attorney was due in 1928 and the front-runner, John A. Swanson, a "clean government" advocate and ally of Thompson's archenemy, Senator Charles S. Deneen, seriously threatened his power base.

The Swanson campaign was marked by a new gangland terrorist weapon, the pineapple bomb — so much so that it became known as the "pineapple primary." There were sixty-two bomb outrages in six months, two of them wrecking Deneen's and Swanson's homes. Thompson blamed it all on Prohibition "agents provocateurs." "There'll always be bombing as long as there is Prohibition," he told the press. Campaigning against Deneen's man, he gave his anti-Prohibition rhetoric a new twist: if whiskey was now so costly, he told crowds, it was "all the fault of King George and his rum-running fleet." Once more, he resurrected the campaign slogan "Whack King George on the snoot." Thompson also repeatedly threatened to resign if his archenemy Swanson was elected. Swanson won, and Thompson changed his mind.

With many former friends leaving the bandwagon, he now faced another calamity: a much-delayed investigation into his campaign finances had revealed irregularities on a huge scale, and a judge ordered him to pay $2,245,000 back to the city. A shocked Thompson suffered a nervous breakdown and went on a prolonged vacation. His influence further diminished as his minions got used to running the town without him. On his return, he appeared to have lost his taste for political infighting. Increasingly frail and confused, he was now little more than a figurehead.

Two sets of killings brought Chicago — and its mayor — into further disrepute. The first was the Saint Valentine's Day massacre (February 14, 1929), which would inspire countless Hollywood movies, including the unforgettable beginning of Billy Wilder's *Some Like It Hot.*

Although it was to become a mythic event, it is worth recalling that the Saint Valentine's Day massacre was nothing more than the routine settling of a banal commercial dispute. "Bugs" Moran — prominent gangster, owner of speakeasies, and would-be Capone challenger — received his regular consignments of whiskey from the Detroit Purple Gang, a bootlegging organization under Capone's control. Although the Old Log Cabin brand Moran purchased was popular with drinkers, it was expensive, and he let Capone know he would seek supplies elsewhere.

Capone did not react when Moran switched to another brand, but Moran's customers did: they hated the stuff. Moran asked Capone to resume supplies, and was shown the door. Good whiskey was in short supply, and Capone had found more lucrative customers.

Moran's men retaliated by hijacking Old Log Cabin consignments, until Capone decided something had to be done. Moran received a message that a consignment of hijacked Old Log Cabin whiskey was for sale, and could be picked up at the North Clark Street garage on the following day. At the appointed time, the killers (including two men in police uniform) entered the garage, gunning down all those inside. (The only reason Moran survived was that he was late for his appointment.) Capone had a cast-iron alibi: not only was he in his Miami home on the day of the massacre, but he had been on the telephone to a Miami district attorney at the very time of the killings. There were no convictions.

Sixteen months later, another killing again made headlines around the world. This time the victim was Alfred J. ("Jake") Lingle, thirty-eight, a *Chicago Tribune* police reporter.

Although his editors at first portrayed him as a martyr, fallen in the course of duty while on a secret investigation, this did not last. As rival newspapers soon pointed out, "Jake" Lingle, on a weekly salary of $65, had a millionaire life-style, gambled heavily, and had been very close to Capone (he died wearing a diamond-studded belt Capone had given him). They also revealed he had acted as intermediary between the police and the underworld for almost as long as he had been a reporter. The *Tribune* was compelled to acknowledge he had "engaged in practices contrary to the code of its honest reporters." Although the motive for the killing was never proved, the likeliest explanation was that Lingle had arranged for police protection of Capone-controlled greyhound racing tracks and speakeasies but had failed to pass on underworld funds, gambling with them instead. It was also believed that Capone, by this time under belated investigation by the IRS, feared that Lingle might give investigators details of Capone's financial empire, about which he knew a great deal. A minor gunman, who may or may not have been responsible for his murder, was sentenced to fourteen years in jail.

Thompson responded to the Lingle scandal by firing his police chief, but his cry to "drive the crooks and criminals out of Chicago" was singularly ill-timed. Shortly afterward, "Big Bill" Thompson's wife was attacked while in her chauffeur-driven car, and relieved of jewelry worth $10,000.

Thompson failed to secure a fourth term in office, and lived on in relative obscurity until his death on March 19, 1944, when he made headlines one last time. Although he left an estate worth only $150,000 and no will, safe deposit boxes in his name were found to contain cash, stocks, and gold certificates worth over two million dollars.

14

REMUS ON TRIAL

When last in the news, George Remus was in Washington, providing the Senate Investigative Committee on former attorney general Daugherty with startling examples of corruption at the highest levels of the Harding administration. Remus became an Atlanta penitentiary inmate in January of 1924, along with his twelve-man team and several other noted bootlegger millionaires. By this time, the drop in America's prison population that had so encouraged the drys was over. Numbers had risen sharply — in all, between 1920 and 1933, some 500,000 people would go to prison for offenses against the Volstead Act — and Atlanta, like all other American jails, was overcrowded.

But Remus was no ordinary prisoner. Money talked. His cell was a small but comfortable apartment, with its own kitchen and bathroom, in a separate building known to the inmates as "millionaire's row." Imogene, who helped him furnish it, and made arrangements for his privileged treatment with John Sartain, the prison governor, regularly visited him, bringing him delicacies, cooking and cleaning for him, and occasionally spending the night. She also acted as his business courier. In her absence, Remus took most of his meals with the governor or the chaplain. These arrangements — which also included the right to unlimited phone calls (Remus called his wife almost daily for 15 to 30 minutes at a time) and permission to go on shopping trips, even spending occasional nights out with Imogene in luxurious Atlanta hotels when she tired of the prison apartment — cost him $1,000 a month.

Franklin N. Dodge was a Justice Department agent working directly for Deputy Attorney General Willebrandt on Prohibition cases of exceptional importance, infiltrating bootlegging rings, posing as a wealthy potential investor. Despite his outstanding record, Remus's friend Willie Haar, another millionaire row inmate, thought that Dodge might be persuaded to use his influence to get Willebrandt to grant them both a pardon. Dodge, he told Remus, would certainly be a useful man to know — and who could sound him out more effectively than Imogene? Remus wrote her (sometime between March 16 and May 1, 1925): "Why do you not look up Dodge?"

Dodge came regularly to Atlanta to debrief other prisoners on separate cases (he had not been involved in the Remus case). Imogene got in touch with him, and it was in Atlanta, but outside the jail, that she and Dodge first met.

It was an immediate "fatal attraction." Imogene fell head over heels in love with the tall, handsome agent. Whether Dodge, a known womanizer, fell for her too, or simply used her, remains unclear. Nor is it clear whether, subsequently, Imogene initiated some of the moves against Remus herself, or blindly followed Dodge's instructions. In any event, shortly after that first meeting, Imogene started playing a devious, dangerous game.

Coached by Dodge, who abruptly resigned from the Justice Department shortly after Imogene became his mistress, she kept up her visits to Atlanta — ever the loyal, loving wife — but now did so on Dodge's instructions. Behind Remus's back, Imogene and Dodge embarked on a perfect crime. Not only did they set about appropriating his fortune (this was relatively easy, in that Imogene had power of attorney), but plotted to have him deported as an illegal alien. If that failed, they even considered having him murdered.

Given the straitlaced atmosphere of the time, their behavior was singularly careless. Not only did they travel together, staying in hotel rooms with communicating doors, sometimes even in the same room as a married couple under an assumed name, but Dodge moved into the Price Hill mansion with Imogene for weeks at a time, sleeping in Remus's bed, even appropriating Remus's hats, tiepins, and cufflinks — everything but his suits and shoes, which did not fit.

While Remus was serving the last months of his Atlanta sentence, Imogene, by stages, emptied his bank accounts, transferring the money into four separate accounts in Dodge's name in Lansing, Michigan, Dodge's home town. She also made over some of Remus's distillery certificates to Dodge, selling the rest at a loss and transferring the money into the Lansing accounts.

Imogene's infatuation with Dodge was total. Remus maintained charge accounts in various Cincinnati stores, and here Imogene bought Dodge clothes and jewelry, also making him a gift of Remus's personal jewelry, worth $100,000. Some of her tokens of love were childishly romantic. As George Remus's housekeeper, William Mueller, would later testify in court, Imogene had the initial R removed from the silver cutlery in the Remus mansion, substituting a D, similarly changing the initials G. R. on the door of Remus's Lincoln to F. D.

Shortly before Remus was released from jail, she stripped the mansion of all its valuable contents, leaving behind only some basic furniture. The costly paintings, and Remus's collection of George Washington's letters, of which he was inordinately proud, were discreetly sold or pawned. All of the valuable fittings and furniture, including the chandeliers, were stored in Cincinnati warehouses and garages.

While dismantling the Price Hill mansion, Imogene ordered Mueller to take a clock down from a sitting room wall. Mueller refused. "That's the master's clock," he said.

"Why, don't be afraid," Imogene told him. "Mr. Remus will never come back. We're going to have him deported. We have it all arranged. He'll go back the same as he came, with a little bundle." All this would eventually come out in court.

When Remus had testified against Daugherty in Washington, Imogene had been in the audience, very much the loyal, supportive wife. But two days before his release from jail, a lawyer he had never previously heard of came to see him, notifying him of Imogene's demand for divorce proceedings on the grounds of "cruelty." Remus would find out later that he was her third choice: two lawyers, consulted earlier, had refused to take her case, saying there were no grounds for divorce.

It was his first intimation of her betrayal — and its impact was devastating. He flew into a blind rage, smashing up the cell furniture until restrained by guards. Subsequently, between catatonic spells, the outbursts returned, to begin with, several times a day. "She's driving me mad," Remus told the *Post-Dispatch*'s John Rogers shortly after his release. "She has outraged me. After all I've done for her." He burst into uncontrollable sobs, shrieking that he was "being persecuted beyond endurance." George Conners, his trusted aide, and John Rogers, who were with him a great deal of the time, would later tell the court that it was their conviction that Imogene's conduct had driven Remus insane.

His rage returned when, in the company of a newspaper cartoonist, he came back to the now empty Price Hill mansion. Its windows and doors were boarded up, and Remus had to break in. As he surveyed the stripped, dilapidated rooms, he became aware of his full predicament for the first time. Entering the swimming pool compound, he shouted "She hasn't taken the water, I've still got the water!" bursting into a fit of hysterical laughter.

He was soon to learn that Imogene had planned everything extremely thoroughly. Her last fifteen affectionate letters to him in jail prior to the lawyer's visit had been written at one sitting, then posted at intervals by a friend, while she and Dodge were in Lansing and meeting with immigration authorities in Atlanta — all part of their plan to get Remus deported. Dodge, though no longer a member of the Justice Department, used his influence to get Remus returned to prison for another year, on other charges related to his original conviction. Remus served this extra term not in Atlanta, but in Troy, near Dayton, Ohio, where, for the first time, he was treated like an ordinary inmate.

Mabel Walker Willebrandt agreed to his eventual release but extracted a singularly vengeful price: she compelled him to testify that he had paid large sums of money to prison governor John Sartain. Millionaire's row was closed down and Sartain eventually went to jail. Under pressure from her peers, she also threatened to send him back to jail unless he withdrew his charges (made before the Senate Investigating Committee) concerning Daugherty. Remus would later confess his shame at having done so, but there were so many other independent witnesses (including Jess Smith's ex-wife) with lurid accounts of Daugherty's corrupt, predatory ways that this vindictive measure was virtually ignored. In the media and in Senate circles, no one doubted that Remus had told the truth.

It was Imogene's betrayal that led him, shortly after his release from Troy, to cooperate with prosecutors in the Jack Daniel's case. Accompanied by the faithful Conners, and John Rogers, who was researching the series about him in the St. Louis *Post-Dispatch,* he went to Indianapolis with one purpose in mind: to reveal Imogene's part in the conspiracy. Not only had she invested $20,000 of her own money in Jack Daniel's whiskey certificates, but had been influential in persuading the rogue syndicate to empty the Jack Daniel's warehouse fast — and cut the whiskey with water. To Remus — ruined, disgraced, and betrayed — this was the ultimate perfidy: not only was he a cuckold, but — through sheer greed — Imogene had destroyed his reputation as America's finest quality bootlegger.

To his dismay, the charges against Imogene were dropped. Although she had filed papers for a divorce, she was still legally his wife and he was unable to testify against her. While the Jack Daniel's case proceeded with the other accused, Imogene and Dodge even showed up in Indianapolis as interested spectators, living in a hotel as man and wife. There was one unexpected confrontation, witnessed by Rogers. A scared Imogene threw up her hands, shouting "Daddy, don't kill me, don't hurt me." Remus ignored her and turned away.

It was in Indianapolis that Remus learned that Imogene — who had found proof of his entry into the United States and of his citizenship in the Price Hill mansion and destroyed them — was trying to have him deported. While in Indianapolis, Remus also discovered that his life was in danger. Rogers learned that Dodge had contacted some gunmen in St. Louis, members of a gang called the Regan Rats, and promised them $15,000 to have him killed. Remus applied for, and received, a gun permit.

At the Indianapolis railway station, Conners caught sight of one of the gang, and persuaded Remus to take a later train. The gunmen, Conners found out later, intended to take Remus's train, stage a brawl, and kill him on board. Conners too was in danger, he would later tell the court, for Dodge and Imogene had also taken out a contract on him.

At times, Remus's attitude toward Imogene was ambiguous. Although his outbursts of rage remained an almost daily occurrence, he sometimes found excuses for her. "I knew the little woman wouldn't do this of her own free will," he told Conners on one occasion. Most of the time he was in a less forgiving mood. "I picked her out of the gutter and tried to make a lady out of her, but she didn't have it in her," he said. He would ask Conners repeatedly: "Did you think she was doing anything like this?" Conners replied that "everyone in Cincinnati was expecting something like this to happen." "My God, I must have been blind," Remus replied.

Conners had also been present when Imogene had telephoned Remus, listening in on their conversation. Imogene asked him: "You won't hurt me if I come in to see you?" Remus told her she had nothing to fear, adding: "You know I would have done the right thing by you if you had let me know." Remus asked if she was still seeing Dodge. "I've been going around with Mr. Dodge, Daddy," she said, "but there's nothing wrong morally. I've got to see him again because he has something very valuable and I must get that."

But later she called to taunt him. "Hello, Daddy, still waiting? You certainly are a mighty good waiter. I may be in tomorrow." Remus had had enough. "You aren't Mrs. Remus any more," he told her. "I'll file a cross-petition, and if you think you're going to get my property, I'll follow you to China if necessary." Rogers had been with Remus when Imogene had phoned once more. Remus asked her to name a single instance of his mistreatment of her. There was a pause, and then she said: "Your kind treatment of Romola" (her step-daughter). Remus replied: "Well, she *is* my daughter."[1]

Because Conners and Remus were convinced their lives were in danger in the Price Hill mansion, they moved into a downtown Cincinnati hotel, the Sinton. Apart from Conners, two of Remus's former staff had remained close to him: George Klug, his driver, and his secretary, Blanche Watson. All four had dinner together on the evening of October 5, 1927 — the eve of Imogene's divorce proceedings, and, as it turned out, her death.

On the morning of October 6, Remus ordered Klug to drive him to the Alms Hotel, where Imogene was staying. "There's something I want to discuss with her before we go before the judge," Remus told him. It was a ruse, to allay any suspicions Klug might have, for he did not attempt to talk to her as she left the hotel. According to a later police report, when he shot and killed her she was wearing "a black silk dress, silk stockings and a small black hat from Paris."

The meeting with Judge Dixon was at eight A.M. While he waited in vain in his chambers for them to show up, a dying Imogene was on her way to Bethesda Hospital, and Remus, having given himself up, was in police custody. The police asked him if he wanted to make a statement. "I'm at peace now after two years of hell. I'm satisfied I've done right," he told them.

In the Hamilton County Jail, Remus got special treatment once again. He kept a sizeable wardrobe (twenty suits, according to the *Cincinnati Enquirer*), and was allowed unlimited visitors, including reporters and photographers — cooperative wardens even brought him liquor for his "hospitality bar." He was photographed doing his morning exercises on the prison rooftop, and was given an additional cell, which he used as an office.

Charged with first-degree murder, which carried the death penalty, Remus was determined to defend himself. Surprisingly, for his conviction should by rights have disbarred him, Judge Chester R. Shook agreed to let Remus act as co-counsel to Robert Elston, an aristocratic-looking former district attorney and the best legal talent in Cincinnati.

This in itself ensured that the Remus trial would be a cause célèbre. Even before it began, it was attracting considerable media attention. Reporters were expected from all over America, as well as from Canada, London, and Berlin. At the Hamilton County courthouse, a courtroom was earmarked for the press. A note to them from County Clerk Frank Lewis banned the use of "artificial lights" but stated that "within reasonable limits, hand cameras can be used."

By today's standards, preliminary procedures were remarkably swift: jury selection took only four days, and a mere thirty-nine days after the murder, the Remus trial began. If it failed to make headline news that day, this was only because of an even more compelling story: the day Remus's trial began — November 14, 1927 — was also the day Charles Lindbergh was given a hero's welcome in Washington after his Atlantic crossing.

The prosecution team was an almost caricatural illustration of the gulf between America's patrician establishment and "new Americans" such as Remus. The chief prosecutor, Charles P. Taft II, whose brother ran the *Cincinnati Enquirer*, was a member of Ohio's most famous political family. Their father, former United States President William

Howard Taft, was currently serving his country in another prestigious capacity, as chief justice of the Supreme Court. In an early altercation with prosecutor Taft, Remus pointedly referred to "this young man's father." "It has been the pleasure of this defendant to appear before the High Chief Justice, but the specimen as given by the offshoot of that great renowned character is pitiful, if the Court please."

The other prosecutors, though from less prestigious backgrounds, were also from well-connected Ohio families. Taft let Walter K. Sibbald do the bulk of the talking, while Remus reserved much of his venom for Harold Basler, the most aggressive member of the prosecution team.

As is often the case in American jury trials, jury selection marked the first clash between prosecution and defense. Remus, a convicted bootlegger, was eager to discover whether any of the potential jurors were fanatical drys or otherwise prejudiced against him. The prosecutors objected to a defendant cross-examining them at all. As they knew he would, Remus lost his temper, alleging harassment.

Remus particularly resented the prosecution's attempt to discredit him as a lawyer. Basler based his allegations on an incident in Chicago years ago, in a case opposing employers and the Chicago Machinists' Union. Remus had acted for the unionists, and his court opponents had appealed to the Chicago Bar Association in an unsuccessful effort to have him disbarred. This led to the first of his many violent clashes with Basler and Taft.

> REMUS: Five hundred judges and members of the Chicago Bar have volunteered to come down here as character witnesses, and just because the son of the Chief Justice in this wonderful United States makes that kind of assertion — man, if I had you in the corridor, I would wreck you physically.
>
> BASLER: How much of this stuff is the court going to stand, this personal vilification? There is absolutely no excuse for it.
>
> REMUS (to Basler): When you were on the Eastern trip you drank two pints of whiskey — you did so!
>
> BASLER: Is that so?
>
> REMUS: That will be shown. Yes, sir, I will show you up.
>
> BASLER: Now then, your Honor sees what kind of vilification is going to be permitted here if this man indulges in such liberties as this.

REMUS: Murder is the charge. My life is at stake, and I will show that you drank liquor by the pint, not by the ounce.

BASLER: There is no occasion for this, as you can see.

REMUS: My life is at stake, not yours.

BASLER: He is turning around to talk to the newspapermen and it is not for the benefit of the court at all.

JUDGE SHOOK: I am ready to pass on the matter. Sit down, Mr. Remus. The court will disregard everything stated by Mr. Remus of any personal character.

The clash had been more violent than the official court proceedings inferred. At one point, Remus rose and strode menacingly over to Basler, waving his fists. Basler (overheard by newsmen, but not, apparently by the court stenographer) hissed: "Get back to your side, or I'll punch you."

Judge Shook allowed Remus to continue cross-examining potential jurors, but cautioned him against any more "spectacular outbursts." It was widely assumed that Remus knew so much about Basler's drinking habits because back in 1921 he had regularly supplied him with liquor.

As it turned out, most of the excused jury members were dismissed because they opposed the death penalty, not because of their attitude toward Prohibition. One juror was excused because he was a machinist, and might therefore be prejudiced in Remus's favor. Another Afro-American juror, described as "Ben Boner, negro," was also dismissed for prejudice of a different type. "I had a wife who ran away with my money too," he told the courtroom, to loud laughter, in which Remus did not join. The twelve-person jury ended up all-white. Ten were men. Its youngest female member, Mrs. Ruth Cross, was twenty-three; the oldest, Mrs. Anna Ricking, sixty-three.

Remus had rashly announced before the trial that he would not plead temporary insanity, but changed his mind after a talk with Elston, who also persuaded him not to intervene too often in the course of the trial. His more dispassionate, polished co-counsel dominated the proceedings from the very start. This was, to a large extent, the prosecution's own fault.

In his opening statement, Walter Sibbald not only accused Remus of "cold-blooded, deliberate and premeditated murder," but claimed "Remus had the assistance and the encouragement of others of the Remus gang," and that even his secretary, Blanche Watson, "was in on the conspiracy." Remus's prompt objection to the word gang was sustained.

Why the prosecution advanced the conspiracy theory is a mystery. It certainly added nothing to the case against Remus, for a conspiracy was not required to prove his own premeditation. Perhaps Taft assumed that with Remus's conviction practically a foregone conclusion, this would enable him, in a subsequent trial, to indict Conners and Klug as well. Instead, he only weakened what, on the face of it, appeared to be an open and shut case.

Subsequently, the Remus trial was scrutinized almost as relentlessly as the O. J. Simpson proceedings some seventy years later, and in retrospect it was clear the conspiracy charge harmed the prosecution's case by detracting from Remus's own dramatic role as executioner. It was in any case impossible to sustain, for there was not a shred of evidence to back it up. Conners, Klug, and Blanche Watson all insisted, in court, that there had been nothing at their dinner with him the night before to indicate that Remus intended to kill his wife. They also recalled their shock at the news of Imogene's death with such conviction the jury clearly believed them.

More damaging still to the prosecution was its unsuccessful attempt to dismiss as irrelevant any of Imogene's behavior prior to her murder. "The State doesn't think that the evidence should go back further than twenty-four hours," Sibbald said in his opening statement.

Elston, in *his* opening statement, argued against this. "Insanity is our defense," he announced, "and insanity that dates back two years, brought about by a conspiracy on the part of his wife and this Franklin L. Dodge — a conspiracy to divorce Remus, keep him in jail, get his property and then deport him." He outlined a conspiracy of a very different type — "a conspiracy to deprive the defendant of every last cent of the fortune he possessed, to keep him in prison as long as possible, and when all his sentences had been served, to deport him." Imogene Remus

. . . used the defendant's money to hire assassins to take his life. . . . Insanity may show itself in different ways. We will show that after his spell in Atlanta penitentiary there was a very great deterioration in his mental faculties. We expect to show his mind snapped because these things bore down so heavily on him, because, after all, he is only human.

Judge Shook decided evidence of this type was relevant, and would be heard. Remus had requested that all of Dodge's and Imogene's financial records be produced as evidence, and this too was granted — a huge advantage for the defense, though no reporters, at this stage, were prepared to bet on the trial's outcome.

The facts themselves were beyond dispute, for Remus had indeed gone straight to the police after the shooting, and other direct evidence was overwhelming. But, from the start, the prosecution behaved with singular incompetence. Ruth, Remus's stepdaughter, was questioned about his attitude toward her after his release from Atlanta — and although she referred to his "disagreeableness," she admitted under cross-examination by Elston that Remus was only trying to recover his property, including Ruth's car — which he had paid for.

The prosecution was equally inept in its handling of George Klug, Remus's driver. Under cross-examination by Elston, Klug told the court that he had been threatened with jail unless he confessed to his part in the conspiracy, but was told "You won't go to jail if you admit to driving Remus to the railway station." Klug, treated like a hostile witness, admitted that prior to driving Remus to the Alms Hotel, he had spent the entire night gambling, only returning to the hotel at five thirty in the morning.

The absurdity of the conspiracy allegation became apparent when another witness, William Hulvershorn, took the stand. Hulvershorn told the court how, at the wheel of his car in Eden Park, "I saw this man hurrying in the park like he was trying to make a train or something and I gave him a lift." The man jumped in, and asked to be taken to the central station. On the way, he said: "You don't know who I am?" Hulvershorn said no, and he replied "I'm George Remus." "The famous George Remus?" Hulvershorn asked. "Glad to know you." When the car arrived at the railway station, Remus appeared disconcerted. "I meant the central police station," he said, adding, "I shot someone in the park." A titter ran through the courtroom when

Hulvershorn added: "I didn't believe him when he told me who he was."

Witness after witness came forward with descriptions of Remus's hysterical grief after his return from Atlanta. Mueller told the court of the clock incident. Rogers recalled Remus's phone conversation with Imogene. He had also, in the course of his reporting, met with Imogene on her own. Imogene had told him: "Remus will never hurt me, but please don't let him hurt Mr. Dodge."

"Remus's conduct convinced me he was insane," Rogers told the court. "I went so far as to report to my managing editor, in the summer of 1926, that he had lost his mind." Another defense witness was Judge Beston S. Oppenheimer, who had earlier been involved in Imogene's divorce, but had handed the case over to another judge at an early stage. He had come to the conclusion, after hearing Remus in his chambers, that the man was "crazy." Rogers also told the court that the U.S. commissioner of immigration in Atlanta "told me that Remus was an alien, which was the reason for seeking deportation."

Although the prosecution did its best to discredit the testimony of Willie Haar, the millionaire's row convict and bootlegger, he too made an impact on the jury. In Indianapolis after his release during the Jack Daniel's trial, he told the court of parties he had attended. "Dodge and Imogene Remus were fondling, hugging and caressing one another and using profane language." In an aside, he added: "It was funny that a lot of Prohibition officials supposed to be enforcing the laws were having liquor themselves."

Thomas Berger, no ex-bootlegger but a wealthy industrial fair organizer (and a boyhood friend of Remus), was another valuable defense witness. He testified how, some months before the murder, Remus had asked him to act as mediator. He began an account of their conversation: "I said to Remus," Berger recounted, "your wife wants nothing whatever to do with you. She is in love with Franklin Dodge. She would not refund to you any of the property. . . . She didn't want a few hundred thousand dollars, but wanted to keep all she had." The judge asked Berger whether, in his opinion, Remus was sane "despite the fact that Dodge was still alive." "He ought to be where she is," Berger replied, to loud, appreciative laughter. He also confirmed that Imogene had tried to have Remus deported.

"I told Remus that the chief immigration officer at St. Louis had told me the department wanted to deport Remus," he continued. "I told Remus I asked the immigration officer to find out who was back of it, and two weeks later I told Remus the officer came to see me and said that Uncle Sam would not be a party to deport an individual for private gain of individuals like Dodge and Mrs. Remus." Again, Remus had flown into such a rage that "I thought he was going to tear one of his ears off. He wanted to go after Dodge and his wife."[2]

George Conners described his first visit to Price Hill mansion after Remus's release. "The only thing in the house was a bed and a pair of shoes, which didn't belong to Remus."[3]

By this time it was clear to reporters that the jury was on Remus's side, but if any doubt remained, it vanished on December 8, when Elston called a surprise witness, Harry Truesdale. It was to be the turning point of the trial.

15

REMUS REDUX

Elston's purpose in calling the witness, he told the judge, was to establish whether Remus had been insane. But it became increasingly clear, as Truesdale's story unfolded, that his real purpose was very different.

Truesdale's voice was so low that the court stenographer had to repeat some of his statements to the jurors. Only a verbatim account can adequately convey the tense drama of those few minutes.[1]

TRUESDALE: I followed him [Remus] several times and talked to him on October 5. [The day before the murder.]

ELSTON: When was the first time you saw him?

TRUESDALE: Sometime during the latter part of the summer. A man called Marcus pointed him out to me. [Marcus's name had already come up. Conners had alleged that Marcus had been offering $15,000 to anyone who would kill Remus]. I saw him around four-five P.M. on October 5.

ELSTON: Did you talk to him?

TRUESDALE: I went there for that purpose.

ELSTON: Did you form an opinion about sanity or insanity?

TRUESDALE: I did, on that afternoon, when I told him what I knew.

ELSTON: Now tell us what you said to him and what he said and did that causes you to form that opinion.

TRUESDALE: I told him that out at Springdale dog track a man by the name of John Marcus told me he knew how I could make $10,000 and I asked him how it would be and he told me that if I would kill a man I could get that much money.

JUDGE SHOOK: Did you tell this to Mr. Remus?

TRUESDALE: Exactly. Marcus told me he would introduce me to the party that would give me the money.

BASLER: *Did* you tell Mr. Remus this?

TRUESDALE: Exactly. Marcus said he could not take me up right away so Marcus went over to see her and came back and said she would not see me right away.

ELSTON: Who?

TRUESDALE: Mrs. Remus. Three or four days later, in Cincinnati, Marcus told me she would see me and took me to the Alms Hotel, room 708.

He introduced me to Mrs. Remus by the name of Charles and we didn't stay there long that afternoon, because she had people in the next room.

But she told me to come back the next day at three, which I did. She then told me that I would get $10,000 if I would kill Remus. She told me she would give me $5,000 and another person would give me $5,000.

I wanted some kind of surety but she would not give it me. I asked her who the other party was. She said "I will vouch for him, his money is all right."

She didn't state his name right at the time, but after a while she said his name was Franklin Dodge. She was very bitter against Remus and said she wished someone would beat his brains out.

She gave me $250 for expenses. Mrs. Remus told me Remus was at the Sinton Hotel, room 327. I went to the hotel and sat on the left side of the elevator.

Once I passed his room which was open — one time I thought of killing him in his room, but too many people went in and out. He always had a lot of callers. I kept on following him till a few days before the Dempsey-Tunney fight.

It was at this juncture that Remus burst into a flood of tears. His sobs got louder and louder until Truesdale could no longer be heard.

His daughter Romola, by his side that day, was also in tears. So was Mrs. Gabriel Ryerson, Remus's sister, and several other spectators. Both women jurors started crying too. "The jurors," the *Cincinnati Enquirer* noted, "were highly sympathetic." All eyes were on Remus, shaking spasmodically, bent over his desk, head in hands.

Between sobs, Remus asked the judge: "Will you adjourn the court for a minute, Your Honor?" Judge Shook ordered Remus removed from the courtroom. He was still sobbing as marshals escorted him out, brushing away photographers. "No, no," he told them. Turning to the judge, he said: "I am sorry, Your Honor, I . . . cannot . . . help . . . it."

The court remained in session for another thirty minutes, with Truesdale impassive in the witness box. Remus's sobs could be heard from behind the door leading to the judge's quarters. Finally Judge Shook adjourned the court.

The following morning a perfectly composed Remus entered the courtroom. "I wish to apologize, Your Honor, to you and the jury, for my unmannish [sic] conduct yesterday," he said, and Truesdale resumed his testimony.

> She said she wanted to see me at her hotel. Her bags were packed. She said she was going away. She told me I would have to hurry as it wouldn't be long before the divorce case. She said she would be gone for ten days to two weeks. After this I saw Remus in Hamilton but had no opportunity to kill him.
>
> Then on October 2 I called at the Alms Hotel. Mrs. Remus said she had been in Chicago for the Dempsey-Tunney fight. She said she was very anxious as the time was running short. She said she would meet me at midnight at the Rentschler building. I noticed a man on the corner and she said he was Dodge, the man who would give me the other $5,000.

Truesdale said Imogene and he walked to the Grand Hotel. She wanted to find out whether Remus was registered there under his name. There was a car outside, with three men inside, one of them Dodge, and Imogene and Truesdale followed at walking pace. "I was a little afraid of this," Truesdale told the court. Imogene said: "If I see him tonight, I'll kill him myself," and showed him a pearl-handled revolver in her bag. By this time Truesdale had had enough. He left. "I never got in touch with Mrs. Remus again."

When he finally met Remus, the following day — October 5 — and told him what he had just told the court, Remus broke down. "I felt he was insane." Truesdale added he had sought out Remus "because I feared I was being set up and would go to jail for something."

The prosecution did its best to discredit his story. Truesdale had a "Bertillon" — that is, a major criminal record — and Sibbald made the most of it.

SIBBALD: You're just a petty thief. You'd do anything if you got your price, right?

TRUESDALE: Yes, I would if I got the money for it.

SIBBALD: You'd come here and give perjured testimony if you got enough money out of it?

TRUESDALE: No, I don't give perjured testimony.

SIBBALD: You'd commit murder for money but you wouldn't commit perjury for money?

TRUESDALE: That's a different thing.

SIBBALD: You know the woman is dead.

TRUESDALE: She must be. [laughter in court]

The prosecution tried to show that Imogene had never asked him to kill Remus, but simply to set him up with a woman, so that Imogene could burst in on him in flagrante.

Truesdale denied this. Sibbald abruptly changed his line of questioning.

SIBBALD: Did you divide the two hundred dollars with your partners?

TRUESDALE: No.

SIBBALD: Who were your partners?

TRUESDALE: Who were my partners? I don't see why it's necessary
to bring . . .

Elston objected to the question.

TRUESDALE: I have no partners.

Truesdale denied he had been paid to testify, but, under further
questioning, admitted staying at the Grand Hotel under the name of
Harry Truelabe. Truesdale's appearance had been carefully planned.
Just prior to his testimony, William A. Hoefft, the cigar stand manager
of the Sinton Hotel, had taken the stand. Hoefft had been seen with
Remus the day before the murder.

"My God, Hoefft," Remus told him, "I just had information I
was going to be killed." Hoefft told the court: "He sat with his head
in his hands. I stayed with him for forty-five minutes. After quieting
him down, Remus apologized. . . . In my opinion he was insane."

Afterward, Elston told reporters Truesdale had agreed to testify
because "he adhered to an underworld code that you make a clean
breast of things when capital punishment is involved." "I've checked
his story," Elston said. "There are witnesses, we can verify it."

Elston was now quietly confident. Truesdale's testimony, he believed, had made a huge impact on the jurors, turning Remus into
the victim and Imogene into the executioner. The prosecution did its
best to fight the tide, with evidence that relations between George
Remus and Imogene had been far from idyllic long before Remus was
released from jail, but their witnesses — Imogene's daughter Ruth
and Elizabeth Felix, a friend of Imogene's — failed to shake the jury,
in that they recalled instances of minor spats that occur among the
most devoted couples. Ruth said Imogene had often been in tears
after seeing Remus in Atlanta jail "because he had been brutal and
unkind." In the light of the earlier testimony, Felix's claim that Imogene had been "morally irreproachable" was, to say the least, unconvincing.

Remus's character witnesses had far greater impact. The most
prominent was Clarence Darrow, the criminal lawyer whose brilliant

advocacy and showmanship had long turned him into a superstar. Slipping into his co-counsel role, Remus could not resist making the most of this, referring to Darrow as "the sage of the twentieth century. . . . How proud am I to know that this great humanitarian takes up his time to testify for me." Judge Shook cut him short with a curt "That's enough."

Darrow praised Remus as a man and as a lawyer, and said he knew nothing of his investigation by a grievance committee of the Chicago Bar Association, but "if he was investigated, I would not regard an indictment as affecting peace and quiet."

Taft did his best to turn Remus's emotional outburst to the prosecution's advantage. "Don't you know he was known [in Chicago legal circles] as the weeping, crying Remus?" he asked. "I knew he was a very emotional fellow, somewhat unstable," Darrow said.

Taft tried again. "Would you regard Remus as characteristic of a law-abiding citizen?" Elston objected, and the question was withdrawn.

The jury probably missed the point. In legal circles, Darrow's anti-Prohibitionist views were well known, and almost certainly explained his presence in court.

Taft brought up Remus's bootlegging past with another character witness, also a well-known Chicago attorney, Thomas S. Hogan. Again, his questions backfired.

Had Hogan been aware of Remus's conviction on liquor charges? "That's a moot question, whether it's moral turpitude," Hogan replied, anticipating Taft's next question. "While I'm a dry myself I wouldn't consider that a heinous offense against the law."

Remus could not resist making himself heard. "The defendant has never hijacked liquor," he told the court, "and the defendant has no apologies to make for having sold good liquor since 1919."

At the close of the trial, Dr. E. A. Baber, superintendent of Cincinnati's Longview psychiatric hospital and one of the panel of psychiatrists who had examined Remus, testified that he was sane. Remus subjected him to repeated questioning. It was "the peculiar situation of a man claiming insanity for his defense, cross-examining an expert on insanity" the *Cincinnati Enquirer* noted, adding that Remus "gave Dr. Baber some uncomfortable moments," as when

Remus asked him: "Sanity is the reverse of insanity, is it not, Dr. Baber?"

BABER: Yes.

REMUS: Insanity is an abnormal condition of the mind, isn't it?

BABER: Not necessarily.

Elston delighted the audience with excerpts of some of the inane tests the panel had subjected Remus to. "Didn't he say at the time that he was on trial for murder, and didn't have time to bother with this nonsense?" he reminded the court.

Taft's lackluster summing up differed little from the prosecution's opening statement, though he did his best to portray "the weeping, whining Remus" as a cynical play-actor. He also reminded the jurors that Truesdale, a convicted felon, must have known that he was immune from prosecution. Under the Ohio state laws, it was not a punishable offense to conspire to commit a crime if no crime was subsequently committed.

Remus came into his own on December 19 with an emotional summing up. "Here before you stands Remus the lawyer. In the chair there [gesturing] is Remus the defendant, charged with murder. Remus the defendant does not desire any sympathy or compassion in any shape or form whatsoever. If you feel the defendant should go to the electric chair, do not flinch. The defendant will not flinch. He stands before you in the defense of his honor and the sanctity of his home."[2]

Thanking the judge for his "fairness and squareness," Remus reminded the jury that insanity [Dr. Baber notwithstanding] in his opinion was "nothing more than the abnormal condition of the mind." He also reminded the court that Franklin Dodge, "that ace of the Prohibition department, that deuce with women, that moral leper, this human parasite with whom County Prosecutor Charles Taft traveled the country" had not been called on to testify. He made a final crack at prosecutor Basler ("Look at his profile and say whether it has the look of hypocrisy?"), ending with a reference to the Volstead Act, " . . . one of the greatest criminal and legal abortions of all time. Why, but for the act, the defendant would not have been here!" Whatever the outcome, Remus told them, "I thank you. Happy Christmas to you."

Elston's summing up was equally passionate, but on a different note.

Was there ever a woman in history, in fiction, who treated a man worse or more shamefully than Imogene Remus? Was there ever a woman who had less reason for doing so? And yet they say he was in a normal state of mind, that October 6 when he had the faith of a little child. . . . Turn him loose for Christmas. Bring peace of mind to the man who has suffered the tortures of hell for more than two years. We are not asking for mercy, we say this man is not guilty.

Just before the jury retired, on December 20, Judge Shook took the unusual step of reminding them that outright acquittal would be "against the law," but the jury was almost certainly more receptive to his ambiguous acknowledgment of Imogene's behavior. "The law," Shook went on, "does not justify one person taking the life of another because the latter may be of a bad character."

As reporters later ascertained, their verdict was determined within two minutes, on a single ballot, but the jurors stayed out for three hours after informing the judge they had come to a decision, enjoying a long, celebratory lunch — aware that the bulk of the press would not be back in the courtroom until four P.M. As a juror later told the *Cincinnati Enquirer,* "We felt: let's go out and give him a Christmas present. He has been persecuted long enough."

"We find the defendant not guilty on the sole ground of insanity," Harry G. Byrd, the jury foreman, announced, to wild cheering, when the court reconvened. "That's American justice!" Remus shouted. Surrounded by reporters in the hubbub that followed, he extended his "deepest appreciation" to the jury, the court, the prosecutors, the sheriff and jailer. "God knows what is in my heart at the moment. The rest of my life I will dedicate to stifle the insult that is upon our statutes, known as the National Prohibition Act." Had there been no Prohibition law "to fill the coffers of a class that seeks and practices only venality," he would not have been in court in the first place, he said.

There was a party in his cell suite that night, attended by Elston, his close circle of friends, his daughter Romola, and two of the jurors.

The following day, the jury presented a unanimous petition to Judge Shook, asking him to free Remus, "if possible, in time for Christmas." A furious Judge Shook promptly ordered them to apologize to the court, which they did. But for a long time afterward, at Taft's instigation, they remained under investigation for improper conduct, facing possible jail sentences.

Remus's troubles were not over either. Taft told the press that despite the verdict, which had been "a gross miscarriage of justice . . . , [we] are not through with all the angles in this case."

A more skillful behind-the-scenes manipulator than prosecutor, Taft worked relentlessly to have Remus committed for life to an insane asylum. He successfully petitioned for a "lunacy hearing" before a probate judge. Remus was confident he would emerge a free man. Had not a panel of psychiatrists, chosen by the prosecution, proclaimed him sane?

But Taft also persuaded two members of the panel to change their minds. A Dr. David A. Wolfstein now determined that Remus was "ruthless, reckless, selfish, eccentric — the kind of man who takes the law into his own hands. . . . He has shown he can be dangerous." Over Dr. Baber's objections, the judge ruled that a two-to-one opinion was sufficient to have Remus confined to the Lima insane asylum. On January 6, 1928, an ambulance took a strait-jacketed Remus to the dreaded Kentucky "prison-hospital."

Elston promptly appealed for a habeas corpus writ on the grounds of illegal confinement, and to the Ohio Supreme Court, while Remus — for all his alleged emotional instability — displayed singular resilience in Lima, soon becoming a hero to the warders there. As reported in the *Cincinnati Post* on January 28, "Wife-slayer George Remus saved the life of a hospital guard who had been overpowered by a giant negro patient."

An appeals court was now convened to review the case, and a fresh panel of six psychiatrists again submitted him to extensive tests, which he passed with flying colors. "Remus is sane beyond a doubt," said Dr. Shelby Mumaugh, a former Longview consultant. "He is not a psychopath." "I wish I had his brain," said Dr. W. L. Neville, a Florida specialist.

Two Lima officials disagreed. A supervisor told the appeals court that Remus had "recently violated standing orders." His offense was "having in his possession a book on insanity." Lima's superintendent, W. H. Vorbau, in frequent touch with prosecutor Sibbald, cited as evidence of Remus's insanity "his persistent refusal to wear underwear."

A more insidious attempt to brand him as insane was disclosed by the *Cincinnati Post*. Prosecutor Sibbald, sent by Taft to Lima to argue in favor of his continued incarceration, intended citing Franklin Dodge as witness at the new hearing — almost certainly to provoke Remus and cast his sanity in doubt. Cornered, Sibbald admitted as much. "We want to see how Remus acts when he meets Dodge" he was foolish enough to admit to the *Post*. Dodge denied his visit had anything to do with the Remus case. He was only in Lima to sell distributors an automatic cigarette lighter whose patent he had acquired, he told the press. The judge decided Dodge's presence was not relevant to the case.

The hearing did not go Sibbald's way. Remus was the calm, dispassionate one, refusing to rise to the prosecutor's bait, and the judge ended up reprimanding Sibbald for his "intemperate language." In many respects, his cross-examination of Remus was a rehash of the murder trial, with Sibbald embarking on a scathing, interminable review of Remus's past, alleging he had always had criminal tendencies. He conspicuously failed to prove his case, succeeding only in antagonizing the court — and revealing his anti-German bias. Remus came across as an archetypal example of the new American in search of the American Dream — a compulsive workaholic and a loving, caring son, as Remus's old mother, seventy-eight, speaking in German through a translator, confirmed. (She had been called as a witness on the spur of the moment after Sibbald alleged that, after becoming rich, Remus had neglected his family). On March 30, the court declared Remus sane.

Taft did not give up even then. Invoking "irregularities," he announced he would appeal to the Ohio Supreme Court to get the decision annulled. A motion for a new trial was denied, but the Ohio Supreme Court took an inordinately long time to make up its mind while Remus appealed for release from what he described as "this dumping-ground of hell."

Finally, on June 20, 1928, he arrived at Cincinnati's Union Station, a free man at last. A small crowd of well-wishers, including some members of the jury, was there to greet him. So were Elston and

Conners. He looked tanned and fit from his work on the Lima farm, and seemed no worse for his six months there. "I shall remain in the city where people have been so kind to me," he told the *Cincinnati Post.*

Remus never returned to bootlegging, and never salvaged his fortune. He sold the Price Hill mansion (it was later pulled down), married Blanche Watson, his former secretary, and tried — but failed — to make another fortune, first in patent medicine, then in real estate.

His death, on January 20, 1952, was the occasion for a series of obituaries recalling a fabulous era. In 1995, the Cincinnati Historical Society staged a Remus exhibit. Among the memorabilia: a photograph of the party he gave to celebrate the opening of his $125,000 swimming pool, with Imogene the glamorous bathing belle — demurely by Remus's side, and the revolver he used to kill her.

16

A FATAL TRIUMPH

While Remus remained in Lima "criminal lunatic" hospital awaiting the Ohio Supreme Court's decision on his sanity, a medical controversy of another type gripped America: for the first time, the Volstead Act was being blamed for huge numbers of deaths from poisoned liquor.

It all began on New Year's Day, 1927, with scores of emergency admissions to New York's Bellevue Hospital. There were forty-one deaths there that day, and the Department of Health announced there had been 750 such deaths in New York alone during 1926.

Although no entirely accurate nationwide statistics are available, it is probable that by 1927 such deaths may have exceeded the 50,000 mark — to say nothing of hundreds of thousands more nonfatal cases resulting in blindness or paralysis. In 1930, the Prohibition Bureau reported that in a single, small county in Kansas — an exceptionally dry state — there had been over 15,000 victims of adulterated liquor.

Bootleggers like Remus, Olmstead, and McCoy, who refused to deal in adulterated liquor, were extremely rare. In Roy Haynes's day, fifteen chemists were on hand to examine samples of all seized liquor. In very few cases did they discover genuine brand whiskey, gin, or wine.

At their most harmless, the bootleggers' wares were diluted; in the majority of cases, the chemists found liquor made of pure grain to which coloring and flavoring had been added; moonshine — from corn meal, molasses, fruit, vegetables or sugar — presented graver risks. In some cases denatured alcohol had been redistilled to remove the poison. But in others the hooch was outright poison — wood alcohol. "Of 480,000 gallons of confiscated booze analyzed in New York in 1927, 98 percent contained poisons," said a Prohibition Bureau report. The New York *Telegram* collected over 500 samples of liquor from four hundred speakeasies. Fifty-five of them were found to contain significant traces of wood alcohol, and lesser poisons were found in seventy more.

Under Volstead Act provisions, the manufacture of denatured alcohol was not only legal, but tax exempt. The denaturing substance was usually methanol, and methanol was extremely poisonous. Three glasses could be lethal, explaining the steady rise in the death toll from 1920 onward. The Volstead Act's provisions that industrial alcohol should be made undrinkable included no proviso that its contents should be labeled "poison," and this was nothing more than "legalized murder," wrote Dr. Nicolas Murray Butler of Columbia University.

So, for the first time, in early 1927, Wayne Wheeler, that master manipulator and moral scourge of godless drinkers, found himself on the defensive. Although he denied any liability, it was a fact that the ASL had originally sanctioned the use of methanol when Volstead Act provisions were being drawn up, and had lobbied against any mandatory "poison" labels on denatured alcohol. Wheeler had boasted of the ASL's key role in drafting the act so loudly, and so frequently, that he lacked all credibility now that he denied responsibility for some of its provisions.

In 1927 cartoons and editorials he was depicted as a poisoner, and a callous one at that, for his response to the attacks against him was surprisingly inept. At first he claimed that only one such death had occurred since 1920; then, when this was ridiculed by experts, he suggested, in a press statement, that "the government is under no obligation to furnish people with alcohol that is drinkable when the Constitution prohibits it. The person who drinks this industrial alcohol is a deliberate suicide."[1] This was a monstrously hard-hearted reaction from the leader of an organization heavily subsidized by the Protestant church, leading to further press attacks on him in an admittedly overwhelmingly wet press.

His clumsiness reflected not only his increasingly precarious health but his loosening grip on Congress — and the ASL itself, for Wheeler's prickly arrogance had made him many enemies within the organization. His loss of face, and clout, had begun in 1925: in a move intended to curb Wheeler's inordinate political powers, and his hold on Congress, President Coolidge appointed Lincoln C. Andrews, a forceful retired brigadier general, as assistant secretary of the Treasury, with overall responsibilities for Customs, the Coast Guard, and the Prohibition Bureau.

The nomination undermined the position of Prohibition Commissioner Haynes, a Wheeler appointee and his pliant stooge, but it also eroded some of Wheeler's own authority, for Andrews himself began keeping Wheeler at arm's length, and a number of congressmen, past victims of Wheeler's strong-arm tactics, now began an open revolt against him. And as his own power declined, a number of new, or long-dormant, anti-Prohibition associations began gathering strength.

By 1926, several articulate and increasingly powerful lobbies had emerged, campaigning for a return to pre-1920 state liquor laws and even for outright repeal. These were no easily dismissed lobbies sponsored by former brewing and distilling vested interests. The Association Against the Prohibition Amendment, the Crusaders, and the Moderation League, mostly composed of middle-class professionals, lawyers, and businessmen, had all been in existence since the early 1920s, had no connections with the liquor industry, and were now attracting considerable media attention for the first time — with prominent personalities joining their ranks. Various state bar associations, as well as the powerful American Bar Association, were now also daring to challenge the legality of the Volstead Act, drawing attention to the abuses it occasioned; the American Federation of Labor (AFL), representing the views of all but a tiny minority of factory workers, had never given up the struggle for legal 2.5-proof beer, and in 1927 was making its influence felt in Congress as never before. Anti-German sentiment was receding at last: the American Legion, to which millions of First World War veterans belonged, was also turning against the ASL, and would soon urge an end to Prohibition.

But what worried Wheeler most in 1927 was another "women's war" phenomenon, waged this time by the wets, and headed by America's most prominent female Republican. Pauline Morton Sabin, granddaughter of a Republican governor and daughter of President Theodore Roosevelt's secretary of the Navy, was a dyed-in-the-wool, mainstream Republican. After marrying a wealthy banker (himself a prominent anti-Prohibition campaigner), she had risen through the Republican ranks to become president of the Women's National Republican Club and the first female ever appointed to the previously all-male Republican National Committee. As a vocal anti-Prohibitionist, she sacrificed her long-standing Republican convictions for her new cause, exploiting the growing, nationwide resentment at corruption and two-tier justice, displaying formidable debating and organizing skills.

Wheeler was by now a very sick man, with severe heart and kidney afflictions, but was refusing to let up. On April 23, 1927, he confronted Clarence Darrow in a contradictory debate on Prohibition at Carnegie Hall. So weak was he that his opening statement had to be read by an underling, and the audience, overwhelmingly pro-Darrow, interrupted him with cruel catcalls. Wheeler responded with considerable bravado. "According to the wets I am dangerously ill and about to quit prohibition work," he told them. "This is unmitigated bunk. My health is better than the wets wish it was and it is getting better every week." In fact, he only had another five months to live, and in the brief period left would face increasingly serious challenges.

That same April, Wheeler had advance warning that Andrew Mellon, Coolidge's closest cabinet colleague, intended letting both Haynes and Andrews go, and the following month, though in constant pain, he lobbied Congress and the White House to get the decision overthrown. But he was no longer the dreaded "big boss," and Coolidge ignored his entreaties, replacing Haynes with James M. Moran, who was no friend of Wheeler's.

The ASL was now in danger of splitting into pro-Wheeler and pro-Moran factions, and had lost the cohesion that had made it so powerful. The crisis was compounded by a growing cash crisis: affluent sympathizers were now more reluctant to give as much to the ASL as they had in the past. For the first time, the league's public relations and publishing budget had to be trimmed.

Wheeler returned one last time to Oberlin, his alma mater, for graduation exercises, to bask in the adulation he knew he would always find there. This was where his ASL career had begun, and he was still an icon to present and past students. He then decided to rest up in his small summer house in Little Point Sable, Michigan, to prepare for the grueling 1928 presidential campaign that lay ahead.

Tragedy continued to dog him. A few weeks after his holiday began, a gasoline stove exploded in the kitchen, inflicting horrible, lethal burns on his wife. At the sight of her in flames, his father-in-law, Robert Candy, dropped dead of a heart attack. Wheeler attempted to resume his ASL career, but he was a broken man.

In early September Wheeler lapsed into a coma and died. The "dry boss" was duly eulogized by the very ASL personalities who had turned against him. There would be "no successor to Wheeler," the ASL pledged. This was deliberately ambiguous praise, for though it consecrated his role in bringing the Volstead Act into being in the first place, it also implied that Wheeler, especially in the last few years, had misused his powers, overstepped his role, and offended too many people. Bishop James Cannon, the head of the Methodist Church and a prim hypocrite who had frequently clashed behind the scenes with Wheeler, immediately did his best to assume the "big boss" mantle.

Wheeler had been looking forward to the 1928 presidential nomination campaigns. He wanted to make sure that — as in 1924 — he would prevent Al Smith, still the veteran governor of New York State, from gaining the nomination. But times were changing, and so had the party's mood. Its delegates to the 1928 Democratic Convention in Houston were well-behaved, with not a drunkard in sight. William Jennings Bryan, the indefatigable Democratic Prohibitionist, was dead, and Cannon lacked Wheeler's political skills.

In a series of ASL meetings and press articles just before the convention, Cannon did his best to imply that Al Smith, if elected, would turn out to be a "cocktail President." Again and again, he quoted an article in the *Nation*. "Do you believe in electing to the Presidency a man who drinks too much for his own good, and is politically a rampant wet? Does Al drink, and does he drink too much? I am reliably informed that he drinks every day, and the number of his cocktails and highballs is variously estimated at from four to eight."[2]

Slurs of this type were only moderately effective: public opinion was now far more blasé. Besides, though it was known that Al Smith was no teetotaler, he had been a popular, competent governor, and unlike many politicians — some of them toeing the dry line — had never been seen the worse for drink.

With the support of up-and-coming Democratic personalities such as Franklin D. Roosevelt and Henry Morgenthau, to say nothing of Tammany Boss George Olvany — a rough, tough, hard-drinking Irish thug — Smith easily won the nomination.

Almost half of his telegram accepting the Democratic nomination dealt with Prohibition — proof that it remained America's most crucial political issue. Whoever won, he wrote, would have to deal with a situation "entirely unsatisfactory to the great mass of our people." Without formally calling for its repeal, he urged a return to "democratic principles of local self-government and state's rights" — in other words, a return to pre-1920 local option laws. There were reports that Smith himself would have preferred a stronger statement but was advised against it by Roosevelt, aware of the lasting importance, especially in rural areas and in the South, of the dry vote.

Once the presidential contest between Herbert Hoover and Al Smith began, Bishop Cannon concentrated all his efforts on another issue he knew prejudiced, narrow-minded (and as they were then called) "nativist" voters would respond to — the Democratic candidate's Catholic faith.

Because the Vatican's *Observatore Romano* had referred in an editorial to Prohibition's ineffectiveness ("it has become so useless not to say dangerous that it would be better to abolish it"), Cannon argued — first in an article for *Outlook* magazine, then in innumerable speeches around the country — that should Smith become president, "he is likely to be tremendously influenced by the views of the Pope and the Romish cardinals," even suggesting that, if elected, he would turn part of the White House into a permanent guest house for the Pope.

His blatant bigotry emphasized the gulf between "old" and "new" Americans and the latent hostility of the former. In Cambridge, Maryland, he told a rally that Smith courted

... the Italians, the Sicilians, the Poles and the Russian Jews. That kind has given us a stomach-ache. We have been unable to assimilate such people in our national life, so we shut the door on them. But Smith says "give me that kind of people." He wants the kind of dirty people that you find today on the sidewalks of New York.[3]

Mabel Willebrandt also joined in the fray, though she avoided any racist invective. Addressing mass meetings of her own Methodist Episcopal church, she urged Protestants to show their support for Hoover by writing in and pledging their vote to him.[4]

Prohibition and the Catholic issue dogged Al Smith's campaign from start to finish. In Oklahoma City, a dry stronghold, he expected a hostile reception, for Ku Klux Klan crosses had lined the railroad tracks of his campaigning train. The KKK was almost as anti-Catholic as it was anti-black, and was one of the most uncompromising advocates of a dry America.

Decidedly nervous, he met the challenge directly. "An effort has been made to distract the attention of the electorate and fasten it on malicious and un-American propaganda; I specifically refer to the question of my religion," he told a large crowd inside the Oklahoma City Coliseum. "I can think of no greater disservice to this country than to have the voters of it divide upon religious lines. It is not only contrary to the spirit of the Declaration of Independence, but of the Constitution itself."

Referring to Mabel Willebrandt's canvassing of Methodist voters, he asked the overwhelmingly Protestant crowd: "What would the effect be upon these people if a prominent official of the government of the State of New York under me suggested to a gathering of the pastors of my church that they do for me what Mrs. Willebrandt suggests be done for Hoover?" Contrary to his expectations, he got a rousing reception from the Oklahomans present.

In cities with large ethnic minorities, especially where Prohibition had made brewery and distillery workers obsolete, the public response to Smith was ecstatic. In Milwaukee, his last major electioneering venue, he focused almost exclusively on Prohibition. "If there is any one subject above all others concerning which the welfare of the country requires plain speech and constructive leadership, it is the Volstead Act," he told the crowd. He not only suggested that it be amended "to allow each state to determine for itself what it wants to do about the question of local habits," but for the first time proposed a referendum on Prohibition. "The cure for the ills of democracy," he told them, "is more democracy. Hand this back to the people. Let them decide it."

He also got in a sly dig at Mabel Willebrandt. "I shall let the Republican campaign managers worry about her. From comments in the public press all over the country, they have abundant reason to do so. We all have something to be grateful for. I haven't got Mabel on my hands."[5]

Herbert Hoover, in his memoirs published twenty-three years later, claimed that "the Prohibition issue was forced into the campaign by Governor Al Smith" but made no reference to the religious polarization that was its most distinctive feature. Whatever his private misgivings may have been (in his memoirs he also claimed, with hindsight, "a reverse of enthusiasm" for the Volstead Act), he knew that in the eyes of the dry rural voters he was one of them — he had spoken out often enough on the evils of alcohol ("one of the curses of the human race") to gain their lasting support.

In the last resort, the anti-Catholic, anti-minority, nativist themes proved compelling. Hoover won by 22 million votes to Al Smith's 15.5 million, and by 444 electoral votes to 87. The election also resulted in the highest percentage of acknowledged drys ever returned to Congress. Even in New York, America's wettest state, up-and-coming Democratic star Franklin D. Roosevelt only won the New York governorship (which Al Smith had vacated) by a small (25,000) majority.

Mabel Willebrandt was right: once again, the Prohibition issue had proved a deciding factor in politics. For all the needless tragedies it provoked, the corruption and damage to the body politic it generated, the myth of a God-fearing, prosperous, hard-working dry America was more attractive to a majority of voters than Al Smith's realistic, more tolerant approach.

There were other reasons for Smith's defeat. Hoover had been a popular secretary of Commerce, untainted by scandal. America was unprecedentedly prosperous, riding a stock market boom. More important, as Al Smith himself noted shortly afterward, "the time hasn't yet come when a man may say his Rosary beads in the White House."

Not only was the leading anti-Prohibitionist contender beaten, and removed from the presidential race for all time, but dry advocates were able to claim that a new millennium was at hand, that after nine fumbling years the Volstead Act would at last come into its own.

Newly elected President Hoover did nothing to disappoint them. "I do not favor the repeal of the 18th Amendment," he said in his acceptance speech. "I stand for the efficient enforcement of the laws enacted thereunder." He described Prohibition as

> a great social and economic experiment, noble in motive and far-reaching in purpose. It must be worked out constructively. Common-sense compels us to realize that grave abuses have occurred — abuses which must be remedied. . . . There are those who do not believe in the purposes of several provisions of the Constitution. No one denies their right to seek to amend it. . . . But the Republican Party does deny the right of anyone to seek to destroy the purposes of the Constitution by indirection.

The day after Hoover's victory, anti-Prohibitionist Pauline Sabin resigned from the Republican party. In fact, repeal was only four years away.

Although the grounds for this dramatic change in mood would be overwhelmingly economic, one reason for the continued decline of the ASL involved Wheeler's self-appointed propagandizing successor and perennial rival for ASL leadership, Bishop James Cannon. Doubts began to be cast on his fitness for the role even before Hoover became president.

A Virginian, nominal Democrat, prominent member of the Methodist Episcopal church, and member of the ASL executive since 1902, Bishop Cannon was a difficult man to like. Even his closest Methodist colleagues considered him a cold fish who had never been known to laugh and seldom smiled. This puritanical Protestant Aya-tollah disapproved of most if not all pleasurable activities, including gambling. He was against dancing, theatricals, and any games, sports, or art that provided glimpses of "the female person." He inveighed against Sarah Bernhardt ("an actress of brilliant powers but unsavory moral ideals") when she came to America to perform *Camille,* and against Marie Curie, the world-famous physicist, for allegedly living in sin with her equally famous scientist companion (to whom she was in fact married), claiming that "she has lost forever her claim to a place among the great men and women of the world." And, of course, he considered Roman Catholicism "the mother of ignorance, superstition, intolerance and sin." New York, his pet hate, was "Satan's beat."[6]

A scrutiny of Bishop Cannon's financial dealings, begun in the press almost accidentally following routine inquiries into the failure of a brokerage firm with which he was associated, revealed questionable, and perhaps indictable, practices on his part. The firm, a bucket shop, had bought $477,000 worth of stocks for him, selling them for $486,000, and Cannon's profit — $9,000 — had been nearly four times what he had actually invested ($2,500). In pre-crash America, this would normally have attracted little attention — but Bishop Cannon was one of the nation's foremost anti-gambling scourges, and his own investment had been nothing less than a prodigious gamble.

As always in America, once the media had trained their sights on a target, they started delving into his past. Reporters discovered that while administering a girls' school during the First World War, Bishop Cannon had hoarded flour, then sold it on the black market at a considerable profit, narrowly escaping prosecution. His biographer, Virginius Dabney, the Richmond *Times-Dispatch* editor, would also show that he had made false income tax returns to conceal the transaction.

Reporters now embarked on a full-scale investigation of his private life, and what they found was hilarious: the narrow-minded bigot turned out to have feet of clay. The scourge of innocent pleasure-lovers was a modern equivalent of Molière's *Tartuffe*.

On one of his frequent trips to New York during the presidential campaign, Cannon had made the acquaintance of Helen McCallum and Joan Chapman in the lobby of the McAlpin Hotel in New York, where he was staying. He introduced himself as "Stephen Trent, writer," gave McCallum twenty dollars, and would subsequently pay her rent.

It was the beginning of a beautiful friendship. Despite the fact that Bishop Cannon's wife was terminally ill with cancer, he came to New York to see McCallum with increasing frequency, even leaving Washington on November 25, 1928, the day after his wife suffered a paralytic (and eventually lethal) stroke, to be with his new friend, spending the night in New York. He returned just in time for his wife's death, and funeral, but returned to New York — and McCallum — the following day.

Subsequently, Helen McCallum became an almost, but not quite, constant companion: she was with him in Jerusalem in 1929, and during an extensive trip to Europe in 1930, both times masquerading as his secretary on all-expenses-paid junkets. Rumors that Bishop Cannon was also dating a friend of McCallum's, Cary McTroy, and might even have married her secretly, made Helen seek out the press and show them some of the bishop's intimate letters to her.

Bishop Cannon and McCallum would eventually marry, but in the meantime he got into trouble of another type: this time he was charged with mishandling Republican campaign funds. He had allegedly received $65,000 but had accounted for only $17,000. Cannon dismissed the allegations as a "popish plot," but never offered a satisfactory explanation to the investigating Senate Lobby Committee. Nor did its members press hard for an answer: a majority were prominent drys, and several were on the ASL payroll.

A final indignity was in store: on their honeymoon in Brazil, after a hasty wedding in London, Bishop Cannon learned that members of his own Methodist church had formally accused him of "gross moral turpitude." He managed to overcome this hurdle as well, but only by invoking irregularities in the way his accusers had invoked the "Methodist Discipline."

The Cannon story became a favorite ongoing topic in the American press, and the ASL's reputation suffered in consequence. An unrelated, but devastating ASL scandal broke with the indictment of the league's New York state superintendent William Hamilton Anderson, eventually convicted for embezzlement.

Another prominent Prohibition personality, the incorruptible Mabel Walker Willebrandt, was also very much in the news just after Hoover's election. For all the new president's public praise (he kept her on as deputy attorney general), she resigned her post in May of 1929.

Although there were rumors she had fallen foul of her new boss, Attorney General William D. Mitchell, and that congressmen with bootlegging connections and prominent Catholics had also lobbied for her removal, the truth was far simpler: after eight years on an inadequate government salary as the single mother of an adopted daughter, the "Prohibition Portia," as Al Smith called her, craved a more financially rewarding life.

Fruit Industries, Inc., a conglomerate representing most of the California grape growers, promptly hired her as its legal counselor on a huge retainer. It proved a wise move. Thanks to Willebrandt's Washington connections, grape farmers, in the first year of Hoover's presidency, obtained large government subsidies and federal loans.

Willebrandt was useful to her new employers in other ways. Fruit Industries manufactured raisin cakes called Vine-glo, a popular raw material ingredient for homemade wine. Willebrandt's appointment was sufficient to deter Prohibition agents from prosecuting the company for infringing the Volstead Act, and Vine-glo sales boomed. A direct competitor — Vino-Sano Inc. — was not as fortunate. Its warehouses were raided and its raisin cakes confiscated, to such an extent that its president asked Willebrandt to be *its* legal counsel as well. She primly refused.

Although there was never any proof that Willebrandt herself encouraged her former Prohibition agents to persecute a business rival, she had shown, in her dealings with Remus, a ruthlessness that was peculiarly suited to the business world. She was also among the first of America's top government servants to set a much-abused precedent: crossing over into a lucrative private sector job to take advantage of expertise acquired in government service.

For all his public support of the Prohibition status quo, Hoover was fully aware of its destructive potential. To give the impression that he was sensitive to advocates of change, he did what all governments do to avert criticism: he set up a nongovernmental organization to deal with it.

The Wickersham Commission, named after its president, a distinguished lawyer, was supposed to assess the worth of the Volstead Act. Its terms of reference were, however, deliberately vague, and by the time its ambiguous findings were published, in 1931, America had been shaken by a cataclysmic event that would leave its imprint on the country right up to entry into the Second World War — the stock market crash of October 1929, triggering the Depression.

It was not just that disposable income shrank to such an extent that people could no longer afford bootleg liquor prices, and that many speakeasies lost their clients — though fashionable clubs such as the Twenty-One and the Stork Clubs still enjoyed affluent show business crowds. Far more important was the growing awareness among economists and business leaders, as well as private citizens, that by banning liquor, the government had, since 1920, cut itself off from extremely valuable tax revenue. In the affluent 1920s, this had not been of over-riding importance. But as one depression year followed the next, with no sign of an upturn, with rival government departments scrambling for shrinking federal funds, and with states cutting back on essential expenditures because widespread unemployment was leading to huge shortfalls in tax revenues, the folly of it all struck home.

The irony was that some of the new sponsors of repeal had been, in the past, the staunchest advocates of a totally dry America. The Du Ponts, one of America's most powerful families, had been as uncom-promising as Henry Ford in enforcing a "no drink, no saloon" rule wherever there were Du Pont munitions factories. New converts in their wake included Elihu Root, a prominent corporation lawyer, the CEOs of Standard Oil and Macy's, and influential bankers such as Paul ine Sabin's husband. Their membership in the AAPA — the American Anti-Prohibition Association — was not simply another nail in what was fast becoming an ASL coffin: it signified that the pendulum was in motion, and that the "establishment" was preparing to burn what it had worshipped for so long.

The Depression accelerated the swing away from Prohibition — it did not initiate it. The change of mood among the Du Ponts, and other like-minded ex-Prohibitionists, had been gradual. Moral and religious considerations were conspicuously absent, and an altruistic concern for the new unemployed was farthest from their minds. What motivated them was exclusively self-interest. Taxes had increased dramatically be-tween 1916 and 1921, and had continued to rise since. Canvassing heavily taxed fellow millionaires, Pierre Du Pont now spoke for many disgruntled CEOs when he claimed that if Britain's liquor tax system were applied to America, this would "permit the total abolition of income tax, both personal and corporate."

A number of millionaires fell for this unlikely, simplistic the-sis — and their new anti-Prohibition zeal got a new boost when Prohi-bition Commissioner James M. Moran told Congress that any attempt to enforce the Volstead Act would cost at least $300 million. Nor were the new zealots all wealthy: newspaper polls, from 1927 on, revealed a growing majority (from 75 to 81 percent) in favor of repeal.

If any single public statement sounded Prohibition's death-knell, it was John D. Rockefeller's open letter to Columbia University Presi-dent Nicholas Murray Butler, published in the *New York Times* on

June 6, 1932, announcing his endorsement of repeal in almost tearful terms. "I was born a teetotaler," he wrote. "All my life I have been a teetotaler on principle. . . . My mother and her mother were among the dauntless women of their day, often found with bands of women of like mind, praying on their knees in the saloons."

He described his enthusiastic support of the Volstead Act (he had been a major ASL contributor for many years before that, though he did not mention this). But "drinking has generally increased," as had crime. "The speakeasy has replaced the saloon; a vast army of law-breakers has been recruited and financed on a colossal scale." For all these reasons he now favored immediate, total repeal. His arguments were all moral ones. The tax issue was unmentioned. Hypocrisy takes many forms.

The 1932 presidential contest between Hoover and Roosevelt illustrated the American propensity to downgrade the importance of issues once regarded as of the utmost gravity when newer, more dramatic issues come to the fore. There had been several historical precedents, the most important swing of the pendulum occurring just before the outbreak of the Civil War. In the mid-1800s, as the debate on abolitionism became more critical, with the threat of a Southern breakaway increasingly dividing the nation, the seemingly unstoppable Prohibitionist movement had faltered, and then practically disappeared as a vocal force in politics. Prohibition would not become a serious issue again until long after the Civil War had ended.

What happened then was happening again in 1932. Jungians might argue that while history never repeats itself, archetypal behavior patterns do not go away, even if they may fade into the woodwork for a long, long time. There is a simpler explanation: leaving psychological jargon aside, let's say that in both centuries Americans had belatedly realized that there were more important things to worry about.

In 1932, the ongoing Depression was the major, perhaps the only, issue at stake, exacerbated by Hoover's repeated (and increasingly unconvincing) claims that there was light at the end of the tunnel. Unlike the 1924 and 1928 presidential contests, Prohibition was no longer part of the political debate. In fact, it was seldom mentioned as an issue, except by Roosevelt, who told a delighted St. Louis crowd that he would "increase the federal revenue by several hundred million dollars a year by placing a tax on beer," indicating his support of repeal.

Much was made of his exchange with Fiorello La Guardia, asking him whether there was a way of enforcing Prohibition in New York. La Guardia replied that not only would this compel disbanding the existing force and recruiting 250,000 men but the raising of a separate force of 250,000 inspectors to monitor police activities.

As La Guardia well knew, the question had been rhetorical: Roosevelt had already made up his mind. He knew he could promise repeal without losing more than a fraction of the popular vote.

The leading underworld bootleggers already knew what Roosevelt planned because an emissary had told them. "Lucky" Luciano, in his posthumous "Testament," even accused Roosevelt of welshing on a deal. New York's Mafia bosses initially intended to use their considerable clout to get the local politicians under their control to cast their votes for Roosevelt's rival, Al Smith, in the forthcoming presidential Democratic nomination contest. Luciano claimed that the Roosevelt emissary told them that if they switched their support, Roosevelt would soft-pedal investigations against them being conducted with exemplary honesty and zeal by Judge Samuel Seabury. After the Roosevelt nomination, Al Smith, according to Luciano, told "Lucky": "You fellas are crazy. I would've murdered Seabury for you. . . . He looked me square in the face and shook his head and said: Frank Roosevelt'll break his word to you. This is the biggest mistake you ever made in your entire life, by trustin' him. He'll kill you."

Luciano may have twisted some of the facts to suit himself, but Al Smith was right: Roosevelt, as soon as he became president, urged Seabury to get even tougher with the mob. In 1936, "Lucky" Luciano was sentenced to twenty-five years in jail.[7]

Even in that dry sanctuary of America, its rural heartland, farmers were beginning to respond favorably to pro-repeal arguments. Here too the reason was self-interest. They were among the hardest-hit Depression victims of all, aware of the grain and hops they could expect to sell to breweries and distilleries. Roosevelt was certainly under no illusion: he knew that for all their new anti-Prohibitionist zeal, the Du Ponts and other members of the AAPA would never vote for someone branded as a "dangerous socialist."

Repeal, after Roosevelt's election, turned out to be a surprisingly easy process. On December 6, 1932, a resolution was tabled to void the Eighteenth Amendment, and this took a mere three days, including a one-day filibuster by Texan Senator Morris Sheppard, whose lone voice only emphasized the impotence of the depleted dry lobby. Although it required, as the previous amendment had, a two-thirds ratification by the states, this would occur within a year. Utah, in December of 1933, became the thirty-sixth state to vote for the Twenty-first Amendment, which declared the Eighteenth Amendment null and void.

In the meantime Roosevelt had already taken steps to placate the AFL, and other advocates of real beer. One of his first decisions, as President, was to ask Congress to modify the Volstead Act to increase its alcoholic content to 3.2 percent, and Congress speedily complied. The protests of WCTU spokespersons and once-famous dry propagandists such as Billy Sunday now had a distinctly archaic flavor.

The two-step repeal — first legalizing real beer, then, a few months later, wine and hard liquor — meant that celebrations, the second time around, were less frenzied than expected. It was the return of real beer in the spring of 1933 that provoked hysteria. There were parades, floodlights, and torchlit processions in St. Louis, home of the Anheuser-Busch brewery, and in Milwaukee, and much ecstatic beer-tasting in packed former near-beer bars, now preparing for their new status, for they would no longer be "saloons" (the word remained anathema).

The evening of December 5, 1933 — marking the return of the legal consumption of hard liquor — began as a carnival but soon degenerated into frustration. Owing to the Depression, many of the former speakeasies had closed, and some had not yet obtained their legal licenses. In a sudden excess of legalism, they were unwilling to risk penalties by serving liquor without a permit. All over America, wines and reputable hard liquor were in short supply, and those establishments that had obtained stocks soon ran out of whiskey, gin, and champagne. New Jersey Governor Harry Moore solved the problem by announcing that "liquor has been sold illegally (in the state) for thirteen years and it will not hurt if this is done a few days more."

Prohibition had become a joke.

17

THE AFTERMATH

In Studs Terkel's *Hard Times*, a Depression survivor recalled the mood of the people on his street when Roosevelt's first Civil Works Administration paychecks arrived, shortly after his election.

> Everybody was out celebrating. It was like a festival in some old European city. . . . You'd walk from tavern to tavern and see people buying ponies of beer and sharing it. They had the whole family out. It was a warm night as I remember. Everybody was so happy. . . . I never saw such a change of attitude. Instead of walking around feeling dreary and looking sorrowful . . . it was like a feast day. They were toasting each other.

It could have been a description of Cincinnati's pre-Prohibition "Across the Rhine" neighborhood. It certainly proved the fallacy of the narrow-minded extremists who had claimed there was no such thing as moderate drinking. Even on the night of December 5, 1933, reporters noted there was very little actual drunkenness on the streets. Even if shortages of supplies — and of cash — were partially responsible, America appeared to have come of age.

Roosevelt's "New Deal" helped to dissipate memories of the previous thirteen years. In the new, more hopeful ambiance, there was less concern for the immediate past, and more interest in the immediate future. The Prohibition era had been a singularly unedifying, shameful thirteen-year-long hangover. It was as if most Americans were eager to forget it entirely, wiping its memories from their individual consciousness. It is significant that this period has attracted less attention, among professional historians, than almost any other epoch in American history.[1]

One of the most consistent critics of the Prohibition era had been H. L. Mencken, the prolific *Baltimore Sun* columnist and uncompromising scourge of other people's prejudices (though he was blind to some of his own). Once a humorist as revered by the American public as Will Rogers or Art Buchwald, Mencken has largely gone out of fashion because his Swiftian irony is no longer appreciated, or even understood, by present-day critics. They fail to grasp that when Mencken proposed that defeated presidential candidates be hanged, on the grounds that they would otherwise remain an intolerable nuisance for the rest of their lives, or that the world would be a safer place if the human race remained in a perpetually drunken state, he did not mean this literally.

What infuriated him most was the mediocrity of all those concerned with Prohibition. William Jennings Bryan had been "a charlatan, a mountebank, a zany without any sense of dignity," Harding "a numbskull," Coolidge "a dreadful little cad," and Hoover "a pious old woman, a fat Coolidge." Mencken's distrust of all those involved in good works was total: to him any reformer was "a prehensile Methodist parson, bawling for Prohibition and its easy jobs."

On its repeal, he wrote: "Prohibition went into effect on January 16, 1920, and blew up at last on December 5, 1933 — an elapsed time of twelve years, ten months and nineteen days. It seemed almost a geologic epoch while it was going on, and the human suffering that it entailed must have been a fair match for that of the Black Death or the Thirty Years War."[2]

Was the Prohibition balance sheet *that* overwhelmingly negative? The answer must be yes. Mencken may have deliberately exaggerated the number of dead and physically maimed — but in all sorts of ways, there was a fatal impact. Walter Lippmann, the famous liberal columnist and critic, whose career began during the Prohibition years, denounced the "circle of impotence in which we outlaw intolerantly the satisfaction of certain persistent human desires, and then tolerate what we have prohibited."[3] His remarks could well apply to certain current by-products of "political correctness."

Like ex-President Taft, Lippmann also pointed out the dangerous consequences of attempting to stamp out later "tolerated vices," thereby "turning over their exploitation to the underworld." For Prohibition was not the end of organized crime in America but only its beginning.

Perhaps the most ominous consequence of Prohibition had to do with a change in American attitudes toward organized crime in general. Even today, awareness of its ravages goes hand in hand with a certain passivity. Americans admire the quixotic qualities of a Serpico, the New York cop who waged a one-man war on his corrupt colleagues, but are not surprised that he ended up a loser. In the fight between good and evil, in real life as in "films noirs," good now seldom prevails over evil, and this is unsurprising, for Americans have been conditioned to believe that criminal vested interests are so powerful that the fight against them is inevitably rigged. In other words, they have lost the capacity to react.

For all his caricatural exaggeration, Mencken was right when he first spotted this tendency. Writing while Prohibition was still in force, he noted that

> It no longer astonished anyone when policemen were taken in evildoing. . . . If, before that time, the corps of Prohibition enforcement officers — i.e. a corps of undisguised scoundrels with badges — had been launched against the populace, there would have been a great roar of wrath, and much anguished gnashing of teeth. People would have felt themselves put upon, injured, insulted. But with the old assumption about policemen removed from their minds, they met the new onslaught calmly and even smilingly. Today no one is indignant over the fact that the extortions of these new *Polizei* increase the cost of potable alcohol.

Mencken went on to argue that there was no such thing as an honest politician, cop, public relations person — or journalist, for that matter. Current American perceptions are not so very different, even if measures have since been taken to limit election campaign contributions. Organized crime no longer openly funds politicians — as it did in Chicago during the Prohibition years. But the log-rolling persists, as do the expectations of major contributors.

That Prohibition helped to shape such prejudices is not surprising. Those who failed to apply the Volstead Act provisions were not necessarily deeply corrupt: they simply did not regard breaking them to be a crime. But even benign neglect of these provisions had the effect of encouraging organized crime — the financial rewards simply being too huge.

The major bootleggers rapidly completed their reconversion into the legitimate liquor business. Joe Kennedy, Sr., father of JFK, became the official distributor of Haig and Haig and Pinchbottle whiskey and Gordon's gin even *before* Prohibition's repeal; Samuel Bronfman, Canada's biggest bootlegger (and "Lucky" Luciano's biggest supplier) founded Seagram's; Frank Costello and his underworld partners set up Alliance Distributors, selling the same brands of Scotch (King's Ransom, House of Lords whiskey) they had smuggled into the United States during Prohibition. They also acquired a controlling interest in J. Turnley and Sons, another Scotch distributor. Meyer Lansky — with Luciano, "Bugsy" Siegel, and others — set up the Capitol Wine and Spirits firm, and became leading importers of vintage French wines, Scotch, and Canadian whiskey. Even in jail — and after (he was deported to Italy in 1946) — Luciano continued to receive a large share of the profits.

As students of organized crime well know, racketeers simply found new targets. After December of 1933, New York's underworld bosses began extending their protection activities to bakeries, restaurants, laundries, limousine services, the garment industry, and New York's Fulton Fish Market. Today, underworld bosses in New York's Chinatown display a businesslike ruthlessness that Al Capone could well have envied. More ominously, from time to time evidence surfaces of a form of gangland-police collusion (at least in Chinatown) that was so prevalent during Prohibition.

The relationships forged during those years did not vanish overnight. When Mafia leaders staged their much-publicized conference in the Appalachians in 1957, it was discovered that many of their pistol permits had been signed by New York and New Jersey po-

lice officials. In 1958, Paul W. Williams, a U.S. district attorney
for the southern district of New York, was the first to refer to "the
Invisible Government," tracing its origins back to the Prohibition
era. And just as corrupt law enforcement officials had been able to
call a halt when overly zealous policemen and Prohibition agents
threatened the livelihood of politically powerful underworld bosses, so
a notorious post-Prohibition politician-entrepreneur like New York's
James J. Hines was able to put a stop to the NYPD's attempt to
crack down on gambling operations, using his clout to have honest
cops transferred and gambling cases dealt with by "friendly" magis-
trates.

Even a hugely respected, influential anticrime crusader such as
Mayor La Guardia could not prevent the election of William Copeland
Dodge as Manhattan district attorney, whose links with organized
crime were an open secret.[4] And his repeated attempts to rid the Fulton
Fish Market of racketeering elements were only temporarily successful:
in 1995, an investigative report in the *New York Times* revealed that
the mob was still as active there as ever.

It would of course be overly simplistic to put the blame exclusively on Prohibition for the shifting patterns of post-1933 organized crime. But there can be no doubt that the laxity of the law
enforcers during the Prohibition years encouraged underworld crime
bosses in their belief that anyone could be bought. "I just couldn't
understand that guy [La Guardia]," "Lucky" Luciano told his ghost-
writers. "When we offered to make him rich he wouldn't even listen. . . . So I figured: what the hell, let him keep City Hall, we got
all the rest, the D.A., the cops, everything."[5]

Prohibition may not have initiated, but it certainly underlined,
the two-tier element in American justice so dramatically illustrated in
1995 by the O. J. Simpson case. As court records from 1920 to 1933
show, Prohibition agents concentrated their efforts on those they could
not shake down; that is, the poor, the barely literate, the recent immigrants least able to defend themselves. With a few exceptions (George
Remus was one of them), the wealthy were virtually immune from
prosecution, as were bankers and wealthy entrepreneurs responsible for
establishing lucrative contracts with bootlegging investors, often with
the complicity of congressmen.

The methods used to enforce Prohibition anticipated those of the DEA in its war on drugs. Although it would be ridiculous to compare the DEA to the Prohibition Bureau — the former a highly professional, motivated organization staffed by high-caliber agents of the greatest integrity; the latter a motley crew of venal political appointees — the *results,* in both cases, are startlingly similar. At no time did Prohibition law enforcers seize more than 5 percent of the quantities of liquor illegally entering the United States. The DEA's record of drug seizures, though higher (around 10 percent), is comparable, inevitably raising all sorts of questions. Should drugs be legalized? Are not current antidrug laws responsible for perpetuating organized crime? With over half of America's current prison population in jail for drug-related offenses, a drastic overhaul of antidrug legislation is not just in order, it is badly overdue.

But perhaps the least-learned lesson of Prohibition is that legislation alone is no answer to America's problems. The moralists and evangelical pioneers without whom Prohibition would have remained a dead letter believed that enactment of the Eighteenth Amendment would be sufficient to change the habits of American society as a whole. They were quickly proved disastrously wrong.

The cart-before-the-horse mentality is the same, as is the strident vocabulary of the new "moral majority." The reason the evangelist Billy Sunday became the popular hero of the twenties, among so many millions of God-fearing households, was that he was the very incarnation of the belief in an endearing, yet hopelessly naive panacea. Today's new repressive penal measures (chain gangs, "three-strikes-you're-out" sentences for habitual offenders, and so on) are not so very different from the special prisons for alcoholics advocated in the early 1800s, or indeed the whole array of laws contained in the Volstead Act.

The thinking in both cases is that such measures (either federal in nature or passed by different state legislatures) can radically reform a sick society, or at least make it tolerable to its law-abiding majority. Only the handful of intellectuals left on the political scene (foremost among them Senator Daniel Patrick Moynihan) are aware of this fallacy, and campaign against it: they know from experience that repression is like morphine — it masks the pain, but in no way cures the sickness.

The Prohibition disaster should have made this clear, but most

American decision-makers are singularly indifferent to the lessons of the past. The American educational system has become highly selective where the teaching of history is concerned. We tend to forget an important lesson: that those who know no history condemn themselves to repeat it, either as tragedy or as farce.

NOTES

INTRODUCTION

1. Andrew Sinclair, *Prohibition: The Era of Excess,* Atlantic, 1962.
2. John J. Rumberger, *Profits, Power, and Prohibition,* State U. of New York Press, 1989.
3. Norman H. Clark, *Deliver Us from Evil,* W. W. Norton, 1976.
4. "Drug War Two," January 30, 1995.

CHAPTER ONE: THE GOOD CREATURE OF GOD

1. Herbert Asbury, *The Great Illusion,* Doubleday, 1950.
2. This practice was known, from the seventeenth century on, as "eleven o'clock bitters." There was a similar break at four P.M.
3. Nine cents a gallon for liquor distilled from grain (whiskey), eleven cents for rum.
4. *The Great Illusion.*
5. The term originated from early smuggling habits, when contraband was hidden in the tops of then-capacious boots.
6. Norman H. Clark, *The Dry Years,* U. of Washington Press, 1965 and 1988.
7. Edwin M. Lemert, *Alcohol and the Northwest Indians,* U. of California Press, 1954.

CHAPTER TWO: FERVOR AND FANATICISM

1. For these and other quotes from nineteenth-century documents, diaries, and sermons I am indebted to the Rev. W. H. Samuels, *Temperance Reform and Its Great Reformers,* A. M. Cincinnati, 1879.
2. *The Great Illusion.*
3. Published by the American Tract Society, New York, in 1847.
4. My italics.

CHAPTER THREE: THE WOMEN'S WAR

1. John Kobler, *Ardent Spirits: The Rise and Fall of Prohibition,* Putnam, 1973.
2. It was part of Carry Nation's eccentricity to believe that Freemasons did the "devil's work."
3. She reproduced them, later, in her rambling autobiography. Her favorite:

This is a joint [as saloons were called]
Touch not, taste not, handle not!
Drink will make the dark, dark blot
Like an adder it will sting!
And at last to ruin bring
They who tarry at the drink!

CHAPTER FOUR: THE LINEUP

1. Norman H. Clark, *The Dry Years,* U. of Washington Press, 1965 and 1988.
2. *The Dry Years.*
3. Nov. 10, 1883, and Jan. 19, 1884.
4. *The Dry Years.*
5. Justin Stewart, *Wayne Wheeler: Dry Boss,* Fleming H. Revell Company, 1928.
6. *Wayne Wheeler: Dry Boss.*
7. *Wayne Wheeler: Dry Boss.*
8. *New York Times,* March 29, 1926.
9. *Wayne Wheeler: Dry Boss.*

CHAPTER FIVE: PROHIBITION'S FIRST VICTIMS

1. I am indebted to Dr. Don Heinrich Todzmann of the U. of Cincinnati for his help and expert advice in this chapter, and for allowing me to consult his Ph.D. thesis: "The Survival of an Ethnic Community: The Cincinnati Germans" (Ph.D. dissertation U. of Cincinnati, 1983).

CHAPTER SIX: AMERICA GOES DRY

1. Examples: The "Prohibition Battle Hymn"
We've played the Good Samaritan
But now we'll take a hand
And clear the road to Jericho
Of the robbing, thieving band;
Distillers and Saloonists
Shall be driven from the land
As we go marching on.

And "The Anti-Saloon War Song"
Tramp, tramp, tramp the States are marching
One by one to victory;
But we cannot win the fight
Until thirty six are white
So we'll press the battle on from sea to sea.
2. *The Great Illusion.*
3. *Ardent Spirits.*

CHAPTER SEVEN: THE PROVIDERS

1. Although his byline does not appear, the series was also researched by a Pulitzer Prize–winning reporter, John T. Rogers, who also spent considerable time with Remus after his release from jail.
2. The land on which it stood is now part of densely populated Cincinnati suburbia.
3. St. Louis *Post-Dispatch,* Jan. 4, 1926.

CHAPTER EIGHT: HARDING AND THE RACKETEERS

1. F. L. Allen, *Only Yesterday: An Informal History of the 1920s in America,* Penguin, 1931.
2. Francis Russell, *The Shadow of Blooming Grove,* McGraw-Hill, 1968.
3. Samuel Hopkins Adams, *The Incredible Era: The Life and Times of Warren Harding,* Houghton Mifflin, 1930.
4. Nan Britton, *The President's Daughter,* Elizabeth Anne Guild, 1927.
5. Charles Mee, *The Ohio Gang,* Evans and Co., 1981.
6. Alice Roosevelt Longworth, *The Crowded Hours,* Scribners, 1933.
7. Among the more absurd changes, Judges ix, 13 became: "Shall I leave my juice that gladdens gods and men," and "He distributed to the whole assembled multitude a roll of bread, a portion of meat, and a cake of raisins."

CHAPTER TEN: THE ADVENTURERS

1. Everett S. Allen, *The Black Ships,* Little, Brown, 1965.
2. Moet et Chandon exports to Canada:

$$
\begin{array}{ll}
1923 - & 22,400 \text{ cases} \\
1924 - & 20,600 \text{ cases} \\
1925 - & 6,900 \text{ cases} \\
1926 - & 11,700 \text{ cases} \\
1927 - & 11,600 \text{ cases} \\
1928 - & 1,200 \text{ cases} \\
1929 - & 13,100 \text{ cases}
\end{array}
$$

Amounts fell markedly after the 1929 crash. After Prohibition ended, they only exceeded 1,000 cases for the year 1938.
3. Roy A. Haynes, *Prohibition Inside Out,* Doubleday, 1926.
4. Studs Terkel, *Hard Times,* Pantheon Books, 1970.
5. *The Great Illusion.*
6. *The Black Ships.*
7. Ibid.
8. New Bedford *Evening Standard* series on McCoy, August 9–12, 1921.
9. David Kahn, *The Code Breakers,* Macmillan, 1967.
10. *The Black Ships.*
11. Aug. 13, 1927, issue.

12. *The Black Ships.*
13. Interview with author.

CHAPTER ELEVEN: "PROHIBITIONS WORKS!"

1. *Cincinnati Enquirer,* Sept. 8, 1921.
2. "Booze" owed its name to an enterprising manufacturer called Edmund C. Booze, who for the 1840 presidential campaign marketed whisky in bottles shaped like log cabins.
3. *Prohibition Inside Out.*
4. Mabel Willebrandt, *The Inside of Prohibition,* Current News Features, 1929.
5. Izzy Einstein, *Prohibition Agent Number 1,* Frederick Stokes Co. 1932.
6. Slang term for French World War I soldier.

CHAPTER TWELVE: "PROHIBITION DOESN'T WORK!"

1. Current News Features, 1929.
2. My italics.
3. My italics
4. My italics.
5. Although sometimes the "little people" got their own back. In Studs Terkel's *Hard Times,* a working-class woman's son reminisced: "A cop started coming around and gettin' friendly. She knew he was workin' up to a pinch. So, she prepares a bottle for him. He talked her into sellin' it to him. He pinches her, takes her to court. He said: 'I bought this half a dog of a booze. Half a pint.' The woman said: 'How do you know it's booze?' The cop takes a swig of it and spits it out. It was urine. Case dismissed."
6. *Collier's,* Sept. 10, 1949.
7. *Wayne Wheeler: Dry Boss.*
8. Thomas Kessner, *Fiorello La Guardia,* Penguin, 1989.
9. Kenneth Allsop, *The Bootleggers,* Arlington House, 1968.

CHAPTER THIRTEEN: CHICAGO

1. Fletcher Dobyns, *The Underworld of American Politics,* Fletcher Dobyns Publishing, 1932.
2. He owed this nickname to his diminutive size.
3. Lloyd Wendt and Herman Kogan, *Lords of the Levee,* Garden City Publishing, 1943.
4. In Chicago, Prohibition became effective in 1919.
5. Martin A. Gosch and Richard Hammer, *The Last Testament of Lucky Luciano,* Little, Brown, 1974.
6. Lloyd Wendt and Herbert Kogan, *Big Bill of Chicago,* Bobbs-Merrill, 1953.
7. Ibid.

CHAPTER FOURTEEN: REMUS ON TRIAL

1. *Cincinnati Enquirer,* Dec. 1–17, 1927.
2. *Cincinnati Enquirer,* Dec. 1927.
3. *Cincinnati Enquirer,* Dec. 1927.

CHAPTER FIFTEEN: REMUS REDUX

1. *Cincinnati Enquirer,* Dec. 1927.
2. Years later, a *Cincinnati Times-Star* columnist, Jame L. Kilgallen, who had covered the trial for the International News Service agency, claimed that he had suggested this dramatic opening to Remus. He also recalled that there was, in fact, no empty chair: Conners's wife was sitting in it.

CHAPTER SIXTEEN: A FATAL TRIUMPH

1. *Wayne Wheeler: Dry Boss.*
2. Oswald Garrison Willard in *Nation,* Nov. 30, 1927.
3. Virginius Dabney, *The Dry Messiah: The Life of Bishop Cannon,* Knopf, 1949. The speech, and an interview, appeared in the *Baltimore Sun.*
4. In later life, she became a Catholic convert.
5. Willebrandt herself had confirmed that on the night of Al Smith's nomination, she had ordered extensive raids on New York's major nightclubs and speakeasies.
6. *The Dry Messiah.*
7. *The Last Testament of Lucky Luciano.*

CHAPTER SEVENTEEN: THE AFTERMATH

1. The swing against Prohibition was not total. Pockets of resistance, the dry counties in what was once rural America, still exist; so does a tiny "Prohibition Party," and drivers caught on certain Alabama or Georgia highways with liquor in their cars face huge fines unless the liquor is stored in the trunk, with the cap or seal intact.
2. H. L. Mencken, *A Choice of Days,* Knopf, 1980.
3. Quoted in Francis Ianni and Elizabeth Reuss-Ianni's *Crime Society,* New American Library, 1976.
4. *Fiorello La Guardia.*
5. *The Last Testament of Lucky Luciano.*

BIBLIOGRAPHY

Adams, Samuel Hopkins. *The Incredible Era: The Life and Times of Warren Harding.* New York: Houghton Mifflin, 1930.

Allen, Everett S. *The Black Ships.* New York: Little, Brown, 1965.

Allen, F. L. *Only Yesterday: An Informal History of the 1920s in America.* New York: Penguin, 1931.

Allsop, Kenneth. *The Bootleggers.* London: Arlington House, 1968.

Asbury, Herbert. *The Great Illusion.* New York: Doubleday, 1950.

Britton, Nan. *The President's Daugter.* New York: Elizabeth Anne Guild, 1927.

Clark, Norman H. *Deliver Us from Evil.* New York: W. W. Norton, 1976.

———.*The Dry Years.* Seattle: University of Washington Press, 1965, revised ed. 1988.

Dabney, Virginius. *The Dry Messiah: The Life of Bishop Cannon.* New York: Knopf, 1949.

Dobyns, Fletcher. *The Underworld of American Politics.* New York: Fletcher Dobyns Publishing, 1932.

Edwards, Rev. Justin. *Temperance Manual.* New York: American Tract Society, 1847.

Einstein, Izzy. *Prohibition Agent Number 1.* New York: Frederick Stokes Co., 1932.

Gosch, Martin A., and Richard Hammer. *The Last Testament of Lucky Luciano.* Boston: Little, Brown, 1974.

Haynes, Roy A. *Prohibition Inside Out.* New York: Doubleday, 1926.

Ianni, Francis, and Elizabeth Reuss-Ianni. *Crime Society.* New York: New American Library, 1976.

Kahn, David. *The Code Breakers.* New York: Macmillan, 1967.

Kessner, Thomas. *Fiorello La Guardia.* New York: Penguin, 1989.

Kobler, John. *Ardent Spirits: The Rise and Fall of Prohibition.* New York: Putnam, 1973.

Lemert, Edwin M. *Alcohol and the Northwest Indians.* Los Angeles: University of California Press, 1954.

Longworth, Alice Roosevelt. *The Crowded Hours.* New York: Scribners, 1933.

Mee, Charles. *The Ohio Gang.* New York: Evans and Co., 1981.

Mencken, H. L. *A Choice of Days.* New York: Knopf, 1980.

Rumberger, John J. *Profits, Power, and Prohibition.* New York: State University of New York Press, 1989.

Russell, Francis. *The Shadow of Blooming Grove.* New York: McGraw-Hill, 1968.

Samuels, Rev. W. H. *Temperance Reform and Its Great Reformers.* Cincinnati: A. M. Cincinnati, 1879.

Sinclair, Andrew. *Prohibition: The Era of Excess.* Boston: Atlantic, 1962.

Stewart, Justin. *Wayne Wheeler: Dry Boss.* New York: Fleming H. Revell Co., 1928.

Terkel, Studs. *Hard Times.* New York: Pantheon Books, 1970.

Todzmann, Dr. Don Heinrich. "The Survival of an Ethnic Community: The Cincinnati Germans." Ph.D. diss., Cincinnati University, 1983.

Wendt, Lloyd, and Herman Kogan. *Big Bill of Chicago.* New York: Bobbs-Merrill, 1953.

———. *Lords of the Levee.* New York: Garden City Publishing, 1943.

Willebrandt, Mabel. *The Inside of Prohibition.* New York: Current News Features, 1929.

INDEX

abolitionism (alcohol), 28, 38–39
abolitionism (slavery), 29, 31, 234
absenteeism, 149
Adams, John, 10–11
advertising, 80
African Negroes, 53–54
alcohol, harmful effects of, 14–16, 23–27, 59
Alcohol Education Act (AEA), 51
alcoholism, deaths from, 147–48
Allen, Everett S., 134, 139–40, 142
America:
　cynicism about politicians, 239–41
　history of drinking in, 7–11
　old and new, tensions between, 3, 63, 226–27
　See also United States
American Anti-Prohibition Association, 233
American Bar Association, 160, 223
American Federation of Labor, 223, 236
American Legion, 223
American Temperance Society, 27

Ames, Fisher, 16
Anastasia, Albert, 173
Anderson, William Hamilton, 231
Andrew, John A., 31
Andrews, Lincoln C., 153–54, 223, 224
anti-Prohibition Congress (1922), 158
anti-Prohibitionists:
　character of, 47–48
　organizations of, 159, 223, 233
　politicians, 171, 226–28
Anti-Saloon League (ASL), 4, 32, 49, 52–61, 67, 68–75, 83, 149, 154, 164, 170, 222–27, 229–31
Appleton, Gen. James, 28
Arends, Abie, 189
armed forces, drinking in, 19, 70–71, 74
Arthur, Timothy Shay, 30
　Six Nights with the Washingtonians, 30–31
　Ten Nights in a Bar Room and What I Saw There, 26, 52

Association Against the Prohibition
    Amendment, 159, 223
Astor, Lord, 158
Atlanta (Georgia), 158

Baber, Dr. E. A., 214–15, 217
Bahamas, 131–32
Baker, Dr. M. W., 27–28
Baker, Newton D., 70–71
Baltimore (Maryland), 30
bar, new word for *saloon,* 236
Basler, Harold, 202
Beck, Charley, 37
Beecher, Rev. Lyman, 18, 22
beer, 12, 65, 236
behavior, regulation of, 3, 4, 242
Benchley, Robert, 88
Benezet, Anthony, 14
Berger, Thomas, 206
Beringer Vineyards, 86
Bible, passages praising liquor, 8
Bielaski, A. Bruce, 142–43
Billard, Frederick C., 144
Billingsley, Sherman, 87, 88
Black, James, 48
blacks, 53–54, 182
"black ships," 144
"blind pigs" (speakeasies), 30
boats, smugglers', 132, 134–35,
    140–41
Boehm, Jacob, 66
Bolsheviks, 71–72
bombings, 191
bootleggers:
    perils facing, 152, 177
    protection of, 163
    revenues and expenses, 103–4, 147
    typical stories of, 92–104
bootleg liquor, 85
    deaths from, 89, 159, 221–22
    manufacturing methods, 187
brewers, 58, 65, 178
    vs. distillers, 60, 68
bribes, 152–54
Bridge Whist Club, 167–68
Brisbane, Arthur, 69–70
Britain, drinking in, 9–10
Britton, Nan, 109–11

Brogan, Delis, 63
Bronfman, Samuel, 240
Brookhart, Smith W., 117
brothels, 176
Brotherhood of Locomotive Engi-
    neers, 149
Bruckman, John Caspar, 65
Bryan, William Jennings, 57, 73–74,
    82, 225, 238
Bureau of Industrial Alcohol, 157
Butler, Nicolas Murray, 222, 233–34
Byrd, Harry G., 216

California, 37, 158
Canada, 84, 130, 137, 151, 240
Candy, Ella Bell, 55, 225
Cannon, James, 225–27, 229–31
Capone, Al, 91, 95, 103, 130, 173,
    179, 184, 185–86, 187, 188,
    189, 190, 192, 193
Capone, Frank, 186
Carnegie Institute, 150
Carroll, John A., 183
Cary, Shepherd, 29
Cass, Lewis, 19
Catholics, 226–27
Cermak, Anton J., 182
champagne, 158
Chapman, Joan, 230
Charles Krug winery, 86
Cherrington, Ernest H., 52, 74
Chicago (Illinois), 64, 84, 88, 94–95,
    173, 175–93
children, prohibition campaign directed
    at, 39–40
Christian, George B., 108
Cicero (Illinois), 185–86
cigar makers, 157
Cincinnati (Ohio), 37, 43, 58, 64–70,
    82, 88, 95–103, 158, 160
cities, 51, 165
Civil Service, 83, 115, 154
Civil War, 31–32, 234
Clark, Norman, 51, 59
clergy, 8, 11
Cleveland (Ohio,) 37, 38, 56
Clifford, Edward, 143–44

Coast Guard (U.S.), 132, 134–36, 140–45, 151
  collusion with smugglers, 142–45
cocktails, 89
coded messages, smugglers', 141–42
Collins, Sam, 104, 125–26
Colosimo, "Big Jim," 177, 182, 183
Columbus (Ohio), 168
Congo, 53–54
congressional investigations, 68–69
congressmen:
  drinking habits of, 164
  dry, 228–29
  wet, 142
Connecticut, 12, 30
Conners, George, 97, 99–100, 126, 178, 198, 199–200, 204, 207
conservatives, 48
Consolidated Exporters' Company, 141–42
Coolidge, Calvin, 3, 142, 169, 190, 223, 224, 238
Cordeaux, Sir Harry, 131
Costello, Frank, 87, 172, 240
Coughlin, "Bathhouse John," 176–77
Country Club, 88
Cox, George "Boss," 107
Cox, Ross, 17
crime:
  organized, Americans' tolerance of, 239–41
  relation to Prohibition, 83, 148
criminals:
  gangs, 177–78, 186, 188, 192
  police protection of, 144, 173, 178, 183, 240–41
  political protection of, 162–63
Crowe, Dorsey R., 189
Crusaders (lobby), 223
Customs Bureau, 145, 164

Dabney, Virginius, 230
Daily News (New York), 78–79
Darrow, Clarence, 95, 183, 213–14, 224
Dater, George, 100
Daugherty, Harry Micajah, 60–61, 108–9, 111, 116–19, 122–24,

153, 159–60, 161, 163, 195, 198
Davis, John, 113
Davis, John W., 171
DEA, 242
Dealey, Edwin, 116
Death Valley Farm, 100–103, 125–26
Delaware, 30
de Marmon, Dr. Paluel, 27
Democratic party, 57, 73, 169–71, 225–26
de Mun, Count Albert, 158–59
denatured alcohol, 163, 222
Denby, Edwin, 71
Deneen, Charles S., 191
Denison, Everett, 164
Denny, Arthur, 18
Depression, 234, 237
Detroit (Michigan), 151, 192
Dever, William E., 185, 189
diplomatic immunity, 156–57
Diplomatic Service, 130
distillers, 60, 68, 70, 80, 235
  during Prohibition, stock and production of, 96
Dobyns, Fletcher, 176
Dodge, Franklin N., 2, 196–98, 218
Dodge, William Copeland, 241
Doheny, Edward, 116–17
Doherty, Jim, 188
Doran, James M., 224, 233
Dow, Neal, 28–29, 31
Draper, Arthur, 113
drinking:
  evils of, 21
  history of, in America, 7–19
  liquor vs. beer, 16
  literary treatments of, 26
  medical evidence against, 22
  popular in Prohibition era, 89
  regulation of, 12–13
  as release for desperate souls, 26
  sinfulness of, 21
  spontaneous combustion myth, 22–23, 25
Drucci, Vincent "The Schemer," 189
drunkenness:
  vs. moderate drinking, 13
  prison and fines for, 27–28

dry cities, counties, etc. (local option), 28, 51, 55, 57–58
Duffy, Tom, 188
Du Pont, Pierre, 233
Dwyer, William "Big Bill," 87, 172

East Coast, 135
Edison, Thomas, 149
Edwards, Edward I., 84
Edwards, Rev. Justin, 21, 23–27
Eighteenth Amendment:
    final repeal of, 235–36
    lobbying for, 4, 58–61
    passage of, 77–80
    repeal movement, 163–64, 169, 233–34
    See also Volstead Act
Einstein, Izzy, 154–57, 170
El Fay Club, 88
Eller, Morris, 184
Elston, Robert, 201–18
Enemy Appropriations Act, 118
England, 158
Europe:
    attitudes toward liquor, 10
    temperance movement in, 45–46
Everett (Washington), 51
Everleigh, Minna, 176

Fall, Albert, 116–17, 119
family morality, 51
Farley, John H., 56
farmers, 51, 235
Fay, Larry, 87, 173
FBI, 136, 175
federal judiciary, 166
Felder, Thomas, 114
Felix, Elizabeth, 213
Fielding, Henry, 9–10
Fitzgerald, F. Scott, 91, 99
    The Great Gatsby, 91, 99
flags of convenience, 132
Fleischmann Distilleries, 96
Flora, Robert E., 125–26
Foraker, Joe, 107
Forbes, Col. "Charlie," 115–16
Ford, Henry, 59, 149–50
Forel, August, 59

France, 158–59
Franchere, Gabriel, 17
Frankel, Max, 5
Franklin, Benjamin, 14
Friedman, Elizabeth Smith, 142
Friends of Temperance, 31
Fruit Industries, Inc., 231–32
Fulton Fish Market (New York City), 240–41
funerals, gangsters', 177–78

gang warfare, 177–78, 188, 192
    number of casualties, 177, 186
Gehrum, George, 100, 126
Genna brothers, 173, 187–88
Georges de Latour winery, 86–87
Georgia, 13
German-American Alliance, 68–70, 82, 182
Germans, 47, 49, 52, 63–72, 182
    hostility toward, 60, 71, 223
Gerstacker, Friedrich, 64
gin, 9, 12
"Gin Act" (Britain), 9
"Gin lane" (Hogarth), 9
Gloyd, Charles, 41
Godman, Thomas, 134–35
Goldman, Nathan J., 125
grain, ban of sales to distillers, 70, 235
Grant, Ulysses S., 32, 48
grape growers, 85–86, 231–32
Greendale distillery, 96
Guinan, "Texas," 88
Guzik, Jake, 181, 190

Haar, Willie, 167, 196, 206
Hancock, John, 129
Hanly, J. Frank, 58
hard cider, 12
Harding, Florence Kling, 107, 108
Harding, Warren Gamaliel, 60–61, 83, 105–16, 153, 161, 169, 184, 238
    administration, 83, 92, 104, 105–19, 159, 169, 195
    nomination and campaign, 111–13
Harvey, George, 111
Haskell Local Option Bill, 55

hatchetization, 42–44
Hayes, Rutherford B., 48
Haynes, Roy A., 223, 224
 Prohibition Inside Out, 131, 151–54, 157–59, 161
Healey, Charles, 183
health, Prohibition and, 147–48
Herrick, Myron T., 57, 114
hijackers, 101, 137, 178
Hines, Alfred J., 173
Hines, James J., 241
Hogan, Thomas S., 214
Hogarth, William, 9
Holinshed chronicles, 23
Holmes, Ruth, 1–2, 94, 205, 213
Hoover, Herbert, 106, 113, 226–29, 232, 234, 238
Hoover, J. Edgar, 175
Howard, Sir Esm ,156–57
Hudson's Bay Company, 17–18
Hughes, Charles Evans, 113
Hughes, Michael, 186
Hunt, Nicholas, 183
hyphenism issue, 67

immigrants, 3, 47–49, 51, 63–72, 227
Independent Order of Good Templars, 31
Indiana, 30, 38, 104
Indian tribes, destruction of, by liquor, 17–18
industrial alcohol, 163
industrialists, support of Prohibition, 149–50, 233
industrialization, 4, 49, 50
informers, 136
International Order of the Grand Templars, 51
international relations, Prohibition and, 130–31
International Workers of the World (IWW), 47
Irish, 30, 32, 47, 49, 52, 66, 172–73
Italians, 47, 49, 52, 172–73

Jack Daniel's, 127, 199
Jews, 65, 157, 173
Jim Beame, 66

Johnson, William E., 56
Jones, W. N., 55
Jones Act, 166
judiciary, federal, 166
justice, two-tier, 172, 241
Justice Department, 83

Kansas, 41–43
Kenna, Michael "Hinky Dink," 176–77
Kennedy, Joe Sr., 133, 240
Kent, Dr. Charles Foster, 115
Kentucky, 104
Kilman, Gen. Marvin, 14
King, John, 119
Klenha, Joseph Z., 186
Klug, George, 1, 200, 204, 205
Knox, John C., 81
Konvalinka, Ed, 185
Kraeplin, Emil, 59
Kraus, Lillian, 94
Ku Klux Klan, 143, 227

labor unions, 46, 149
La Guardia, Fiorello, 171–73, 176, 235, 241
Langley, John, 104
Lansky, Meyer, 173, 240
left wing, 3–4, 48
legislation, for social problems, 242
Lewis, Dr. Dioclesian, 36–37
Lewis, Frank, 201
Lincoln, Abraham, 32–33
 temperance address (1842), 32
Lincoln Legion, 32–33
Lingle, Alfred J. "Jake," 192–93
Lippmann, Walter, 238–39
liquor:
 vs. beer, 16
 called "good creature of God," 7
 condemnation of, 23–27
 consumption figures, 12, 28, 147, 148, 158
 as currency, 9
 defense of, 23, 31
 dire effects of, 14–16, 23–27, 59
 homemade, 89
 new brands of, 85

liquor (*continued*):
  poisoned, 221–22
  and politics, in America, 10–11
  sale of, illegalization, 29
  stocks of, 80, 96
  taxes on, 33, 47, 233
  watered, 127, 222
liquor industry, 26–27
  lobbyists, 47–48, 68
Livingstone, Belle, 88
Locke, John (of Ohio), 55
Loesch, Frank J., 189
London, Jack, 26, 49–50
Long Island (New York) , 140–41
Longworth, Alice Roosevelt, 114
Lorimer, William, 180–81, 182
Luciano, "Lucky," 99, 173, 178, 235, 240, 241
Lundin, Fred, 181, 182–84

Madeira, 12
Madison, James, 16
Mafia, 173, 235, 240
Maine, 28–29, 31
Malaga, 12
Mannington, Howard, 112, 114
Marcus, "John Jew," 100
Marsh, Rev. John, 31
  Hannah Hawkins, 31
Marxists, 3–4
Massachusetts, 12, 13, 28, 30, 31
Mather, Increase, 13
Mather, Cotton, 13
Matthews, Rev. Mark, 22
McAdoo, William Gibbs, 170
McCallum, Helen, 230–31
McCoy, Bill, 136–37, 139, 221
McGhee, Jimmy, 140–41
McKinley, William, 43
McLean, John R., 115
McLean, Ned, 115
McSorley's saloon, 88
McSwiggin, William, 188
McTroy, Cary, 231
medicinal liquor, 84–85, 96–97, 100, 133
Medicine Lodge (Kansas), 41–42
Mellin, Bill, 168–69

Mellon, Andrew, 113, 224
Mencken, H. L., 73–74, 107, 238–39
methanol, 222
Methodists, 13
Mexico, 130
Michigan, 30, 165
middle class, 46
Midwest, 37, 172
Milwaukee (Wisconsin), 64, 236
Minnesota, 30, 77
Mississippi, 80
Mitchell, William D., 231
moderation, 13, 38–39
Moderation League, 223
Moerlein, Kristian, 65
Moët Chandon, 130
Mondi, Jimmy, 181, 190
Montana, 166
moonshine, 222
Moore, Harry, 236
Moran, "Bugs," 192
Morgan, Burt, 104, 124–26
Morgan, Harry, 48
Morgenthau, Henry, 226
Mortimer, Elias and Kate, 115
Moynihan, Daniel Patrick, 5, 242
Mulhouse (ship), 135
Mumaugh, Dr. Shelby, 217
Murphy, "Big Tim," 189

Napa Valley (California), 85–87
Nation, Carry, 40–44
Nation, David, 41
Nebraska, 30, 80
Nevada, 166
Neville, W. L., 217
New Bedford (Massachusetts) 139–40
Newell, William, 50–51
New England, 37
New Hampshire, 30
New Jersey, 84, 158, 166, 167, 236, 240
New York (city), 43, 63, 81–82, 87–88, 154–57, 167, 169, 173, 176, 178, 221, 240–41
New York (state), 30, 165, 166, 169, 172, 228, 240
New York Times, 66

nightclubs, 88
Norfolk (Virginia), 169
Northwest (region of the U.S.), 135
Norwegian smugglers, 135
Nott, Dr. Eliphalet, 22–23

O'Banion, Dan, 186–87
Oberlin College, 53–54, 225
O'Donnell, Myles, 188
Ohio, 36–38, 54–61, 108
"Ohio gang," 106
Old Lexington Club, 96
Olmstead, Roy, 137–39, 221
Olvany, George, 226
opium, 16
Oppenheimer, Beston S., 206
Oregon, 30, 48
organized crime, 239–41
Ormsby-Gore, W. G. A., 131
Orr, Bill, 114

Pacific Fur Company, 17
Palm, Fred, 165
Palmer, A. Mitchell, 69
Pasley, Fred D., 185
Pattison, John M., 57
Pennsylvania, 12, 30
Philadelphia (Pennsylvania), 43
Philanthropist, The, 18–19
Phillips, Carrie, 109, 112
pirates, 135
pledges, 33
police, collusion with criminals, 144,
    173, 178, 183, 240–41
political corruption, 45, 58, 91, 102,
    105–19, 152–54, 158, 175–93
politicians:
  Americans' distrust of, 239–41
  bosses, 176
  campaigns, 55, 56
  and criminals, 162–63
  liquor served and drunk by,
    114–15, 164
  politically "dry" but privately "wet,"
    56–57, 108, 164
  "wet" (anti-Prohibition), 171,
    226–28
port, 12

Porter, Col. Daniel, 84
Portland (Maine), 28–29
Presbyterian Church, 38
priests, 86–87
Prohibition:
  benefits of, 147–60
  constitutional amendment first
    proposed, 58–61
  damaging effects of, 91, 238–43
  failure of, 88–89
  and foreign policy, 130–31
  nationwide, campaign for, 39–40
  as political issue, 45–46, 162, 234
  supporters of, 149–50, 233
  as tool of social control, 3–4,
    51–52
  total, first advocacy of, 28
  worldwide, 74–75
  See also Temperance movement
Prohibition Bureau, 83–89, 136,
    144, 151, 166–67, 169, 242
  agents killed in line of duty, 152
  corruption in, 152–54
  prevented from doing its job, 159
Prohibition era:
  desire to forget, 238
  in novels and films, 91
  as watershed in American history, 3
prohibitionists:
  character of, 48, 143
  lobbying by, 49
  propaganda of, 39–40
  rise and decline of, 28–33
Prohibition party, 28–29, 40, 48,
    52, 57
protection racket, 178
protest movements, nonviolent, 35
puritan ethic, 21, 63
Puritans, 8, 10, 13

rabbis, 87
racism, and prohibition movement,
    50, 226–27
radio, smugglers' use of, 138–39,
    141–42
raids, 29
raisin cakes, 85–86, 232
Rand, Sally, 132

reform movements, 46–47, 49, 224, 239
religion, and temperance movements, 14, 21–22
Remus, George, 92–104, 119, 121–28, 160, 167, 168–69, 221
    fall of, 121–28
    murder case, 1–3
    trial of, 195–219
Remus, Imogene, 1–2, 94, 128, 195
Remus, Romola, 94–95, 211
Republican party, 57, 61, 73, 107, 108, 111, 184, 185, 224
Rhode Island, 30
Rockefeller, John D., 58, 149, 233–34
Rogers, John, 198, 199, 206
Rogers, Will, 172
Roosevelt, Franklin D., 170, 226, 228, 234–35, 237
Root, Elihu, 233
Rothstein, Arnold, 173
Rugby, 96
rum, 10, 12
rumrunners, 129–45
Rush, Dr. Benjamin, 14–16, 22
Russell, Rev. Howard Hyde, 54–55
Ryan, Mike, 183
Ryerson, Mrs. Gabriel, 211

Sabin, Pauline Morton, 224, 229
sacramental wine, 87, 157
St. Louis (Missouri), 43, 236
St. Pierre and Miquelon, 130
Saint Valentine's Day massacre, 192
saloons, 151, 236
    condemnation of, 22, 27
    hours of, 28, 50
    owned by breweries, 58, 178
    political involvement of, 10–11, 165
    social function of, 49–50
    taxes and licenses, 50, 58
Sartain, John, 195, 198
Scaife, Capt. H. L., 118
Scandinavia, 45
schools, evils of drink taught in, 39–40
Schultz, "Dutch," 141, 173
Schwaab, John, 67
Scotland, 45

Scottish-Americans, 32
Seabury, Samuel, 235
sentences, mandatory, 165
Serritella, Daniel A., 189, 190
Sewell, Dr. Thomas, 22
Sheppard, Morris, 236
Shevlin, James, 154
Shook, Chester R., 201–17
Sibbald, Walter K., 202, 218
Siegel, Benjamin "Bugsy," 173, 240
Simpson, Sir George, 17
Sinclair, Andrew, 3
Sinclair, Harry, 116–17
slavery, 29
Slovick, Joseph, 144–45
Small, Len, 184, 187
Small, Rev. Sam, 72–73
Smith, Al, 166, 169–71, 225–28, 235
Smith, Jess, 108–9, 112, 117–18, 119, 122, 127, 160
Smith, Mal, 119
Smith, Rev. Matthew Hale, 30
Smith, Moe, 154–57
smugglers, 84, 129–45
    as folk heroes, 129, 134
    interception of, at sea, 142–45
    profits of, 130–33, 136
    tricks of, 132
Society for the Suppression of Intemperance, 12
"Song of the Moonshiners," 131
Sons of the Soil, 31
South, 172
South Carolina, 13
Spanish Marie, 134
speakeasies, 87–88, 165–67, 236
Spiegel, Frederick S., 65, 67
Spokane (Washington), 84
Sprague, Albert A., 186
Squibb distillery, 96
Stanley, Owen, 131
states:
    lax enforcement of Prohibition, 166
    statewide prohibition laws, 30
Stevens, Walter, 187
Stinson, Roxy, 109, 118
Stork Club, 87, 88, 232
Stowe, Harriet Beecher, 18

Stratton, Harry, 101
Stuart, Frank J., 143
Stuyvesant, Peter, 9
Sullivan, Mark, 106
Sunday, Billy, 82–83, 236, 242
Swanson, John A., 191
Sweitzer, Robert M., 182, 186

Tacoma (Washington), 48
Taft, Charles P., 66
Taft, Charles P. II, 201–18
Taft, William Howard, 80, 116, 161,
    201–2
Tammany Hall, 169, 171, 172,
    176, 226
taverns, 10
taxes:
    on liquor, 33, 47, 233
    on saloons, 50, 58
Teapot Dome scandal, 116–17
"Temperance Manual" (Edwards),
    23
Temperance movement:
    in colonial times, 13–14
    in Europe, 45–46
    international, 72–75
    in nineteenth century, 21–33
    organizers of, 36
    as political issue, 10
    religious motive of, 14, 21–22
    social class concerns in, 46–47
    See also Prohibition
Temperance Recorder, 21
Temperance societies (voluntary),
    18–19, 30–31
Terkel, Studs, 237
    Hard Times, 237
territorial waters, 132, 139
third party movements, 48
Thompson, "Big Bill," 112, 173,
    176, 177, 179–78, 179–93
Thompson, Elizabeth "Mother,"
    36–38
Times (Seattle), 149
Times Square, 88
Times-Star (Cincinnati), 66
tobacco, 41
Tom August (ship), 134–35

Torrio, Johnny, 95, 173, 177, 184,
    185–86
travelers, drinking abroad by, 158–59
Treasury Department, 83
Tresca, Carlo, 173
Tribune (Chicago), 181, 192–93
Truesdale, Harry, 207–13
Twenty-One (club), 87, 232

United States:
    political system, flaws of, 162–63
    smugglers' role in history of, 129
    See also America
United States Brewers Association,
    47–48, 68–70
"untouchables," 124
Untouchables, The (TV series), 175
urbanization, 49
Utah, 236

van Pelt, John Calvin, 37
Vermont, 30
Versailles Peace Conference, 74
Veterans Administration, 115–16
vineyards, 85–87
visitation bands, 36–38
Volstead, Andrew J., 77, 159, 171
Volstead Act, 77–80
    damaging effects of, 3, 80, 221–23
    enforcement of, 83–84, 154–60,
        166, 171–72, 195
    flouting of, 84–89
    last night before going into effect,
        81–82
    penalties for violation, 78, 165, 166
    political resistance to, 158
    reason for failure, 79
    See also Eighteenth Amend-
        ment
Vorbau, W. H., 218
Votaw, Carolyn, 115
voting fraud, 176, 181

Walker, Jimmy, 171, 176
Walnut, T. Henry, 153
War on Drugs, 5, 131, 133, 142,
    167, 242
Washington (D.C.), 169

Washington, George, 13–14
Washingtonian Revival, 30–31, 32
Washington (state), 48, 50, 51, 84, 137
Washington Times, 69–70
WASP establishment, 3
Watson, Blanche, 200, 204, 219
Watson, Thomas B., 88–89
Weber, Joe, 118
Weeks, John, 113
Welliver, Jud, 113
Werner, "Hippy," 136
West Coast, 158
Whalen, Grover, 178
Wheeler, Burton K., 117, 122
Wheeler, Mrs. Charles, 37
Wheeler, Wayne, 4, 52–61, 68–71, 77, 83, 148, 155, 164, 170–71, 222–25
whiskey, 12
whiskey certificates, 81, 96
Whiskey Rebellion, 12
White, James A., 72
Wickersham Commission, 232–33
Willard, Frances Elizabeth, 38–39
Willebrandt, Mabel Walker, 139, 150–51, 196, 198, 227, 228, 231–32
The Inside of Prohibition, 161–69

Williams, Paul W., 241
Wilson, Woodrow, 60, 67, 70, 78, 83, 111, 115, 170
Winchell, Walter, 87, 88
wiretaps, 139, 167–68
Wisconsin, 166
Wittenmayer, Mrs. Annie, 37
Wolfstein, Dr. David A., 217
Woman's Christian Temperance Union (WCTU), 38–40, 46, 236
women:
    benefits of Prohibition to, 150–51
    as reformers, 46–47, 224
Women's Crusade (E. Thompson's), 37–38
"Women's War," 35–44
wood alcohol, 222
Woods, Rev. Leonard, 8
working class, 4, 46–47
    drink of, 12, 223
World League Against Alcoholism, 56
World War I, 60–61, 66–72, 142
World War II, 142
Worldwide Prohibition Congress, 72–74

Zola, Emile, 26
Zoline, Elijah, 122
Zuta, Jack, 189